P9-DVJ-481

The Power *for* True Success

How to Build Character in Your Life

The Power *for* True Success

How to Build Character in Your Life

Institute in Basic Life Principles

Oak Brook, Illinois

The Power for True Success: How to Build Character in Your Life

Published by the Institute in Basic Life Principles, Inc.
Box One
Oak Brook, IL 60522-3001
Tel: 630-323-9800
Fax: 630-323-7271
www.iblp.org

The Institute in Basic Life Principles is a Biblically based, not-for-profit, nonsectarian training and service organization dedicated to serving families, youth, and leaders worldwide, through training in Biblical principles that bring true success in life.

Copyright ©2001 by the Institute in Basic Life Principles

All rights reserved.

All Scripture verses are quoted from the King James Version of the Bible.

No part of this publication may be reproduced, stored in a retrieval system, or transmitted, in any form or by any means—electronic, mechanical, photocopying, recording, or otherwise—without the prior written permission of the publisher.

Special thanks to the following contributing photographers:
Rowan Gillson, Tanya Hart, Kristen Hoopes, Matthew Hoopes, Joy Jensen, Samuel Martin, Phil McCracken, Meta Thur Olson and Kenneth Olson, Bronwyn Pellascio, Jim Perkins, Janel Reid, Nathan Stone, Anna Storm, Matthew Tabbut, Will Thornton

International Standard Book Number: 0-916888-19-3 (hardbound)

Recognizing the importance of preserving what has been written, this book is printed on pH neutral paper.

Printed in the United States of America
First Edition
01 02 03 04 05 06 — 10 9 8 7 6 5 4 3 2 1

Dedicated to

all those who are of the household of faith and members of the Body of Christ—that we "may grow up into him in all things, which is the head, even Christ" (Ephesians 4:15), "being rooted and grounded in love" (Ephesians 3:17); that we may be one in our love for Him and for each other; and that our love will convince the world that God sent His Son into the world. "Now unto him that is able to do exceeding abundantly above all that we ask or think, according to the power that worketh in us, Unto him be glory in the church by Christ Jesus throughout all ages, world without end" (Ephesians 3:20–21).

This introductory edition is primarily designed for the families enrolled in the Advanced Training Institute; we invite each family to make comments and suggestions for future editions to charactercomments@iblp.org.

$\mathscr{C}$ontents

Character Qualities
explained from Scripture

How to Use This Book

1. Trace Conflicts to Character Deficiencies

Every conflict in life can be traced to the neglect, violation, or misapplication of one or more character qualities. For example, conflicts that a teenager has toward his parents may be traced to a lack of honor, obedience, or forgiveness. The conflicts that a wife has because of her circumstances may be traced to the need for contentment, gratefulness, or joyfulness. A father who is harsh toward his family would need to "camp" on the qualities of patience, gentleness, wisdom, flexibility, humility, self-control, and genuine love.

Every character quality also needs balancing qualities. For example, flexibility must be balanced with responsibility and decisiveness, and attentiveness needs to be practiced with alertness and discernment.

2. Understand the "Impossibility" of True Character

The more we understand the true nature of character, the more we realize how humanly impossible it is to fully carry it out. For example, we may think that we are grateful, but are we grateful to everyone and for every situation, even tragedies? Are we fully grateful to God? Do others regard us as grateful people, and do we have the right motives for expressing gratefulness?

Furthermore, every character quality is a practical expression of genuine love. True love springs from a heart that is willing to give, not from a heart focused on personal gain. One who has genuine love will demonstrate all character qualities all the time.

3. Learn How to Gain the Power for Character

The very situations that cause most people to become discouraged and bitter and to violate character qualities are actually designed or allowed by God to help us realize our need for Him and His power in our lives. It is only by the power of God that we will be able to achieve genuine love and all its related qualities.

There is a process by which we can gain this power of genuine love. It begins by being indwelt, filled, and controlled by the Holy Spirit of God. Then this process includes a time of testing as guided by the Holy Spirit. Our responses to each trial or tribulation must include:

- Thanking God for all things—even trials
- Rejoicing in all things by finding benefits in them
- Engrafting and using the *rhemas* of Scripture
- Crying out to God when necessary
- Doing good works for all people—even our enemies

To the degree that we carry out these responses, we will experience the power of genuine love and every other related character quality.

What Is Good Character?

- Character is the inward motivation to do what is right according to the highest standards of behavior in every situation.

- Character consists of the stable and distinctive qualities built into an individual's life which determine his or her responses, regardless of the circumstances.

- Character is the wise response to the pressure of a difficult situation and what we do when we think that no one is watching. It is the predictor of good behavior.

The Greek word for *character* is *charakter*. It is translated in Scripture as "the express image." According to *The Complete Word Study Dictionary New Testament*, the word "originally denoted an engraver or engraving tool. Later it meant the impression itself, usually something engraven, cut in, or stamped, a character, letter, mark, [or] sign. This impression with its particular features was considered as the exact representation of the object whose image it bore." In Hebrews 1:3, Christ is referred to as the "express image" of God.

Why Must We Learn Character?

1. Character reveals the Lord Jesus Christ, since He is the full personification of all good character qualities.

2. Understanding character explains why things happen to us, because all things work together for good to conform us to the character of Christ.

3. Knowing precise character qualities gives us the basis for praising the character of God and others.

What Is the Source of Character and How Is It Accurately Defined?

Values are based on the changing opinions of what people or groups feel is important. However, character is based on universal standards that are time-tested and recognized as being right.

In 1844, the City of Philadelphia was bequeathed a large amount of money and land to establish a school for orphans. The Will of the decedent prohibited the use of clergymen or ministers in teaching the orphans, yet the Will required that the students be instructed in the "purest principles of morality." Over the objection of the heirs, the Supreme Court of the United States ruled that Philadelphia could use the Bible to teach the students, even though clergymen could not be used in the school.

The Court stated: "Where can the purest principles of morality be learned so clearly or so perfectly as from [the Bible and especially] the New Testament?" (Vidal v. Girard's Executors; 43 U.S. 127, 200 [1844]).

George Washington

Noah Webster

James Madison

Patrick Henry

"It is impossible to rightly govern the world without God and the Bible." —George Washington, First President of the United States

"The principles of all genuine liberty, and of wise laws and administrations are to be drawn from the Bible and sustained by its authority. The man, therefore, who weakens or destroys the divine authority of that book may be accessory to all the public disorders which society is doomed to suffer." —Noah Webster, Founding Educator

"The Bible must be considered as the great source of all the truth by which men are to be guided in government as well as in all social transactions." —Noah Webster

"We have staked the whole future of American civilization, not upon the power of government, far from it. We have staked the future of all our political institutions upon the capacity of mankind to self-government; upon the capacity of each and of all of us to government [govern] ourselves, to control ourselves, to sustain ourselves according to the Ten Commandments of God." —James Madison, Father of the United States Constitution

"It cannot be emphasized too strongly or too often that this great nation was founded . . . not on religions, but on the gospel of Jesus Christ." —Patrick Henry, Founding Father, Orator

Why Are "Operational Definitions" Necessary to Define Character?

The precise and accurate definition of a particular character quality is universally recognized and understood because it is based on the Law of God, which is written in every person's heart. Therefore, when a person lies or steals or commits an immoral act, his conscience condemns him, and he knows he has done wrong.

Even though the basic truth of a character quality is understood, there is a need for further clarification on how to apply it in daily situations. This is also true for the Law of God, as illustrated in the days of Ezra.

"And all the people gathered themselves together as one man into the street that was before the water gate; and they spake unto Ezra the scribe to bring the book of the law of Moses, which the LORD had commanded to Israel. . . . So they [Ezra and the Levites] read in the book in the law of God distinctly, and gave the sense, and caused them to understand the reading" (Nehemiah 8:1, 8).

Various definitions for the same character quality are therefore further clarifications of how to apply that quality. Another reason for "operational definitions" of a character quality is that truth needs to be confirmed by two or three witnesses. Each witness will give the same truth in different words. "In the mouth of two or three witnesses shall every word be established" (II Corinthians 13:1).

With various definitions for character qualities, there is always a possibility of an inaccurate definition. This is also true in explaining the meaning of Scripture, and therefore God warns about the false teachers who come as ravening wolves in sheeps' clothing.

Testing the truth of a character definition is the same as testing the truth of a Scriptural interpretation. The first test is discerning the spirit that the definition communicates. Is it consistent with the nature of God and the Lord Jesus Christ and His Holy Spirit?

The second test is in its conformity to genuine love and all the other character qualities. One definition must not contradict other definitions. For example, a definition for tolerance cannot be in contradiction to the qualities of discretion, self-control, honor, or virtue.

The third test of truth is in the results that occur in the lives of those who apply it. Jesus said, "By their fruits ye shall know them" (Matthew 7:20). If a person says he is kind, compassionate, and patient, but justifies bitterness, harshness, and hatred, then he does not understand true character.

How Is Character Distinct From Religion?

Character is not a religion. Character transcends all religions and is a universal standard that is inscribed in the heart and conscience of every person. When God made us in His image, He put within us the capacity to recognize and need His character.

Therefore, when Adam and Eve sinned and their eyes were opened to their nakedness, they did not need anyone to tell them that they were immodest. It was an instinctive response to being in the presence of God.

The True Meaning of the "Separation Clause"

The Founding Fathers of America did not want one church denomination to rule in America as had been the case in England. However, they affirmed their commitment to America's being a God-fearing nation built on Biblical principles. Even today, all United States currency confirms this commitment with the statement, "In God We Trust."

The distinction between God and the Bible on one hand and church and church doctrine on the other hand was clearly understood until the middle of the last century, when courts were convinced to combine all of them under the term "religion" and exclude them from public life. The social chaos that we are now experiencing was predicted by the Founding Fathers if such an action were ever taken.

Character transcends culture, race, age, social status, religion, gender, and nationality, because it deals with the daily struggles of human nature.

Noah Webster stated, "All the miseries and evils which men suffer from vice, crime, ambition, injustice, oppression, slavery, and war proceed from their despising or neglecting the precepts contained in the Bible."

The phrase "wall of separation" is from the early history of our nation and not in the First Amendment, the Constitution, or any other official document. It is actually a partial quote—taken out of context from a message given by Thomas Jefferson to the Danbury Baptist Association in 1802. In this address, he assured the concerned group that the power of government did not reach to religion, but that the government must be based upon moral principles to maintain good order.

Why Is God's Power Needed for Character?

Every person tends to have some addiction, habit, or besetting sin that violates the character he believes in and requires the power of God to overcome.

Ken[1] knew that self-control was a good character quality. He even gave sermons on the subject because he is a minister. However, it was quite obvious to his congregation and to his doctor that he did not have self-control.

One day he attended a birthday party, and one of the gifts for the guest of honor was a floor scale. Each of the other guests took turns on the scale. When Ken stood on the scale, it read "Error." After several more tries, it finally registered 300 pounds!

Ken had tried many practical programs to solve his problem, but nothing worked for him. He even fasted for forty days and lost about forty pounds, but the weight returned in a few weeks. One day, Ken applied a truth that he had been overlooking—a simple yet profound truth that is setting many free from the bondage of various types of addictions.

That was about a year ago. Each day since then he has experienced the power of self-control. He has lost over 100 pounds and is now at his proper weight.

The same truth that is giving Ken the power to have self-control is being used by others to resolve anger, rage, and bitterness and instead experience forgiveness, compassion, and kindness. Others are conquering lust, evil thoughts, and sensual addictions and are enjoying genuine love, joy, and peace. Still others are replacing habitual lying and stealing with truthfulness, sincerity, and generosity.

There was another man who also experienced problems similar to Ken's. He wrote out his dilemma, and millions of people who read it exclaimed, "That is exactly what is happening to me!" This man wrote the following message: "The things that I know are wrong and don't want to do, I keep doing; and the things that are right and I want to do, I don't do! O wretched man! who shall deliver me from this body of death?"

That statement paraphrased from the Apostle Paul in Romans 7 was an introduction to the freeing truths he presented. May they also guide you in discovering and enjoying the power to have God's character and success in your personal life, marriage, family, finances, and vocation.

[1] Pastor Ken Pierpont still marvels at the new power of self-control that he began experiencing in June 2000. He has been happy to share his story with others, and they too are experiencing similar results. You may contact him directly at his web site: www.kenpierpont.com to find out more about how he discovered the secret of self-control.

Is God's Power Needed for All Character Qualities?

In order to break the bondage of addictions such as anger, lust, lying, or stealing, the need for extra power is understandable. But what about other qualities that seem to come more naturally for a person because of his or her gifting or training? Why would he or she need the power of God to carry them out?

Why are some people orderly and punctual by their natural disposition and others kind and compassionate? The answer is that all character qualities are linked together and are the expression of perfect love.

A person may have the quality of punctuality and be everywhere on time; however, that same person may find it very difficult to tolerate those who keep him or her waiting. Or, his motive for being on time may be to impress others with his punctuality—thus violating the quality of humility.

Every quality is a practical expression of perfect love. It takes the power of God to develop and live out such love.

Another person may be generous and give to the needs of the poor. However, their giving may not be led by God and thus be iniquity. Scripture points out the unprofitability of generosity that is not connected to perfect love. "And though I bestow all my goods to feed the poor, and though I give my body to be burned, and have not charity, it profiteth me nothing" (I Corinthians 13:3).

All the qualities are intrinsically related to each other and are expressions of perfect love. It takes the power of God to have this love, because it is not natural for us to demonstrate it. On the other hand, it is natural for us to have and display the opposite qualities such as selfishness, apathy, stinginess, resistance, pride, and anger.

Demonstrating specific character qualities is not possible without a change of heart, and this again requires an act of God's supernatural power.

The "Secret" of Character Building— Knowing It Is Impossible!

God designed life with continuing impossibilities so that we will be aware of our total dependence upon Him and cry out for His supernatural power.

Those who think that they can perfect character qualities or keep the Law of God do not understand that it is humanly impossible to do so.

The fact is obvious with even a cursory review of some of God's commands: "Be perfect" (Deuteronomy 18:13), "Be ye holy for I the LORD your God am Holy" (Leviticus 19:2), "Put off all . . . anger" (Colossians 3:8), "Rejoice when all men speak evil of you" (see Matthew 5:10–12), "Pray without ceasing" (I Thessalonians 5:17), "Bring every thought into captivity" (see II Corinthians 10:5), and "Love your enemies" (Matthew 5:44).

One of the best examples of impossible instructions took place when Jesus told His disciples to row across the Sea of Galilee. (See Luke 8:22–25.) He knew that they could not do it. He knew that a storm would come up that would be so severe that it would be impossible to row through it.

Yet, with this understanding, Jesus climbed into the boat with His disciples, and they began their rowing. While they rowed, Jesus found a sheltered place and went to sleep.

Soon the clouds formed, and the wind and the waves began to rise. The disciples just rowed harder. After all, several were experienced fishermen. They had been through many storms—but none like this!

The wind grew stronger, and the waves became higher and crashed over the boat with unusual fury. Finally, the disciples realized the seriousness of the situation. There was no way for them to row to the distant shore, and in fact, their lives were endangered with imminent drowning.

It was only at that humanly-impossible moment that they did the one thing God wants all of us to do on a regular basis. They cried out to God. Only as they cried out in recognition of their total inadequacy did Jesus rise up and rebuke the storm.

It is significant that Jesus did not save the disciples from their distress until the moment they cried out—not one second sooner!

Why Did God Design Life to be Impossible?

God created us to have fellowship with Him. Think of it! The mind that created the universe wants to communicate with the hearts and minds He created from the dust of the earth.

However, true fellowship is based on genuine love, and love cannot be required—it must be the response to a free choice. Love is strengthened by an awareness of mutual need. Thus, God allows situations and responsibilities to bring us to the point where all we can do is cry out to Him. At that moment, God demonstrates His power and His love to us so that we will glorify Him and grow in our love for Him.

It is important to realize that Jesus did nothing to calm the storm until His disciples cried out— not a second sooner.

How Does Crying Out Initiate the Power for Character Building?

The most important cry of a person's life is the cry for salvation.

Effective character building comes from a changed heart, and a changed heart results from being born again by the Spirit of God. In our day, it is customary to "become a believer" by making a decision to receive Christ as Savior. However, many who make such a decision tend to fall away from their commitment when pressures and temptations come against them.

In contrast to the 5 or 10 percent who follow through on their decision in our day, there was a 75–80 percent follow-through among those who were saved during the revivals led by Jonathan Edwards and Charles Finney in the eighteenth and nineteenth centuries.

It is significant that they did not ask for decisions but instead explained the awesome wrath of God that was upon those who lived in violation of God's commandments and His character.

The people of that day were introduced to a holy God Who requires perfection in order to enter Heaven. They realized that they were not perfect, having broken God's commandments, and were deserving of hell.

Therefore, when they repented, they were urged to cry out to God so that He might make a decision to have mercy upon them. This approach is very consistent with the Scriptures on salvation.

Scriptures That Explain the Power of Salvation

Peter's message on the Day of Pentecost resulted in 3,000 new believers. His message included the following:

"The sun shall be turned into darkness, and the moon into blood, before that great and notable day of the Lord come: And it shall come to pass, that whosoever shall call on the name of the Lord shall be saved" (Acts 2:20–21).

Note: The word *call* is from two Greek words. The first is *epi,* meaning "upon," and the second is *kaleo,* which means "to call aloud; to utter in a loud voice."

When Paul explained salvation to the believers in Rome, he used the same word for *call* when he wrote, "That if thou shalt confess with thy mouth the Lord Jesus, and shalt believe in thine heart that God hath raised him from the dead, thou shalt be saved. For with the heart man believeth unto righteousness; and with the mouth confession is made unto salvation. For the scripture saith, Whosoever believeth on him shall not be ashamed. For there is no difference between the Jew and the Greek: for the same Lord over all is rich unto all that call upon him. For whosoever shall call upon the name of the Lord shall be saved" (Romans 10:9–13).

Why a Cry Is So Effective

1. **It conquers pride**—I will humble myself.

2. **It expresses helplessness**—I am weak.

3. **It is a plea for mercy**—I am unworthy.

4. **It is total surrender**—I will do Your will.

How Crying Out Differs From Praying

Scripture makes a very clear distinction between prayer and crying out. This difference is especially obvious in the Psalms:

- "O LORD, attend unto my cry, give ear unto my prayer" (Psalm 17:1).
- "Hear my cry, O God; attend unto my prayer" (Psalm 61:1).
- "Let my prayer come before thee: incline thine ear unto my cry"(Psalm 88:2).

There is good reason for this distinction. It takes training to pray effectively. Thus, the disciples asked Jesus, "Lord, teach us to pray" (Luke 11:1).

However, a cry takes no training. It is the natural response of a newborn baby. It is the beginning response for salvation and a continuing expression of our need throughout life. David stated, "Evening, and morning, and at noon, will I pray, and cry aloud: and he shall hear my voice" (Psalm 55:17).

A Case Study of Crying Out to God

The owner of a plumbing company in the Chicago area bought a large truck that would hold all the tools he needed for his jobs. Thus, he had a mobile plumbing shop.

One day, he drove his truck up to a local store to take care of a matter. He would be gone for only three minutes, so he left the key in the ignition. When he came out a few minutes later, the truck was gone.

He was stunned and called the police. They informed him that car thieves regularly circle the area, looking for unattended vehicles that are easy to steal. The policeman told him, "If we cannot locate your truck in an hour, you might as well forget about it. The thieves are well organized and quickly dismantle the vehicles and sell the contents."

The owner was heartsick. His entire business was gone. He even had several payments and job orders in the truck. After several hours of searching with no results, it all seemed hopeless.

At that point, the owner asked some friends to pray. On October 13, 2000, a group of his friends cried out to God on his behalf. Their cry was simple: "Abba Father, cause the thief to repent and return the truck."

Three days later, the owner received a phone call from someone in Chicago saying, "Come get your truck." He went to the address that he was given, and there it was! It was still intact—checks and job orders, but all the power tools and some of the hand tools were gone.

Several days later, he went to the flea market and found many of his tools for sale in one of the booths. After proving that they were his, he recovered them. The remaining tools were replaced by people in donations to him—*threefold*!

Several other exciting results came from this experience, but the most important was the gratefulness and praise that this owner and his friends had to the Lord because of His response to their cry. They experienced the reality of God's promise in Psalm 50:15: "And call upon me in the day of trouble: I will deliver thee, and thou shalt glorify me."

Further Promises on Crying Out

- "In my distress I called upon the LORD, and cried unto my God: he heard my voice out of his temple, and my cry came before him, even into his ears" (Psalm 18:6).

- "When I cry unto thee, then shall mine enemies turn back: this I know; for God is for me" (Psalm 56:9).

- "Call unto me, and I will answer thee, and shew thee great and mighty things, which thou knowest not" (Jeremiah 33:3).

A Three-Phase Process to

The power for developing character does not come from our ingenuity or willpower. It comes from the Holy Spirit of God. "Not by might, nor by power, but by my spirit, saith the LORD of hosts" (Zechariah 4:6). There are three aspects of the work of God's Spirit in our lives.

1. Being indwelt in my spirit

The moment you call upon the name of the Lord, you are given not only the gift of salvation, but also the gift of God's Spirit. God's Holy Spirit indwells our spirit. "The Spirit itself beareth witness with our spirit, that we are the children of God" (Romans 8:16).

2. Being filled in my soul

The soul involves the mind, will, and emotions. As a child of God, an individual can ask his Heavenly Father to fill every area of his soul with His Holy Spirit. "If ye then, being evil, know how to give good gifts unto your children: how much more shall your heavenly Father give the Holy Spirit to them that ask him?" (Luke 11:13).

3. Being controlled in my body

After salvation, one should dedicate his body to God as a living sacrifice. It is now the temple of the Holy Spirit, and daily we are to yield the members of our bodies as instruments of righteousness (Romans 6:19, 12:1–2).

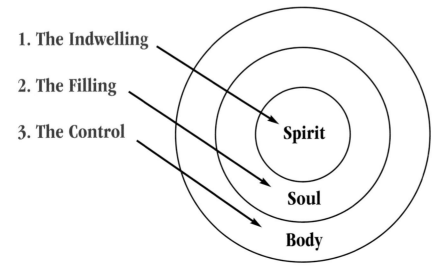

1. The Indwelling
2. The Filling
3. The Control

Spirit
Soul
Body

In the same way that the Holy Spirit led Jesus into the wilderness for testing (see Luke 4:1–14), He will lead us into trials and temptations.

- "Beloved, think it not strange concerning the fiery trial which is to try you, as though some strange thing happened unto you" (I Peter 4:12).

- "My brethren, count it all joy when ye fall into divers temptations; Knowing this, that the trying of your faith worketh patience" (James 1:2–3).

- "Blessed are they which are persecuted for righteousness' sake: for theirs is the kingdom of heaven. Blessed are ye, when men shall revile you, and persecute you, and shall say all manner of evil against you falsely, for my sake" (Matthew 5:10–11).

- "For this is thankworthy, if a man for conscience toward God endure grief, suffering wrongfully. . . . For even hereunto were ye called: because Christ also suffered for us, leaving us an example, that ye should follow his steps" (I Peter 2:19, 21).

Experience the Power of Love

<table>
<tr><td>

God's Spirit

</td><td>

The Power of God's Spirit

</td></tr>
</table>

The Types of Testing

- **Fiery Trials:**
  Sudden surges of anger or lust quenched by the shield of faith (see I Peter 4:12, Ephesians 6:16).
- **Infirmities:**
  Physical limitations and defects that hinder strength or health (see II Corinthians 12:10).
- **Reproaches:**
  Ridicule, scorn, and rejection as a result of living by God's standards
- **Necessities:**
  The pressures and responsibilities that are part of daily life
- **Persecutions:**
  Those who stalk us and do all they can to make life miserable for us
- **Distresses:**
  Situations and circumstances that do not turn out as we had hoped or expected, bringing grief and sorrow

The Required Responses

1. Thank God for all things.
"In every thing give thanks: for this is the will of God in Christ Jesus concerning you" (I Thessalonians 5:18).

2. Rejoice in all things.
"Rejoice in the Lord alway: and again I say, Rejoice" (Philippians 4:4).

3. Cry out to God when necessary.
"Call upon me in the day of trouble: I will deliver thee, and thou shalt glorify me" (Psalm 50:15).

4. Do good to all.
"Be not overcome of evil, but overcome evil with good" (Romans 12:21).

To the degree that we pass the test of the Spirit, we will experience the power (*dunamis*) of God's Spirit.

- "Most gladly therefore will I rather glory in my infirmities, that the power of Christ may rest upon me" (II Corinthians 12:9).

- "If ye be reproached for the name of Christ, happy are ye; for the spirit of glory and of God resteth upon you: on their part he is evil spoken of, but on your part he is glorified" (I Peter 4:14).

- "We glory in tribulations also: knowing that tribulation worketh patience; And patience, experience; and experience, hope: And hope maketh not ashamed; because the love of God is shed abroad in our hearts by the Holy Ghost which is given unto us" (Romans 5:3–5).

- We are "heirs of God, and joint-heirs with Christ; if so be that we suffer with him, that we may be also glorified together" (Romans 8:17).

The Power of the Spirit Is . . .

love, joy, peace, longsuffering, gentleness, goodness, faith, meekness, and temperance. (See Galatians 5:22–23.)

- "That Christ may dwell in your hearts by faith; that ye, being rooted and grounded in love, May be able to comprehend with all saints what is the breadth, and length, and depth, and height; And to know the love of Christ, which passeth knowledge, that ye might be filled with all the fulness of God. Now unto him that is able to do exceeding abundantly above all that we ask or think, according to the power that worketh in us" (Ephesians 3:17–20).

21

How to Pass the Tests to Experience the Power of Love

A large group of teenagers was asked, "How many of you have younger brothers and sisters?" Most of them raised their hands. Then they were asked, "How many of you would be overjoyed if they got into your prized possessions and damaged them?" The entire group broke out with an incredulous laugh. Who would have such a foolish response toward the loss of their possessions?

The answer is: first-century Christians. They realized the superior rewards of experiencing the power of God's love. They also understood that such power came through a proper response to trials and tribulations. Therefore, they took the spoiling of their goods with joy. (See Hebrews 10:34.)

Most people make no connection between the trials, irritations, and distresses of daily life and the fact that they are the tests of the Holy Spirit.

Jesus warned His disciples to "Watch and pray, that ye enter not into temptation" (Matthew 26:41). Peter urged New Testament believers, "Be sober, be vigilant; because your adversary the devil, as a roaring lion, walketh about, seeking whom he may devour: Whom resist stedfast in the faith, knowing that the same afflictions are accomplished in your brethren that are in the world" (I Peter 5:8–9). Periodic fasting with prayer will increase our alertness to pass these tests.

1. The Test of Thanking God in All Things

Scripture instructs us: "In every thing give thanks: for this is the will of God in Christ Jesus concerning you" (I Thessalonians 5:18). This instruction means what it says—thank God for everything that happens in your life.

This directive is confirmed in other Scriptures such as Ephesians 5:20: "Giving thanks always for all things unto God and the Father in the name of our Lord Jesus Christ." We can sincerely thank God for every single thing that happens in our lives because of the following points.

1. All things come from the hand of God—even "bad things."

Job understood this important point, and God said of him, "Hast thou considered my servant Job, that there is none like him in the earth, a perfect and an upright man, one that feareth God, and escheweth evil?" (Job 1:8).

As a result of plundering neighbors, lightning, hailstones, and a great wind, Job lost all of his herds, flocks, and children. Because all this was arranged by Satan, Job could have said, "The Lord has given, and Satan has taken away." Instead, he affirmed "the LORD gave, and the LORD hath taken away; blessed be the name of the LORD." (Job 1:21).

When Satan went even further with God's permission and took away Job's health, Job responded, "Shall we receive good at the hand of God, and shall we not receive evil? In all this did not Job sin with his lips" (Job 2:10).

Paul had similar spiritual insight. After praying three times that his thorn in the flesh might be removed from him, he acknowledged that it was indeed a messenger of Satan but that its ultimate purpose was to allow him to experience more of the power of Christ upon his life.

"For this thing I besought the Lord thrice, that it might depart from me. And he said unto me, My grace is sufficient for thee: for my strength is made perfect in weakness. Most gladly therefore will I rather glory in my infirmities, that the power of Christ may rest upon me" (II Corinthians 12:8–9).

Can you imagine the owner of a plumbing company coming out of the store, realizing that his truck, containing many of his tools, was stolen, and exclaiming, "Thank you, God, for allowing my truck to be taken!"? This may sound ridiculous, but if it had not been done, the potential for experiencing the power of God would not have been achieved. What God did in the following seventy-two hours gave the owner reason to thank God for what had happened.

A woman called the owner of the plumbing company and explained that her husband had been a plumber before he died and that she would like to give this owner all of his tools. Then a man called and offered to give even more tools plus hundreds of copper fittings without charge. Thus, after a few days, the owner had his truck returned plus three times as many tools as he had before it was taken.

2. All things are designed for our good—even "bad things."

Romans 8:28 makes this point very clear, "And we know that all things work together for good to them that love God, to them who are the called according to his purpose."

It would have been understandable for Joseph to question the good of being sold as a slave and then imprisoned after being falsely accused. But through Joseph's testimony and the testimonies of many others, we can easily see that God designs all things for the good of His children. Jeremiah 29:11 states: "For I know the thoughts that I think toward you, saith the LORD, thoughts of peace, and not of evil, to give you an expected end."

3. All things produce character in us—especially "bad things."

When we experience loss, we have the opportunity to develop contentment, patience, thankfulness, and meekness. When we are offended, we can learn the qualities of forgiveness, compassion, and understanding.

Scripture states that Jesus learned obedience by the things he suffered and that we are to have His mind in us by yielding all of our rights to Him.

4. All things reveal to us the ways of God.

David said, "It is good for me that I have been afflicted; that I might learn thy statutes." (Psalm 119:71).

Unfortunately, there are many important things in life that we cannot learn without pain, but these things do need to be learned because our ways are just the opposite of God's ways. God affirmed this when He said, "For my thoughts are not your thoughts, neither are your ways my ways, saith the LORD. For as the heavens are higher than the earth, so are my ways higher than your ways, and my thoughts than your thoughts." (Isaiah 55:8–9).

Even in the matter of ending our sinful ways, there is value in physical affliction. "Forasmuch then as Christ hath suffered for us in the flesh, arm yourselves likewise with the same mind: for he that hath suffered in the flesh hath ceased from sin; That he no longer should live the rest of his time in the flesh to the lusts of men, but to the will of God" (I Peter 4:1–2).

2. The Test of Rejoicing in All Things

Thanking God is an act of our wills, but rejoicing is an expression of our spirits. We can thank God and still not be thankful in our emotions; however, we cannot rejoice in the bad things without an attitude of joy in us.

It is important to note that it is possible to be sorrowful and joyful at the same time, because sorrow is a response of our soul or heart, and joyfulness is an expression of our spirit.

The only way to rejoice in something that appears to be damaging is to see the benefits that come from it. So, what are the benefits of the owner's truck being stolen? Here is a starter list:

- A reminder that the truck has been dedicated to God. Therefore, it was really God's truck that had been stolen.
- Motivation to be a better steward of property belonging to God.
- Urgency to pray for the thief who has obvious spiritual needs.
- Confirmation of the vulnerability of possessions and the need to set our affections on things above and not on things on the earth.
- An opportunity to evaluate priorities and consider whether too much time is being spent on business rather than on spiritual matters.

We can also rejoice in the loss of things because if we respond to it properly, we will be given a far greater reward of the power and glory of Christ. This was one of the great points in Paul's teaching. "But what things were gain to me, those I counted loss for Christ. Yea doubtless, and I count all things but loss for the excellency of the knowledge of Christ Jesus my Lord: for whom I have suffered the loss of all things, and do count them but dung, that I may win Christ." (Philippians 3:7–8).

Paul reaffirmed this truth in Romans 8:17–18 "If so be that we suffer with him, that we may be also glorified together. For I reckon that the sufferings of this present time are not worthy to be compared with the glory which shall be revealed in us."

With the power of the Holy Spirit that we are given to properly respond to sufferings, we will be enabled to accomplish far greater things for the Lord during our lifetime. These achievements will have great reward and will last throughout eternity.

Jesus said to His disciples, "Blessed are ye, when men shall revile you, and persecute you, and shall say all manner of evil against you falsely, for my sake. Rejoice, and be exceeding glad: for great is your reward in heaven: for so persecuted they the prophets which were before you" (Matthew 5:11–12).

3. The Test of Knowing and Using Scripture

Every temptation that Satan brought to Jesus in the wilderness was met with just the right Scripture. When Satan tempted Jesus to turn stones into bread, Jesus answered by saying, "It is written, Man shall not live by bread alone, but by every word that proceedeth out of the mouth of God" (Matthew 4:4).

The Greek word translated *word* is not *logos*, but *rhema*. The *rhemas* of Scripture are the passages of the Bible that the Holy Spirit gives to us for personal application.

These *rhemas* will usually stand out to us in our daily reading of God's Word. When a passage has special significance, we should write it out, memorize it, and meditate upon it because the *rhemas* of Scripture make up our shield of faith. It is through the shield of faith that we are able to quench every fiery dart of the wicked one.

4. The Test of Crying Out When Necessary

There are some trials and tribulations that God does not intend for us to endure indefinitely. He wants to deliver us from these; however, deliverance will not come until we cry out.

David was continually crying out for deliverance from his oppressors, and he gives powerful testimonies of God's faithful deliverance. "When I cry unto thee, then shall mine enemies turn back: this I know; for God is for me" (Psalm 56:9). He also stated, "Evening, and morning, and at noon, will I pray, and cry aloud: and he shall hear my voice" (Psalm 55:17).

Jesus also confirmed the importance and effectiveness of crying out for relief from an unjust situation: "There was in a city a judge, which feared not God, neither regarded man: And there was a widow in that city; and she came unto him, saying, Avenge me of mine adversary. And he would not for a while: but afterward he said within himself, Though I fear not God, nor regard man; Yet because this widow troubleth me, I will avenge her, lest by her continual coming she weary me. And the Lord said, Hear what the unjust judge saith. And shall not God avenge his own elect, which cry day and night unto him, though he bear long with them?" (Luke 18:2–7).

Conditions That Hinder Our Cries

1. Not crying with the whole heart

God heard the cries of David, because David cried out with his whole heart. "I cried with my whole heart; hear me, O LORD: I will keep thy statutes" (Psalm 119:145). In contrast to David, the people of Hosea's time did not cry out with their whole hearts. "They have not cried unto me with their heart, when they howled upon their beds: they assemble themselves for corn and wine, and they rebel against me" (Hosea 7:14).

2. Not crying with sincere humility

Humility is an essential quality for crying out, because "God resisteth the proud, but giveth grace unto the humble" (James 4:6). God promises that "he forgetteth not the cry of the humble" (Psalm 9:12).

3. Not crying with a loud voice

If a little baby whimpers, the mother will probably look over to see if anything is wrong, but if the baby screams, the mother will rush over with a readiness to respond. All the words for crying out involve a loud verbal response to a need. David emphasizes this point. "Evening, and morning, and at noon, will I pray, and cry aloud: and he shall hear my voice" (Psalm 55:17). "I cried unto the LORD with my voice; with my voice unto the LORD did I make my supplication" (Psalm 142:1).

Crying out is very effective; however, there are certain conditions that will hinder God from hearing our cry.

4. Not fulfilling past vows

God refuses to listen to the cries of a man who has broken his marriage vow and has not properly repented. "This have ye done again, covering the altar of the LORD with tears, with weeping, and with crying out, insomuch that he regardeth not the offering any more, or receiveth it with good will at your hand. Yet ye say, Wherefore? Because the LORD hath been witness between thee and the wife of thy youth, against whom thou hast dealt treacherously: yet is she thy companion, and the wife of thy covenant. And did not he make one? Yet had he the residue of the spirit. And wherefore one? That he might seek a godly seed. Therefore take heed to your spirit, and let none deal treacherously against the wife of his youth. For the LORD, the God of Israel, saith that he hateth putting away" (Malachi 2:13–16).

5. Not confessing and forsaking sin

Scripture warns that if we regard iniquity in our hearts, the Lord will not hear us. (See Psalm 66:18.) This was clearly demonstrated in God's dealings with Israel.

"The children of Israel cried unto the LORD, saying, We have sinned against thee, both because we have forsaken our God, and also served Baalim. And the LORD said unto the children of Israel, Did not I deliver you from the Egyptians, and from the Amorites, from the children of Ammon, and from the Philistines? The Zidonians also, and the Amalekites, and the Maonites, did oppress you; and ye cried to me, and I delivered you out of their hand. Yet ye have forsaken me, and served other gods: wherefore I will deliver you no more. Go and cry unto the gods which ye have chosen; let them deliver you in the time of your tribulation" (Judges 10:10–14).

6. Not giving to the needs of the poor

God warns that if we fail to hear the cries of the poor, He will not hear our cries. "Whoso stoppeth his ears at the cry of the poor, he also shall cry himself, but shall not be heard" (Proverbs 21:13). Further warnings are given in the following passage:

- "Ye shall not afflict any widow, or fatherless child. If thou afflict them in any wise, and they cry at all unto me, I will surely hear their cry; And my wrath shall wax hot, and I will kill you with the sword; and your wives shall be widows, and your children fatherless" (Exodus 22:22–24).

In addition to being generous to the poor and needy, we are to be just and compassionate to those who work for us. "Thou shalt not oppress an hired servant that is poor and needy, whether he be of thy brethren, or of thy strangers that are in thy land within thy gates: At his day thou shalt give him his hire, neither shall the sun go down upon it; for he is poor, and setteth his heart upon it: lest he cry against thee unto the LORD, and it be sin unto thee" (Deuteronomy 24:14–15).

7. Not removing bitterness

When Hagar developed contemptuous attitudes toward Sarah and a sharp contention developed between them, God instructed Abraham to send Hagar and her son away.

When their water ran out, Hagar put the child under a bush expecting him to die, and she went on further so she would not hear his cries and wept bitter tears. "And God heard the voice of the lad; and the angel of God called to Hagar out of heaven, and said unto her, What aileth thee, Hagar? fear not; for God hath heard the voice of the lad where he is. Arise, lift up the lad, and hold him in thine hand; for I will make him a great nation" (Genesis 21:17–18). It is significant that God does not mention hearing her cries, but only the cries of her son.

5. The Test of Doing Good to All People— Even Our Enemies

"Be not overcome of evil, but overcome evil with good" (Romans 12:21).

There is great benefit in serving others with good works. In fact, we are instructed to "do good unto all men, especially unto them who are of the household of faith" (Galatians 6:10).

The reactions of people against us are often awkward appeals for help. Therefore, Jesus told His disciples, "Love your enemies, bless them that curse you, do good to them that hate you, and pray for them which despitefully use you, and persecute you; That ye may be the children of your Father which is in heaven: for he maketh his sun to rise on the evil and on the good, and sendeth rain on the just and on the unjust." (Matthew 5:44–45).

Actually, all those who are redeemed ought to be zealous to do good works. (See Titus 2:14). It is also with good works that we silence those who falsely accuse us and cause others to glorify God.

The Rewards of Passing the Tests

1. The Power of Genuine Love

This power will make possible the development of every one of the character qualities. We will not be diverted by the love of things or the hurts of offenders, because the things that would ordinarily cause discouragement or bitterness are actually means by which we can win the far greater prize of the power of God's Spirit.

"We glory in tribulations also: knowing that tribulation worketh patience; And patience, experience; and experience, hope: And hope maketh not ashamed; because the love of God is shed abroad in our hearts by the Holy Ghost which is given unto us" (Romans 5:3–5).

2. The Power of Exceeding Joy

By thanking God for trials and finding benefits in them, we begin the act of rejoicing, and the Holy Spirit energizes it with His power (*dunamis*), which turns it into exceeding joy.

"Beloved, think it not strange concerning the fiery trial which is to try you, as though some strange thing happened unto you: But rejoice, inasmuch as ye are partakers of Christ's sufferings; that, when his glory shall be revealed, ye may be glad also with exceeding joy" (I Peter 4:12–13).

3. The Power of God's Glory

God is greatly glorified in the lives of believers who go through tribulations and persecutions. Since glorifying God is the chief purpose of our lives, it is important to remember the relationship between being reproached for God's name and God's being glorified.

"If ye be reproached for the name of Christ, happy are ye; for the spirit of glory and of God resteth upon you: on their part he is evil spoken of, but on your part he is glorified" (I Peter 4:14).

4. The Power of Christ's Life in Us

All character is personified in Christ. Therefore, to have His power in us is to have all we need for character development.

"That Christ may dwell in your hearts by faith; that ye, being rooted and grounded in love, May be able to comprehend with all saints what is the breadth, and length, and depth, and height;

"And to know the love of Christ, which passeth knowledge, that ye might be filled with all the fulness of God. Now unto him that is able to do exceeding abundantly above all that we ask or think, according to the power that worketh in us" (Ephesians 3:17–20).

How Does Character Bring Success?

Success is determined by relationships, and relationships are determined by character.

Vital relationships require getting along with ourselves, with our families, with our life partner, with our children, with our businesses, churches, communities, and most importantly, with God. True success involves proper relationships in all these areas. If a man is successful in business but a failure in his marriage and family, he can not be identified as truly successful.

This book identifies forty-nine character qualities that are expressions of genuine love. When understood and demonstrated, these qualities will produce true success.

Why Is the Quality of Love First?

The goal of our lives is to experience and share with others the love that God demonstrated by sending His Son into the world for our redemption. Every quality is actually a practical expression of the quality of love. Therefore, it is important for us to understand this quality first.

Love
vs. Selfishness

Love is giving to the basic needs of others so that their authorities get the credit, God gets the glory, and we have the joy of eternal rewards.

Definition

The primary Greek words for love are *agapao* and *phileo*. *Agapao* means "to love dearly, to be well pleased." On the other hand, *phileo* refers to a fondness or friendship. (The Greek word *philanthropia* is a "fondness of mankind, benevolence, and love towards man.") The Greek word for *brotherly love* is *philadelphia*, which means "fraternal affection, brotherly love, and kindness."

When Jesus asked Peter if he loved Him, Jesus used the stronger of these words—*agapao*—but Peter responded with the weaker term—*phileo*. "Jesus saith to Simon Peter, Simon, son of Jonas, lovest [*agapao*] thou me more than these? He saith unto him, Yea, Lord; thou knowest that I love [*phileo*] thee. He saith unto him, Feed my lambs.

"He saith to him again the second time, Simon, son of Jonas, lovest [*agapao*] thou me? He saith unto him, Yea, Lord; thou knowest that I love [*phileo*] thee. He saith unto him, Feed my sheep. He saith unto him the third time, Simon, son of Jonas, lovest [*phileo*] thou me? Peter was grieved because he said unto him the third time, Lovest [*phileo*] thou me? And he said unto him, Lord, thou knowest all things; thou knowest that I love [*phileo*] thee" (John 21:15–17).

Jesus then told Peter about the suffering he would experience.

If we respond to suffering with joy and thankfulness, we receive the power of the Holy Spirit with *agape* love. It is through suffering that our love is perfected and deepened. (See II Corinthians 12:9.) Twenty-seven times in the New Testament, the Greek word *agape* is translated "charity."

How Light Explains the True Expression of Love

In John's epistle on love, he explains that "God is light" (I John 1:5) and "God is love" (I John 4:8). The significance of equating light and love is that neither one determines who will benefit from its service. All who come to the light receive its benefits, regardless of their spiritual condition. Similarly, all who come to us should receive the benefit of God's love through us.

God loves everyone in the world so much that He gave His only begotten Son as full payment for our sin, in order that whosoever believes on Him and receives Him will receive the power to become the sons of God and have eternal life. (See John 1:12; 3:16.)

How Genuine Love Is Demonstrated by Giving

Each time Peter stated that he loved Jesus, Jesus told him to give—"Feed my lambs," "Feed my

Genuine love is giving without any expectation of personal gain.

"For God so loved the world, that he gave his only begotten Son, that whosoever believeth in him should not perish, but have everlasting life."
—John 3:16

"Faith, like light, should always be simple and unbending; while love, like warmth, should beam forth on every side, and bend to every necessity of our brethren."
—Luther

"You can give without loving, but you cannot love without giving."
—Amy Carmichael

*L*ove is the only badge of discipleship that the world recognizes.

"By this shall all men know that ye are my disciples, if ye have love one to another." —John 13:35

"The knowledge that God has loved me to the uttermost ...will send me forth into the world to love in the same way." —Oswald Chambers

*N*o sincere seeker of truth can refute the argument of genuine love.

"[Love] is a weakness in which lies our strength." —C. H. Spurgeon

sheep," and "Feed my sheep." (See John 21:15–17.) Our motivation for giving is that we are actually giving to Jesus. "Inasmuch as ye have done it unto one of the least of these my brethren, ye have done it unto me" (Matthew 25:40).

Love is not complete without giving. "God so loved the world, that he gave" (John 3:16). If we see a person in obvious need and say to him, "Be clothed," or "Be warmed," but do not give to his need, "how dwelleth the love of God in him [us]?" (I John 3:17.)

Love will manifest itself in generous giving through good works. If these are done with pure motives and credit is given to others, God will be glorified. Therefore, we are commanded, "Let your light so shine before men, that they may see your good works, and glorify your Father which is in heaven" (Matthew 5:16).

First-century believers had such powerful love that they claimed nothing as their own but sold their goods and gave the money to care for the needs of other believers. (See Acts 4:32–35.)

The Importance of Love

Genuine love is the most important character quality. Every other quality must be motivated by it, or the quality will be empty and of no benefit. "Though I bestow all my goods to feed the poor [kindness, compassion, and generosity], and though I give my body to be burned [sincerity, boldness, and determination], and have not charity, it profiteth me nothing" (I Corinthians 13:3).

Agape love is greater than faith and hope (see I Corinthians 13:13). It is the greatest commandment given by God (see Matthew 22:36–40). It is

expected of a local church and is the badge of a true disciple (see John 13:35). It is one of the primary requests of Jesus in His final prayer for His disciples. (See John 17:23–26.)

God's Description of Love

Because love is so important and there are many distorted ideas of what it is, God defines exactly what it involves in I Corinthians 13.

1. Love suffereth long.

It does not lose heart. It perseveres with patience and bravely endures misfortunes and troubles. It bears offenses and injuries with joy and confidence that a good reward will come from God's hand.

Related qualities: Endurance, patience, forgiveness, joyfulness, faith, loyalty, flexibility

2. Love is kind.

It looks for ways to be useful and acts benevolently. It is easy to be entreated and has the motivation of giving rather than taking. It focuses on people's needs rather than their faults.

Related qualities: Tolerance, generosity, availability, creativity, compassion, sensitivity, initiative, gentleness, alertness

3. Love envieth not.

It does not boil with desires to have that which belongs to others. It is not possessive of what has been entrusted to it. It is content with basic necessities and rich fellowship with the Lord.

Related qualities: Gratefulness, contentment, resourcefulness, thriftiness, security

4. Love vaunteth not itself.

It does not boast of its abilities or its accomplishments. It does not look for ways to promote itself or extol its virtues with rhetorical embellishments.

Related qualities: Sincerity, meekness, deference

5. Love is not puffed up.

It does not cherish exaggerated ideas of its own importance. It does not look down on others with contempt or disdain. It is not proud.

Related qualities: Virtue, humility

6. Love doth not behave itself unseemly.

It does not flaunt itself to attract attention or to stir up sensual desires in others. It does not act indecently or shamefully. It has good manners.

Related qualities: Self-control, discretion, responsibility

7. Love seeketh not her own.

It does not demand its own way. It does not crave things for its own pleasure or profit. It focuses not on itself but on the needs of others. It is willing to lay down its life for the benefit of others.

Related qualities: Hospitality, dependability

8. Love is not easily provoked.

It does not get irritated or exasperated. It conquers anger and wrath. It is not quickly excited to rivalry but rather to helping others succeed.

Related qualities: Honor, cautiousness, punctuality, orderliness

9. Love thinketh no evil.

It guards its heart and mind and brings every thought into captivity to the obedience of Christ. It distinguishes between good and evil and rejects the evil. It does not retain wrong desires or plans and does not harbor hurtful feelings toward others.

Related qualities: Obedience, thoroughness, discernment

10. Love rejoices not in iniquity.

It grieves when evil people are promoted and unjust laws are made. It does not secretly desire to carry out the lusts of the flesh, the lusts of the eyes, or the prideful goals of life.

Related qualities: Justice, decisiveness, determination

11. Love rejoices in the truth.

It delights in God's Law and meditates on it day and night. It dwells upon thoughts that are true, honest, just, pure, lovely, and of a good report. It is eager to share truth with others and rejoices with all good people when truth prevails.

Related qualities: Truthfulness, boldness, persuasiveness, diligence, enthusiasm, attentiveness, wisdom

This kind of love "beareth all things, believeth all things, hopeth all things, endureth all things" (I Corinthians 13:7). It can outlast anything, because love "never faileth." (See I Corinthians 13:8.)

The male **emperor penguin** demonstrates genuine love by standing almost motionless for over two months in below-zero temperatures to provide the warmth necessary to incubate a single egg. During the nesting sequence, he goes up to 120 days without eating.

The sweetest love is that which is neither sought nor deserved.

"God commendeth his love toward us, in that, while we were yet sinners, Christ died for us." —Romans 5:8

The greatest love is the sacrifice of one life for another.

"Greater love hath no man than this, that a man lay down his life for his friends." —John 15:13

*L*ove is enjoying the fellowship of another and showing it by laying aside personal rights.

"Charity [love] . . . seeketh not her own." —I Corinthians 13:4–5

*L*ove is seeing in others what Christ saw in them when He created them.

"Thou art worthy, O Lord, to receive glory and honour and power: for thou hast created all things, and for thy pleasure they are and were created." —Revelation 4:11

"One of the world's worst tragedies is that we allow our hearts to shrink until there is room in them for little beside ourselves."

—A. W. Tozer

How Love Is Developed

The power of genuine love is a reward of being in fellowship with God's Holy Spirit and successfully passing the tests that He designs for our spiritual growth. When a person becomes a believer by faith in the finished work of the Lord Jesus Christ, the Holy Spirit indwells his spirit. Each believer can then ask his Heavenly Father to fill his soul with the Holy Spirit, based on the promise of Luke 11:13: "If ye then, being evil, know how to give good gifts unto your children: how much more shall your heavenly Father give the Holy Spirit to them that ask him?"

The Holy Spirit then takes believers through times of testing. If believers respond with rejoicing and gratefulness, a powerful spirit of love will come upon them.

This sequence is illustrated throughout the New Testament, beginning with the life of Jesus. And being filled with the Spirit (Luke 4:1), the Spirit immediately led Jesus into the wilderness for testing, and He returned—not in the fullness of the Spirit, but in the power of the Spirit. (See Luke 4:1–14.)

In the same way, the Thessalonian believers received the Holy Spirit at their conversion. Then they endured "much affliction, with joy of the Holy Ghost" (I Thessalonians 1:5–6). The result was that their faith grew exceedingly, and their love for each other abounded. (See II Thessalonians 1:3–4.) This is the pattern described by Paul: "We glory in tribulations also: knowing that tribulation worketh patience; And patience, experience; and experience, hope: And hope maketh not ashamed; because the love of God is shed abroad in our hearts by the Holy Ghost which is given unto us" (Romans 5:3–5).

Personal Evaluation

How genuine is your love?

- Do you tend to get discouraged and want to give up when everything seems to go wrong?
- Do you look for ways to be useful and help out wherever you go?
- Do you tend to envy the possessions or opportunities of other people?
- Do you enjoy telling about your achievements more than listening to the accomplishments of others?
- Do you tend to look down on those who do not live by your standards?
- Do you choose your clothing with a motive of drawing attention to yourself?
- Do you know and practice good manners wherever you are?
- Do you tend to want your own way and argue when you do not get it?
- Do you get irritated or exasperated with the character deficiencies of others?
- Do you harbor grudges against those who have hurt you?
- Do you dwell on secret desires to fulfill the lust of the flesh?
- Do you meditate on God's Word day and night and delight to do His will?

Alertness
vs. Carelessness

Alertness is exercising my physical and spiritual senses to recognize the dangers that could diminish the resources entrusted to me.

Definition

Alertness presupposes that there are dangers that threaten to diminish or destroy the resources God has entrusted to us. Therefore, we must exercise extreme care in protecting these resources. The Biblical words *beware* and *vigilance* define the concept of alertness.

- **Beware**—Three Greek words are all translated *beware*. Each one defines a different intensity of alertness. *Blepo* means to give general oversight. *Phulasso* designates a sentry who is carefully guarding those put under his care lest they escape. The third word is *prosecho*. It means "to pay attention to, be cautious about, beware."

- **Vigilance**—*Gregoreuo* means "to take heed lest through remission and indolence some destructive calamity suddenly overtake one." A church leader must be sober and vigilant. (See I Peter 5:8.)

What to Beware of:

- "Beware [*prosecho*] of false prophets, which come to you in sheep's clothing, but inwardly they are ravening wolves" (Matthew 7:15).

- "Beware [*prosecho*] ye of the leaven of the Pharisees, which is hypocrisy" (Luke 12:1).

- "Take heed, and beware [*phulasso*] of covetousness: for a man's life consisteth not in the abundance of the things which he possesseth" (Luke 12:15).

- "Beware [*blepo*] lest any man spoil you through philosophy and vain deceit, after the tradition of men, after the rudiments of the world, and not after Christ" (Colossians 2:8).

- "Beware [*blepo*] of dogs [men with evil minds], beware of evil workers" (Philippians 3:2).

- "Beware [*phulasso*] lest ye also, being led away with the error of the wicked, fall from your own stedfastness" (II Peter 3:17).

What Must We Protect?

- **Our time:** Time is a valuable asset that attracts many robbers. (See Ephesians 5:16.)

- **Our health:** Energy and vitality will be dissipated through immoral living. (See Proverbs 5:11.)

- **Our purity:** Evil men and women prey upon the unsuspecting and defile the strength and wealth of their purity. (See Proverbs 6:26.)

- **Our fellowship with God:** "Your iniquities have separated between you and your God." (See Isaiah 59:2.)

- **Our family and friends:** Beware of whisperers, for they separate chief friends. (See Proverbs 16:28.)

- **Our good name:** "A good name is rather to be chosen than great riches, and loving favour

*A*lertness is the awareness that we are being stalked by a deadly enemy. (See I Peter 5:8.)

Lions hunt in groups called prides. While part of the hunting party hides in the grass, blocking the escape route of their intended victim, other lions frighten the prey, driving it into the path of the concealed hunters. Those who are truly alert recognize both obvious dangers and hidden dangers. (See James 4:7.)

"Set a strong guard about thy outward senses: these are Satan's landing places, especially the eye and the ear." —William Gurnall

*W*hen did flattery disarm a king and cause him to lose all the treasures of his kingdom? (See II Kings 20:12–18.)

"The price of freedom is eternal vigilance." —Thomas Jefferson

The **ring-necked pheasant** survives by fleeing the attacks of predators. It can easily detect approaching danger through its keen senses of sight and hearing.

*T*ime is a limited resource that is extended only by giving the first part back to God.

"Redeeming the time, because the days are evil." —Ephesians 5:16

"I have ever found it, when I have thought the battle was over and the conquest gained, and so let down my watch, the enemy had risen up and done me the greatest injury."

—David Brainerd

rather than silver and gold." (See Proverbs 22:1.)

- **Our money and possessions**: "A gracious woman retaineth honour: and strong men retain riches." (See Proverbs 11:16.)

- **Our eternal rewards**: "Hold that fast which thou hast, that no man take thy crown." (See Revelation 3:11.)

What Is the Basis of Alertness?

Every physical sense has a corresponding spiritual sense. Through our physical senses we can be alert to the physical world, and through our spiritual senses we are able to understand the spiritual world. A mature believer is one who has exercised all his senses to discern between good and evil. (See Hebrews 5:14.)

Physical Senses and Corresponding Spiritual Senses

Sight

Spiritual sight: "Open thou mine eyes, that I may behold wondrous things out of thy law" (Psalm 119:18).

Hearing

Spiritual hearing: "Of whom we have many things to say, and hard to be uttered, seeing ye are dull of hearing" (Hebrews 5:11).

Taste

Spiritual taste: "O taste and see that the LORD is good: blessed is the man that trusteth in him" (Psalm 34:8).

Touch

Spiritual touch: "Which we have heard, which we have seen with our eyes, which we have looked upon, and our hands have handled, of the Word of life" (I John 1:1).

Smell

Spiritual smell: "We are the savour of death unto death; and to the other the savour of life unto life" (II Corinthians 2:16).

How Can We Develop Greater Alertness?

1. Recognize that we are in perpetual warfare.

Since Satan's fall, there has been a war between good and evil. God's goal is to raise up Godly generations and establish righteousness. Satan's goal is to kill, steal, and destroy. (See John 10:10.)

Scripture urges us to be "good soldiers" of Jesus Christ (see II Timothy 2:3). A soldier gives up his personal desires and comforts for the sake of the cause for which he is fighting. As believers, we also are to forsake worldly pleasures so that we can fight the good fight of faith. (See I Timothy 6:12.)

2. Realize that our enemy is a master of deception.

Jesus warned that Satan is a liar and the father of lies (see John 8:44). The Apostle Paul pointed out that Satan is able to disguise himself as an angel of light. "For such are false apostles, deceitful workers, transforming themselves into the apostles of Christ. And no marvel; for Satan himself is transformed into an angel of light" (II Corinthians 11:13–14).

3. Ask God for spiritual understanding.

When Solomon became king, he asked God for keen spiritual senses: "Give therefore thy servant an understanding heart to judge thy people, that I may discern between good and bad" (I Kings 3:9).

Paul prayed that the believers in Ephesus would be aware of their position in Christ and thus live victoriously. "The eyes of your understanding being enlightened; that ye may know what is the hope of his calling, and what the riches of the glory of his inheritance in the saints" (Ephesians 1:18).

4. Understand that life involves cause-and-effect sequences.

Alertness is motivated by the realization that actions have predictable results and that the laws of the harvest apply to all levels of life. Scripture warns us to not be deceived. Whatever we sow, we will also reap. (See Galatians 6:8–9.) We reap *what* we sow, we reap *where* we sow, we reap *more* than we sow, and we reap in a different *season* than we sow.

5. Have a Biblical response to each danger.

- **Be alert to resist**—Our first line of resistance must be to check every thought that comes to our minds. Satan can put evil thoughts into our minds as he did with Peter (see Luke 4:8) and with Ananias and Sapphira (see Acts 5:3). As soon as we recognize that a thought is not from God, we should resist it and bring it into captivity to the obedience of Jesus Christ (see II Corinthians 10:4–5). "Resist the devil, and he will flee from you" (James 4:7).

- **Be alert to avoid**—Danger can come from association with the wrong people and wrong ideas. Paul wrote, "Now I beseech you, brethren, mark them which cause divisions and offenses contrary to the doctrine which ye have learned; and avoid them" (Romans 16:17). "Foolish and unlearned questions avoid, knowing that they do gender strifes" (II Timothy 2:23). "Avoid foolish questions, and genealogies, and contentions, and strivings about the law; for they are unprofitable and vain" (Titus 3:9).

- **Be alert to escape**—When we recognize temptation, we are promised that there is also a way to escape, if we are alert to recognize it. "There hath no temptation taken you but such as is common to man: but God is faithful, who will not suffer you to be tempted above that ye are able; but will with the temptation also make a way to escape, that ye may be able to bear it" (I Corinthians 10:13).

- **Be alert to flee**—When Joseph was confronted with the evil request of Potiphar's wife, he was alert to the danger and fled. Similarly, we are instructed to flee youthful lusts and situations that would lead to fornication. (See II Timothy 2:22, I Corinthians 6:18).

Be Vigilant!

During times in history, prisoners were entrusted to guards whose very lives depended on their ability to exercise vigilance.

If a prisoner escaped, the guards were put to death! Thus, the Philippian jailer drew his sword to kill himself when he thought that Paul and Silas had escaped. (See Acts 16:27.)

> "A thief can steal in a moment, but the watchman must watch all night. Sin can undo in an unguarded second the character which required years to form."
>
> —Charles H. Spurgeon

Personal Evaluation

How alert are you to dangers?

- Do you daily remind yourself that you are in a spiritual war?
- Do you diligently guard your time from detractors?
- Do you confirm with Scripture everything you are taught?
- Do you guard your daily time with the Lord and His Word?
- Do you reject all whisperers and talebearers?
- Do you protect your good name by doing only what is right?
- Do you ask God for daily guidance and find His will?

*B*y considering the opposite of our natural inclinations, we prepare to hear the voice of God.

"As the heavens are higher than the earth, so are my ways higher than your ways, and my thoughts than your thoughts." —Isaiah 55:9

"There is a way that seemeth right unto a man, but the end thereof are the ways of death." —Proverbs 16:25

*T*hose who listen best learn most.

"Attend to my words; incline thine ear unto my sayings." —Proverbs 4:20

"My sheep hear my voice, and I know them, and they follow me." —John 10:27

Attentiveness
vs. Distraction

Attentiveness is giving a "hearing heart" to the people or projects that need our concentration.

Definition

Several Hebrew words carry the meaning of *attentiveness*. The word *azan* is translated "to give ear" and means "to expand . . . to broaden out the ear." The word *shama* describes our attentiveness to God and means "to hear intelligently." *Qashab* describes the attentiveness a son should give to his father's instruction and means "to prick up the ears, i.e. hearken."

The Greek word for *attentive* is *ekkremamai*, which means "to hang upon the lips of a speaker, i.e. to listen closely." This is the word used to describe the attentiveness of the crowds who listened to Jesus teach. (See Luke 19:48.)

What Is Attentiveness?

Attentiveness is an attitude of readiness to do what is true and right. An attentive person maintains good eye contact, sits up straight, is not distracted, takes notes, and clarifies information that is given.

Attentiveness is much deeper than just listening with the ears—it involves a "listening heart." When Solomon was given the opportunity by God to ask for whatever he wanted, he wisely asked for a listening heart. In his prayer, the Hebrew word translated *understanding* can also be rendered *hearing*. "Give . . . thy servant an understanding [*shama*] heart to judge thy people, that I may discern between good and bad" (I Kings 3:9). God gave Solomon his request, and because he asked for a listening heart, God also promised him wisdom, riches, and honor. (I Kings 3:10–13.)

Commands to Be Attentive

The ear is one of the first organs to develop in the womb, and hearing is one of the last senses to cease as death approaches. It is therefore appropriate to develop attentiveness, because many other character qualities are dependent on it. Without attentiveness, we will not even hear the commands of Scripture or the instructions of parents or authorities.

- "A wise man will hear, and will increase learning; and a man of understanding shall attain unto wise counsels" (Proverbs 1:5).

- "If thou wilt diligently hearken to the voice of the LORD thy God, and wilt do that which is right in his sight, and wilt give ear to his commandments, and keep all his statutes, I will put none of these diseases upon thee, which I have brought upon the Egyptians: for I am the LORD that healeth thee" (Exodus 15:26).

- "My sheep hear my voice, and I know them, and they follow me" (John 10:27).

How Attentive Are You . . .

1. To the voice of God and the direction of the Holy Spirit?

God speaks to us through the Scriptures and the prophets of old: "All scripture is given by inspiration of God, and is profitable for doctrine, for reproof, for correction, for instruction in righteousness" (II Timothy 3:16). "As he spake by the mouth of his holy prophets" (Luke 1:70).

God brings our attention to verses that have significance in our lives. These important *rhemas* build faith and bring true success. (See Matthew 4:4, Romans 10:17, John 15:7.)

If we have been too busy for God's Word, then we have been too busy! Set a time and a place that you can use for private appointments with the Lord in His Word.

Personal Evaluation

How attentive are you to the voice of God?

- Do you spend time each day reading God's Word?

- Do you search out the meanings of key words in your reading?

- Do you ask how you can apply the Scriptures to your daily life?

- Do you turn Scripture into personal prayers?

- Do you give attention to verses that have special meaning and application to your life?

- Do you take time to listen to God speak to you as you pray?

2. To the instructions of your father and mother?

If you have not been attentive to your parents, consider the following Scriptures.

- "My son, hear the instruction of thy father, and forsake not the law of thy mother" (Proverbs 1:8).

- "Honour thy father and mother; which is the first commandment with promise; That it may be well with thee, and thou mayest live long on the earth" (Ephesians 6:2–3).

- "The eye that mocketh at his father, and despiseth to obey his mother, the ravens of the valley shall pick it out, and the young eagles shall eat it" (Proverbs 30:17).

- "Hearken unto thy father that begat thee, and despise not thy mother when she is old" (Proverbs 23:22).

Attentiveness to parents (or any other authority) begins with the understanding that God communicates His will to us through those He places over us. When the children of Israel murmured against Moses, God said, "Your murmurings are not against us, but against the LORD" (Exodus 16:8).

Attentiveness springs from an obedient spirit—a prior commitment and desire to do what authorities ask us to do unless it violates Scripture or is not wise. In such cases we should wisely appeal their requests, maintaining a higher commitment to never do evil.

The **white-tailed deer** constantly listens to what takes place around it. It has extremely acute hearing. Even while grazing, it remains attentive to its surroundings and is on the lookout for danger.

When have attentive listeners saved the lives of great leaders?

- A loyal subject saved the life of a king. (See Esther 6.)

- A lad saved the life of a great apostle. (See Acts 23.)

Both listeners received rewards from which we still benefit.

We hear the voice of God more clearly when we are on our faces crying out for wisdom, than when we are on our feet, asking for help.

"Bow down thine ear, and hear the words of the wise, and apply thine heart unto my knowledge."
—Proverbs 22:17

*A*ttentiveness begins by asking God for a "hearing heart."

Listening is more than hearing words. It is also discerning facial expressions, tonal patterns, body language, and most of all, listening to the spirit of a person.

The Latin root of *attentiveness* is *attendere*, meaning "to stretch," as a horse turns its ears forward. A horse indicates its attentiveness by the position of its ears.

"Whosoever would understand what he hears must hasten to put into practice what he has heard."
—Saint Gregory

We can be attentive to parents by offering them respectful and undivided attention. We do this by sitting up straight or standing when they talk, looking at them rather than at other things, nodding when we understand, and asking polite questions if we do not understand.

Giving such honor brings the rewards of God, including a wise example for our own children.

"Hear, ye children, the instruction of a father, and attend to know understanding. For I give you good doctrine, forsake ye not my law. For I was my father's son, tender and only beloved in the sight of my mother. He taught me also, and said unto me, Let thine heart retain my words: keep my commandments, and live. Get wisdom, get understanding: forget it not; neither decline from the words of my mouth" (Proverbs 4:1–5).

Personal Evaluation

How attentive are you to your parents?

- Would your parents say you have an obedient spirit when they give you instructions?

- When your parents call, do you stop what you are doing and go to them quickly?

- When your parents give directions, do you make sure you understand them?

- Do you confirm instruction with the Word of God?

- When making decisions, do you ask yourself what your parents would say?

3. To the counsel of wise advisors?

By walking with wise men we will become wise (see Proverbs 13:20). One effective way to walk with the wise is to read the biographies of great men and women of faith. As Charles Jones stated, "You will be five years from now what you are today except for two things: the books you read and the friends you make."

We should get wisdom as cheaply as we can. Others have paid a high price for it through lessons learned "the hard way" and will usually share their experience if we ask them. "Hear counsel, and receive instruction, that thou mayest be wise in thy latter end" (Proverbs 19:20). "In multitude of counsellors there is safety" (Proverbs 24:6).

When gathering counsel, we must always check it against Scripture and make sure that there are no cautions from the Spirit of God that our consciences override.

Personal Evaluation

How attentive are you to wise counselors?

- Do you surround yourself with wise and mature counselors?

- Do you ask wise people for counsel and for their insight on lessons they have learned?

- Do you read of great Christians regularly?

- Do you carefully search out a matter before making a decision?

Availability
vs. Self-Centeredness

Availability is simplifying our daily needs so we are ready and able to serve those whom God brings to us.

Definition

When Jesus called his disciples, He used the verb *akoloutheo*, which means "to accompany (specifically as a disciple)." He taught them to not be hindered by personal cares and distractions and explained the sacrifices they would make to serve Him: "If any man will come after me, let him deny himself, and take up his cross, and follow me" (Matthew 16:24). The Greek word for *deny* is *aparneomai*, meaning "to forget one's self, lose sight of . . . one's own interests."

Availability Begins by Choosing One Leader

Availability is impossible to achieve if we try to serve more than one leader. "No man can serve two masters: for either he will hate the one, and love the other; or else he will hold to the one, and despise the other" (Matthew 6:24).

Based on this passage, we must choose to serve the Lord. Otherwise, we will serve ourselves by seeking money, popularity, possessions, or other things. Joshua stated, "As for me and my house, we will serve the LORD" (Joshua 24:15).

Availability Is Basic to Discipleship

When Jesus called His disciples, He called them to a life of availability. The whole concept of discipleship is rooted in being available for training and serving. In the days of Jesus, a person who wanted to acquire knowledge from a master teacher would set aside his personal agenda and literally follow the teacher. Because of this practice, these people were called "followers."

This very same practice is carried out in our day as students leave their homes and go to a place of learning to be taught by experienced teachers.

Availability Is Motivated by Being a "Giver" Rather Than a "Taker"

Jesus made it clear to His disciples that they must have the motivation of being givers rather than takers. "Then said Jesus unto his disciples, If any man will come after me, let him deny himself, and take up his cross, and follow me" (Matthew 16:24).

Jesus then explained this paradox: if someone tries to keep his life for his own goals, he will lose it. "For whosoever will save his life shall lose it: and whosoever will lose his life for my sake shall find it" (Matthew 16:25).

A taker often focuses on getting money. Yet Jesus asked, "What is a man profited, if he shall gain the whole world, and lose his own soul?" (Matthew 16:26).

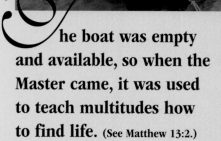

*T*he boat was empty and available, so when the Master came, it was used to teach multitudes how to find life. **(See Matthew 13:2.)**

When we serve God-given authorities as if we are serving the Lord, it is hard to distinguish which voice is calling us. This was the experience of young Samuel. (See I Samuel 3.)

"Put them in mind to be subject to principalities and powers, to obey magistrates, to be ready to every good work." —Titus 3:1

*A*vailability is giving our hearts—not just our hands—to a task.

"I used to ask God to help me. Then I asked if I might help Him. I ended up by asking Him to do His work through me."

—J. Hudson Taylor

*W*e are motivated to be available if we recognize how our tasks accomplish part of a greater objective.

When three bricklayers were asked what they were doing, the first answered, "I am making a living." The second said, "I am building a wall." But the third responded with a smile, "I am building a great cathedral!"

"Let your light so shine before men, that they may see your good works, and glorify your Father which is in heaven." —Matthew 5:16

A **giraffe** travels with a herd and is available to serve its herd by standing guard, providing defense, or watching the young.

Availability Is Based on the Joy of Making Others Successful

True happiness is not in receiving things, but in giving that which will truly benefit the lives of others. Paul praised Timothy for having the quality of availability. "For I have no man likeminded, who will naturally care for your state. For all seek their own, not the things which are Jesus Christ's. But ye know the proof of him, that, as a son with the father, he hath served with me in the gospel" (Philippians 2:20–22).

Jesus is the ultimate example of availability. He lived among people who had needs and served them from early morning until night. He laid down His life that we might have life, and now He makes continual intercession for us. (See Romans 8:34.)

How Can We Develop Availability?

1. By not seeking our own pleasure

The pleasures of the world dissipate time, energy, and assets. Proverbs says, "Give not thy strength unto women, nor thy ways to that which destroyeth kings" (Proverbs 31:3). The futility of seeking our own pleasure is accurately described by the word *amusement*, derived from the root words *a*, meaning "not," and *muser*, meaning "to think."

2. By not seeking great achievements for ourselves

"Seekest thou great things for thyself? seek them not" (Jeremiah 45:5). By seeking our own achievements, we will be distracted from achieving the goals of those whom we serve, and we will tend to use others to serve us and our goals.

3. By developing efficiency in meeting personal needs

The more organized our personal lives and the less we need for ourselves, the more time, energy, and resources we will have for the tasks of those we serve. Paul stated, "I count all things but loss for the excellency of the knowledge of Christ Jesus my Lord: for whom I have suffered the loss of all things, and do count them but dung, that I may win Christ" (Philippians 3:8).

4. By discovering the priorities of those we serve

Availability means knowing when needs occur and which needs should be taken care of first. If we try to decide this for ourselves, we risk making unnecessary sacrifices. "To obey is better than sacrifice" (I Samuel 15:22).

Personal Evaluation

How available are you for service?

- Do you choose to serve God rather than money?

- Do you purpose to be a giver rather than a taker?

- Do you work to make others successful?

- Do you keep your personal responsibilities to a minimum?

- Do you deny yourself distracting pleasures?

- Do you set aside personal ambitions in order to advance the kingdom of God and His righteousness?

Boldness
vs. Fearfulness

Boldness is welcoming any suffering that comes from doing what is right, because it will produce a greater power of love.

Definition

There is rich insight in the Biblical definitions of boldness. Three Greek words translated *bold* each identify a distinct and important aspect of this quality.

1. *Tharrheo*—Boldness in the face of death

2. *Parrhesiazomai*—Boldness to speak the truth

3. *Tolmao*—Boldness to accomplish great things for God

Boldness is the fearless and daring courage to carry out the work God calls us to do. When Joshua was commanded to "be of good courage," he was being told to have boldness—boldness to face death in battle, to speak truth to his own heart and to the nation, and to do great exploits for God.

1. Boldness in the Face of Death

No believer needs to fear death, because of the confidence that to be absent from the body is to be present with the Lord.

Conquering this fear is actually one of the purposes for which Christ died. "That through death he might destroy him that had the power of death, that is, the devil; And deliver them who through fear of death were all their lifetime subject to bondage" (Hebrews 2:14–15).

The Apostle Paul had this type of boldness. He faced beatings, persecutions, and shipwrecks without fear. His secret was the assurance that he was indestructible until his work was done and that death would bring him immediately into the eternal presence of the Lord Whom he served.

Paul stated, "Therefore we are always confident [*tharrheo*], knowing that, whilst we are at home in the body, we are absent from the Lord. . . . We are confident, I say, and willing rather to be absent from the body, and to be present with the Lord" (II Corinthians 5:6–8).

Paul considered the benefits of continuing his ministry on earth or enjoying the rewards of his labors in Heaven. He favored the idea of going to Heaven but knew it would be more beneficial for believers if he continued his ministry on earth. "For to me to live is Christ, and to die is gain. . . . Having a desire to depart, and to be with Christ; which is far better" (Philippians 1:21, 23).

God promised that He will never leave us or forsake us. Therefore, "We may boldly say, The Lord is my helper, and I will not fear what man shall do unto me" (Hebrews 13:5–6).

The most powerful people on the face of the earth are those who have no fear of death.

*T*he righteous are bold as a lion.   —**Proverbs 28:1**

*W*hen did one man's boldness cause empires to fear the Lord?

Daniel came to Babylon as a captive and served four kings. Before he came, he purposed in his heart that he would not defile himself or violate the Law of the Lord. He stood firm, even in a den of lions, causing King Darius to decree, "That in every dominion of my kingdom men tremble and fear before the God of Daniel: for he is the living God" (Daniel 6:26).

"There is nothing more dangerous on this planet than people that are not afraid of dying."   —Josef Tson

"They overcame him by the blood of the Lamb, and by the word of their testimony; and they loved not their lives unto the death."—*Revelation 12:11*

The wolverine illustrates boldness. It is a fearless and tenacious fighter and does not back away from any opponent, even one that is many times its size.

*H*onor is given to those who are bold.

Daniel was bold to speak the truth to King Belshazzar during the drunken feast in which the king used the sacred vessels from God's Temple. After hearing God's judgment upon himself and his kingdom, the king honored Daniel. (See Daniel 5:29.)

**"Dare to be a Daniel,
Dare to stand alone!
Dare to have a purpose firm!
Dare to make it known!"**

—Philip P. Bliss

"Who art thou, that thou shouldest be afraid of a man that shall die, and of the son of man which shall be made as grass; And forgettest the LORD thy maker, that hath stretched forth the heavens, and laid the foundations of the earth." —Isaiah 51:12–13

Personal Evaluation

How bold are you in the face of death?

- Have you purposed to die to self and follow Christ? "If any man will come after me, let him deny himself, and take up his cross daily, and follow me" (Luke 9:23).

- Have you conquered the fear of man by exchanging your reputation for Christ's and choosing to be concerned only that people see Christ in you?

- Have you dedicated your life to fulfill God's calling, and are you determined to make whatever sacrifices God requires?

- What Biblical convictions do you have that you are willing to die for?

- In what specific ways are you dying to self so others can know Christ?

---

2. Boldness to Speak the Truth

Whereas boldness to conquer the fear of death comes through salvation, boldness to speak the truth (*parrhesiazomai* boldness) comes through the prayer of other believers. Even the Apostle Paul requested prayer for such boldness: Pray "for me, that utterance may be given unto me, that I may open my mouth boldly, to make known the mystery of the gospel, For which I am an ambassador in bonds: that therein I may speak boldly, as I ought to speak" (Ephesians 6:19–20).

When the apostles were threatened with harm if they spoke in the name of Jesus, they received boldness through prayer: "And now, Lord, behold their threatenings: and grant unto thy servants, that with all boldness they may speak thy word . . . . And when they had prayed, the place was shaken where they were assembled together; and they were all filled with the Holy Ghost, and they spake the word of God with boldness" (Acts 4:29, 31).

Boldness to speak the truth must begin with a clear conscience toward the Lord and toward others. Nothing stops the freedom of the mouth like the failures of a life. Before Isaiah was commissioned to speak, he was cleansed of his iniquity. (See Isaiah 6:7–9.)

Personal Evaluation

How bold are you in speaking the truth?

- What Christian leaders are you praying for to have boldness to speak the truth?

- Have you asked others to pray that you will have boldness to witness?

- Do you wait for opportunities to witness, or do you make them?

- When people ridicule the Lord, do you defend the truth in a loving way?

- What good treasures are you putting in your heart that will then be spoken by your tongue?

- Have you written out your testimony so that you are prepared to give a ready answer?

3. Boldness to Accomplish Great Things

When a believer has conquered the fear of death and has become bold in speaking the truth, he or she is equipped for *tolmao* boldness. God is able to accomplish mighty things through such a believer. "For the eyes of the LORD run to and fro throughout the whole earth, to shew himself strong in the behalf of them whose heart is perfect toward him" (II Chronicles 16:9).

Doing great exploits for God and His kingdom is the result of knowing God and understanding something of His character and His purposes in the world. "The people that do know their God shall be strong, and do exploits" (Daniel 11:32).

God initiates the boldness to do exploits by giving His people special passages of Scripture that are directly related to what He wants them to accomplish. These passages are *rhemas* and are the basis of faith, for "faith cometh by hearing, and hearing by the word [*rhema*] of God" (Romans 10:17).

As we engraft the *rhemas* of Scripture into our lives and meditate on them, we can claim their fulfillment in bold exploits. "If ye abide in me, and my words [*rhemas*] abide in you, ye shall ask what ye will, and it shall be done unto you. Herein is my Father glorified, that ye bear much fruit; so shall ye be my disciples" (John 15:7–8).

Gideon demonstrated boldness when he pulled down his father's false altar and then led three hundred soldiers against the vast hosts of the enemy's army. David also demonstrated boldness as he went out against Goliath.

The heroes of faith in Hebrews 11 demonstrated *tolmao* boldness. "And what shall I more say? for the time would fail me to tell of Gedeon, and of Barak, and of Samson, and of Jephthae; of David also, and Samuel, and of the prophets: Who through faith subdued kingdoms, wrought righteousness, obtained promises, stopped the mouths of lions, Quenched the violence of fire, escaped the edge of the sword, out of weakness were made strong, waxed valiant in fight, turned to flight the armies of the aliens" (Hebrews 11:32–34).

Personal Evaluation

How bold are you to do exploits for God?

- Is your heart right before the Lord so He can work mightily through you?

- Is it your goal in life to lead as many others as you can to a personal relationship with Jesus Christ and then to disciple them in all the teachings of Christ?

- What special passages of Scripture (*rhemas*) has God given to you, and do you regularly meditate on them? (See Psalm 1.)

- Has God given you a special concern for a certain category of people so that you can meet their needs?

- When you get to the end of your life, what do you want to look back on, of which you can say, "This is what God accomplished through me"?

*F*ear of God will destroy the fear of man.

John Knox was a sixteenth-century reformer. He spoke the truth to his large congregation in Scotland but was arrested for it and chained to the oars of a galley ship.

During long months of pulling on oars, he built not only his physical strength but also strength of fervent prayer. His cry was, "O God! Give me Scotland or I die!"

His life and work for God became so powerful that the Queen of Scotland is quoted as saying, "I fear the prayers of John Knox more than all the assembled armies of Europe."

"Greater is he that is in you, than he that is in the world." —I John 4:4

"We fear men so much, because we fear God so little. One fear cures another. When man's terror scares you, turn your thoughts to the wrath of God."

—William Gurnall

Cautiousness

vs. Rashness

Cautiousness is planning for the success of a venture by following the ways of God rather than my natural inclinations.

*W*aiting on the Lord for guidance forces us to reevaluate priorities and identify the "needful" things of life. (See Luke 10:41–42.)

"But they that wait upon the LORD shall renew their strength; they shall mount up with wings as eagles; they shall run, and not be weary; and they shall walk, and not faint."
—Isaiah 40:31

"Keep thy foot when thou goest to the house of God, and be more ready to hear, than to give the sacrifice of fools: for they consider not that they do evil."
—Ecclesiastes 5:1

"Preparation is not something suddenly accomplished, but a process steadily maintained."
—Oswald Chambers

Definition

Scripture describes the consequences of not using caution when it speaks of the man who is hasty in his words or actions. The Hebrew word *'uwts* is translated as *hasty* and means "to be pressed, confined, or narrow; to insist; to urge." This word is used to describe the man who does not plan, resulting in poverty. (See Proverbs 21:5.) Another Hebrew word, *maher,* is used to warn of speaking rash vows to the Lord and means "quickly; soon; speedily." (See Ecclesiastes 5:2.)

Jesus taught the multitudes to count the cost of following Him, just as a man should count the cost of building a tower in order that he might carry it through successfully and not be mocked by those who stand by. (See Luke 14:25–33.)

What Is Cautiousness?

Cautiousness is recognizing that we have natural inclinations that are opposite to God's ways. These tendencies seem right but lead to destruction and death. "There is a way that seemeth right unto a man, but the end thereof are the ways of death" (Proverbs 16:25). "For my thoughts are not your thoughts, neither are your ways my ways, saith the LORD. For as the heavens are higher than the earth, so are my ways higher than your ways" (Isaiah 55:8–9).

If we act according to our natural tendencies, we will act foolishly and pay a heavy price. "He that trusteth in his own heart is a fool" (Proverbs 28:26). "Lean not unto thine own understanding. In all thy ways acknowledge him, and he shall direct thy paths" (Proverbs 3:6).

When people speak evil of us, it is our natural tendency to speak evil of them. The opposite response of doing good to them is consistent with the teaching of Scripture. "Love your enemies, bless them that curse you, do good to them that hate you, and pray for them which despitefully use you, and persecute you; That ye may be the children of your Father which is in heaven: for he maketh his sun to rise on the evil and on the good, and sendeth rain on the just and on the unjust. For if ye love them which love you, what reward have ye? do not even the publicans the same? And if ye salute your brethren only, what do ye more than others? do not even the publicans so?" (Matthew 5:44–47).

How Does Cautiousness Relate to Iniquity?

Iniquity is simply doing what seems to be right to us. It would seem right, for example, to preach and do many good works, yet if these activities are not motivated and directed by the Spirit of God, they are iniquity.

Jesus said, "Many will say to me in that day, Lord, Lord, have we not prophesied in thy name? and in thy name have cast out devils? and in thy name done many wonderful works? And then will I profess unto them, I never knew you: depart from me, ye that work iniquity" (Matthew 7:22–23).

Acting apart from the life and power of God is iniquity. "All we like sheep have gone astray; we have turned every one to his own way; and the LORD hath laid on him the iniquity of us all" (Isaiah 53:6).

There was no iniquity in Jesus Christ because of His divine nature. He did nothing of His own will but only what His Heavenly Father directed Him to do. Jesus said, "I seek not mine own will, but the will of the Father which hath sent me" (John 5:30). A cautious person will also seek God's will for each situation.

How Do We Develop Cautiousness?

1. Acknowledge that our natural inclinations are often wrong, and cry out to God for His wisdom.

"Call unto me, and I will answer thee, and shew thee great and mighty things" (Jeremiah 33:3). "Call upon me in the day of trouble: I will deliver thee, and thou shalt glorify me" (Psalm 50:15). "Whosoever shall call upon the name of the Lord shall be saved" (Romans 10:13).

"If thou criest after knowledge, and liftest up thy voice for understanding; If thou seekest her as silver, and searchest for her as for hid treasures; Then shalt thou understand the fear of the LORD, and find the knowledge of God"

(Proverbs 2:3–5). "If any of you lack wisdom, let him ask of God, that giveth to all men liberally, and upbraideth not; and it shall be given him" (James 1:5).

2. Learn from the experiences of others.

The biographies that God wrote in the Bible are filled with rich counsel on how to do things God's way—and what happens when God's ways are rejected. "The testimony of the LORD is sure, making wise the simple" (Psalm 19:7).

King David thought that bringing the holy Ark of God to his capital city of Jerusalem would be a good idea. He organized a huge procession and began the venture. However, he failed to exercise the cautiousness of checking Scripture.

The Ark was sacred, and God had given special instructions on how it should be moved. The Philistines, who captured the Ark, put it on an ox-drawn cart to return it to Israel. David thought he could use the same method; however, his idea ended in death.

When the cart was driven on uneven ground, it tipped, and the Ark began to slide off. A priest reached out to steady it and instantly died, because no one was to touch the Ark. (See II Samuel 6:3–8.)

Later, David exercised cautiousness by following God's regulations for carrying the Ark. Two poles were put through the rings on opposite sides of the Ark, and it was carried on the shoulders of four priests. The Ark was safely delivered to Jerusalem, and all the people rejoiced. (See I Chronicles 15:11–15 and Exodus 25:10–14.)

Cautious people are those who have conquered the urge to speak before they get all the facts.

"Wherefore, my beloved brethren, let every man be swift to hear, slow to speak, slow to wrath." —James 1:19

"The thoughts of the diligent tend only to plenteousness; but of every one that is hasty only to want." —Proverbs 21:5

The **prairie dog** builds an earthen dike around the entrance of its burrow to prevent flash floods from destroying its home.

How cautious are you?

- Do you seek God's will for every situation?
- Do you ask for counsel from wise and experienced people?
- Do you learn from the mistakes of others?
- Do you think about what you are going to say before you speak?
- Do you consider the right timing for doing a good deed?
- Do you realize how your actions will affect others?
- Do you plan ahead and count the cost, especially for big endeavors?

*A*llow time to test the credibility of your course and the stability of your steps.

"Also, that the soul be without knowledge, it is not good; and he that hasteth with his feet sinneth."

3. Consider the opposite action of natural inclinations.

Since our natural inclinations are often opposite God's universal principles, it may be helpful to ask, "What would I naturally do?" and then see if the opposite action is confirmed by Scripture.

4. Seek out wise counsel.

A caution sign on the highway usually means that others have not exercised sufficient cautiousness in that spot and have paid a costly price for it. A cautious driver will slow down, make sure he is following all the rules of the road, and be extra alert to danger.

There are similar "caution signs" on the highway of life. Others have failed to heed them and have painful memories to share. They will usually be willing to tell their stories to others who want to avoid the consequences they experienced. We would be wise to listen to their mistakes. Get experience as inexpensively as you can—others have paid a high price for it.

Natural Inclinations	God's Ways
1. Reject unchangeable physical or family features.	Accept these as God's means of developing inward character, and thank Him for them.
2. React to parents and others in authority who do not give us what we want.	Recognize that God has established all human authorities to praise those who do good and punish those who do evil.
3. Cover our secret sins and failures so others will not think less of us.	Humble ourselves by confessing faults, asking forgiveness, and making restitution where appropriate. "Before honor is humility" (Proverbs 15:33), but he that covers his sin will not prosper (see Proverbs 28:13).
4. Reject our offenders and eagerly hope that they will be damaged.	Forgive those who offend us, and look for ways to benefit their lives.
5. Claim ownership of our possessions and use them for our own pleasure.	Dedicate our possessions to God, and use them to advance His kingdom.
6. Reprove those who fail to respect our personal rights.	Yield our rights to God, and thank Him for whatever happens beyond our control.
7. Enjoy the pleasures of sensuality and lust.	Dedicate our bodies to God as "living sacrifices," and daily yield our members to Him.
8. Desire to be rich so we will have security, nice possessions, and the praise of others.	Purpose to be a "giver" rather than a "taker," and learn how to serve others to make them successful.

Compassion
vs. Indifference

Compassion is responding to a deep need with a longing to do whatever is necessary to meet it.

Definition

The phrase "bowels of compassion" comes from the Greek word *splagchnon*. It means "a yearning of our inward emotions, with a tender love and affection." To be "moved with compassion" describes Jesus' response to the deep needs He saw. The Hebrew word *racham* means "to have tender affection; have mercy; love deeply." It is used to describe the tender love that a father and mother have for their children and the mercy that God shows to His people.

Another Greek word for *compassion* is *eleeo*. The wicked servant who was forgiven much had no compassion [*eleeo*] for the one who owed him little. It is from this word that we get the term *eleemosynary*, which describes the benevolent giving of humanitarian aid. Other concepts that describe compassion are "to have pity, to spare from destruction, and to show mercy."

Compassion Is Stirred by an Urgent Need for Help

- **Pharaoh's daughter had compassion on Moses as a baby**— "When she had opened it [the basket], she saw the child: and, behold, the babe wept. And she had compassion on him" (Exodus 2:6).

- **Jesus had compassion on a grieving widow**—When Jesus saw a widow whose only son was being carried to his burial, "he had compassion on her, and said unto her, Weep not" (Luke 7:13), and He raised her son from the dead.

- **The Good Samaritan had compassion on a wounded traveler**—"A certain man went down from Jerusalem to Jericho, and fell among thieves, which stripped him of his raiment, and wounded him, and departed, leaving him half dead. . . . A certain Samaritan, as he journeyed, came where he was: and when he saw him, he had compassion on him" (Luke 10:30, 33).

Compassion Results From Discerning a Deep Need

- **Jesus saw the spiritual needs of the multitudes and had compassion**—"When he saw the multitudes, he was moved with compassion on them, because they fainted, and were scattered abroad, as sheep having no shepherd. Then saith he unto his disciples, The harvest truly is plenteous, but the labourers are few; Pray ye therefore the Lord of the harvest, that he will send forth labourers" (Matthew 9:36–38).

- **Jesus saw the physical needs of the multitude and gave healing**

Some great people make others feel small, but the greatest people of all make others feel tall.

"But whoso hath this world's good, and seeth his brother have need, and shutteth up his bowels of compassion from him, how dwelleth the love of God in him?" —I John 3:17

Sympathy—feeling sorry for people who are hurting

Empathy—feeling the pain with hurting people

Compassion—doing something about the pain

Three men saw a wounded traveler by the side of the road. The first one must have felt sympathy as he passed by. The second indicated empathy as he came over and looked at him, but the third had compassion as he stopped and helped him. He was the Good Samaritan.
—See Luke 10:30–37.

A herd of **zebra** will slow its pace when one member is injured so it can stay together while the wounded member recovers.

*O*ne reason for pain is to help us have compassion on others with similar hurts.

The cries of a baby caused the king's daughter to have compassion, and the cries of a nation caused the King of Kings to have compassion. Then God used the baby who received compassion to give compassion. (See Exodus 2:6, 23–25; 3:9–10.)

"Blessed be God . . . Who comforteth us in all our tribulation, that we may be able to comfort them which are in any trouble, by the comfort wherewith we ourselves are comforted of God. For as the sufferings of Christ abound in us, so our consolation also aboundeth by Christ." —II Corinthians 1:3–5

and food—"Jesus went forth, and saw a great multitude, and was moved with compassion toward them, and he healed their sick. . . . He commanded the multitude to sit down on the grass, and took the five loaves, and the two fishes. . . . And they did all eat, and were filled" (Matthew 14:14, 19–20).

- **Jesus saw the leadership needs of the multitudes and had compassion**—"And Jesus, when he came out, saw much people, and was moved with compassion toward them, because they were as sheep not having a shepherd: and he began to teach them many things" (Mark 6:34).

Compassion Is Activated by Humble Pleas for Help

- **The hopelessly indebted servant begged for patience**—"The servant therefore fell down, and worshipped him, saying, Lord, have patience with me, and I will pay thee all. Then the lord of that servant was moved with compassion, and loosed him, and forgave him the debt" (Matthew 18:26–27).

- **Two blind men cried out for healing**—"And, behold, two blind men sitting by the way side, when they heard that Jesus passed by, cried out, saying, Have mercy on us, O Lord, thou Son of David. . . . So Jesus had compassion on them, and touched their eyes: and immediately their eyes received sight, and they followed him" (Matthew 20:30, 34).

- **A leper knelt and appealed for healing**—"There came a leper to him, beseeching him, and kneeling down to him, and saying

unto him, If thou wilt, thou canst make me clean. And Jesus, moved with compassion, put forth his hand, and touched him, and saith unto him, I will; be thou clean" (Mark 1:40–41).

- **The father of a boy with an unclean spirit cried out for help, with tears**—"Straightway the father of the child cried out, and said with tears, Lord, I believe; help thou mine unbelief. When Jesus saw that the people came running together, he rebuked the foul spirit, saying unto him, Thou dumb and deaf spirit, I charge thee, come out of him, and enter no more into him" (Mark 9:24–25).

- **The Prodigal Son repented and pled for mercy**—"He arose, and came to his father. But when he was yet a great way off, his father saw him, and had compassion, and ran, and fell on his neck, and kissed him" (Luke 15:20).

Compassion Is a Normal Response to an Urgent Need

- **A cry for help indicates humility and dependence**—Most people are reluctant to acknowledge a personal need or ask for help. Thus, a cry for help is humbling and acknowledges a personal inability and inadequacy to meet an urgent need. "God resisteth the proud, but giveth grace unto the humble" (James 4:6).

- **Refusing to meet a need requires us to "shut up" our "bowels of compassion"**—"Whoso hath this world's good, and seeth his brother have need, and shutteth up his bowels of compassion from him, how dwelleth the love of God in him?" (I John 3:17).

- **Wealthy people are urged to distribute to the needy**—"Charge them that are rich in this world, that they be not high-minded, nor trust in uncertain riches, but in the living God, who giveth us richly all things to enjoy; That they do good, that they be rich in good works, ready to distribute" (I Timothy 6:17–18).

Compassion Presupposes an Ability to Meet Needs

- Jesus drew from the power of His divine nature to feed the multitude.
- The Good Samaritan drew from his own resources to provide healing.
- We are to draw from the resources that God has entrusted to us to meet the needs of others. "God is able to make all grace abound toward you; that ye, always having all sufficiency in all things, may abound to every good work" (II Corinthians 9:8). "Be kindly affectioned one to another . . . Distributing to the necessity of saints" (Romans 12:10, 13). "Give, and it shall be given unto you" (Luke 6:38).

Commands to be Compassionate

The character quality of compassion is not a suggestion for those who would follow Christ, but rather a command.

- **Have compassion one of another**—"Finally, be ye all of one mind, having compassion one of another, love as brethren, be

pitiful, be courteous: Not rendering evil for evil, or railing for railing: but contrariwise blessing; knowing that ye are thereunto called, that ye should inherit a blessing" (I Peter 3:8–9).

- **Put on bowels of mercies, kindness**—"Put on therefore, as the elect of God, holy and beloved, bowels of mercies, kindness, humbleness of mind, meekness, longsuffering; Forbearing one another, and forgiving one another, if any man have a quarrel against any: even as Christ forgave you, so also do ye" (Colossians 3:12–13).

- **Have compassion, making a difference**—"Keep yourselves in the love of God, looking for the mercy of our Lord Jesus Christ unto eternal life. And of some have compassion, making a difference: And others save with fear, pulling them out of the fire; hating even the garment spotted by the flesh" (Jude 21–23).

How to Develop a Compassionate Heart

1. Focus on our great debt to God.

It is all too easy to shut up our bowels of compassion to those who have offended us, yet our attitude should be totally different when we realize the huge debt we have toward God.

The wicked servant who was forgiven a huge debt did not have the same kind of compassion on one who owed him a small debt, because he himself was not humble enough to plead for mercy—he asked only for an extension of time. Thus, he did not appreciate the compassionate mercy shown to him, nor could he show similar

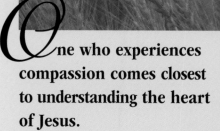

One who experiences compassion comes closest to understanding the heart of Jesus.

Christ's greatest concern was the spiritual state of the lost.

"For the Son of man is come to seek and to save that which was lost."
—Luke 19:10

"Who gave himself for us, that he might redeem us from all iniquity."
—Titus 2:14

"He was wounded for our transgressions . . . and with his stripes we are healed."
—Isaiah 53:5

"But when he saw the multitudes, he was moved with compassion. . . . Then saith he unto his disciples, The harvest truly is plenteous, but the labourers are few; Pray ye therefore the Lord of the harvest, that he will send forth labourers into his harvest."
—Matthew 9:36–38

"We will never know by experience God's richest blessings of comfort and compassion toward others until we ourselves have had trials."
—T. J. Bach

"Finally, be ye all of one mind, having **compassion** *one of another, love as brethren, be pitiful, be courteous: Not rendering evil for evil, or railing for railing: but contrariwise blessing; knowing that ye are thereunto called, that ye should inherit a blessing."*   —I Peter 3:8–9

Personal Evaluation

How compassionate are you?

- Are you "moved to compassion" when you see a group of people in need of Christ?

- Do you pray that God will send forth laborers into His harvest?

- When a neighbor has a need, do you say, "Let me know if I can help," hoping he will not call on you? Or do you find a way to show compassion?

- When you see a disabled person of another race, do you provide practical help?

- Do you have funds or skills that are available to help those who have a need?

- Who was the last person who asked you for help, and how did you help him?

mercy to one who also asked him for an extension of time.

"Therefore is the kingdom of heaven likened unto a certain king, which would take account of his servants. And when he had begun to reckon, one was brought unto him, which owed him ten thousand talents. But forasmuch as he had not to pay, his lord commanded him to be sold, and his wife, and children, and all that he had, and payment to be made. The servant therefore fell down, and worshipped him, saying, Lord, have patience with me, and I will pay thee all. Then the lord of that servant was moved with compassion, and loosed him, and forgave him the debt.

"But the same servant went out, and found one of his fellowservants, which owed him an hundred pence: and he laid hands on him, and took him by the throat, saying, Pay me that thou owest. And his fellow-servant fell down at his feet, and besought him, saying, Have patience with me, and I will pay thee all. And he would not: but went and cast him into prison, till he should pay the debt.

"So when his fellow-servants saw what was done, they were very sorry, and came and told unto their lord all that was done. Then his lord, after that he had called him, said unto him, O thou wicked servant, I forgave thee all that debt, because thou desiredst me: Shouldest not thou also have had compassion on thy fellow-servant, even as I had pity on thee? And his lord was wroth, and delivered him to the tormentors, till he should pay all that was due unto him" (Matthew 18:23–34).

2. Enlarge your heart with a prayer list.

The larger our hearts, the more compassion we will have.

David asked the Lord to enlarge his heart. (See Psalm 119:32.) Paul urged the Corinthian believers to enlarge their hearts toward each other and toward him in the same way that his heart was enlarged toward them. (See II Corinthians 6:1–13.)

One of the obvious ways that Paul enlarged his heart for compassion was to have a detailed and extensive prayer list. (See Philippians 1:4.) He carried the daily responsibility of all the churches and prayed for many of the believers by name. (See II Corinthians 11:28.)

3. Turn personal suffering into compassion for others.

All believers are called to experience suffering. "For even hereunto were ye called: because Christ also suffered for us, leaving us an example, that ye should follow his steps" (I Peter 2:21). One of the purposes for suffering is to learn the compassion of Christ. By understanding how others feel when they go through suffering, we can give them the comfort we receive from the Lord. "God comforteth us in all our tribulation, that we may be able to comfort them which are in any trouble, by the comfort wherewith we ourselves are comforted of God" (II Corinthians 1:4).

4. Look for ways to do good to all people.

Compassion is a practical expression of genuine love, and all believers are commanded to have love toward each other and toward others. Not only is love the credential of being a disciple, but it is also the means by which we fulfill the instruction of Galatians 6:10: "Do good unto all men, especially unto them who are of the household of faith."

Contentment
vs. Covetousness

Contentment is realizing that God has already provided everything I need for my present and future happiness.

Definition

In Hebrew, the word *ya'al* means "to show willingness; to undertake; to agree to or accept." This word is used to describe a person who is resolved to do something or let something be, such as the Levite who agreed to dwell with Micah. "Micah said unto him, Dwell with me . . . . And the Levite was content to dwell with the man" (Judges 17:10–11).

In the New Testament, the words *content* and *contentment* are translated from *arkeo*, which means "to be satisfied; to be strong," and *autarkeia*, which means "to need no aid or support; sufficiency of the necessities of life."

Contentment comes as we realize that God is all we really need and He will never leave us. We can be satisfied in Him, knowing that He is the Supplier of all our physical and spiritual needs. "Be content with such things as ye have: for he hath said, I will never leave thee, nor forsake thee" (Hebrews 13:5).

Contentment Is Contrary to Human Nature and Must Be Learned

We long for a better environment in which to live, assuming that with it we will achieve contentment. Yet Adam and Eve had the perfect environment, and they were not content in it. They had

perfect health, a perfect marriage, a perfect garden, and daily fellowship with God Himself, yet they soon believed the lie that God had not provided everything they needed for their present and future happiness.

If Adam and Eve were not content in the Garden of Eden, what hope is there for the rest of us, apart from the spiritual insight that comes from God? May we, with Paul, be able to say, "Not that I speak in respect of want: for I have learned, in whatsoever state I am, therewith to be content" (Philippians 4:11).

Contentment Begins by Knowing the Purpose of Life

"The chief end of man is to know God and to enjoy him forever" (Westminster Shorter Catechism). Man was created with a God-sized vacuum, and He is the only One Who can fill that void. The Apostle Paul's ultimate aim was to "know him [Christ], and the power of his resurrection, and the fellowship of his sufferings, being made conformable unto his death" (Philippians 3:10).

Contentment Requires Distinguishing Between Needs and Wants

There are few things in life that are really necessary. In fact,

The secret of contentment is enjoying the presence of the Lord.

"Thou wilt shew me the path of life: in thy presence is fulness of joy; at thy right hand there are pleasures for evermore." —Psalm 16:11

The alternative to contentment is boredom with worldly possessions.

"He said unto them, Take heed, and beware of covetousness: for a man's life consisteth not in the abundance of the things which he possesseth." —Luke 12:15

"It is not how much we have, but how much we enjoy, that makes happiness."
—C. H. Spurgeon

$\mathcal{I}$dolatry is trusting people or possessions to do for me what only God can do.

"My God shall supply all your need according to his riches in glory by Christ Jesus." —Philippians 4:19

"If I am not satisfied with what I have, I will never be satisfied with what I want."

—Ralph Guthrie

"For I have learned, in whatsoever state I am, therewith to be content."

—Philippians 4:11

"Next to faith, this is the highest art: to be content in the calling in which God has placed you." —Martin Luther

God identified just two: food and clothing. "And having food and raiment let us be therewith content" (I Timothy 6:8). If we are not content with the basics of food and clothing, we will never be content, no matter how many things we obtain.

God has promised to provide for our needs; however, He has not assured us that we will get all our wants. We have a tendency to spend our resources on wants and then worry about our needs. Jesus warned about such concern. "Therefore take no thought, saying, What shall we eat? or, What shall we drink? or, Wherewithal shall we be clothed? (For after all these things do the Gentiles seek:) for your heavenly Father knoweth that ye have need of all these things. But seek ye first the kingdom of God, and his righteousness; and all these things shall be added unto you" (Matthew 6:31–33).

Contentment Is Based on a Recognition of Mutual Need

One of the great mysteries and wonders of life is that God has a need for each one of us. He desires our fellowship, and He needs our bodies to be the temple of His Holy Spirit. He needs the members of our bodies to be the instruments of righteousness to do His will, because He chooses to work through believers.

In return, God created us to have a daily need for Him. He did not create us to survive on one meal a month but on daily food, and He taught us to pray, "Give us this day our daily bread" (Matthew 6:11). He also pointed out that "man shall not live by bread

alone, but by every word that proceedeth out of the mouth of God" (Matthew 4:4).

Discontentment Begins by Desiring Self-Sufficiency

When either partner in a marriage becomes self-sufficient, the love relationship is damaged, because joy and grace come from giving and receiving. The temptation of Adam and Eve was not simply to taste some forbidden fruit but to be self-sufficient and no longer need God. The subtle serpent told them that if they ate the fruit, they would "be as gods" and be able to decide for themselves good and evil (see Genesis 3:1–6).

Discontentment Leads to Covetousness

When a brother complained about not receiving his fair share of an inheritance, Jesus said, "Take heed, and beware of covetousness: for a man's life consisteth not in the abundance of the things which he possesseth" (Luke 12:15).

Covetousness Produces Idolatry

If we desire what God has not given to us but what He has given to others, we are guilty of coveting. This is a violation of the tenth commandment: "Thou shalt not covet thy neighbour's house, thou shalt not covet thy neighbour's wife, nor his manservant, nor his maidservant, nor his ox, nor his ass, nor any thing that is thy neighbour's" (Exodus 20:17).

When we expect from possessions or people what only God

can give, we turn them into idols and become guilty of idolatry. For example, if we expect security from money, we make money an idol, because only God can give security. Likewise, if we expect fulfillment from wealth or expensive possessions, we make them idols. The same is true if we look to food or diets alone for health.

Contentment Is Achieved by Exchanging Things for More of Christ

Someone has wisely observed that Jesus is all we need, but we will not know it until He is all we have. Paul understood this truth by exchanging things for more of Christ. "Yea doubtless, and I count all things but loss for the excellency of the knowledge of Christ Jesus my Lord: for whom I have suffered the loss of all things, and do count them but dung, that I may win Christ" (Philippians 3:8).

In one sense, life is a continual exchange. We exchange time on the job for money. We then exchange money for food, and we exchange food for strength. A wise person will exchange things of lesser value for things of greater value. Jim Elliot said, "He is no fool, who gives what he cannot keep, to gain what he cannot lose."

Contentment Allows Us to Gain Things of Greater Value

Contentment is setting our affections on eternal treasures rather than on temporal possessions. It is experiencing the qualities of Godliness without the distraction of earthly cares. Jesus warned about the conflict between temporal things and eternal riches when He spoke of the seed falling into different types of soil: "He also that received seed among the thorns is he that heareth the word; and the care of this world, and the deceitfulness of riches, choke the word, and he becometh unfruitful" (Matthew 13:22).

Personal Evaluation

How content are you?

- In what specific ways do you enjoy the presence of the Lord?

- How much time do you spend enjoying your family?

- Are you making practical use of the possessions that have been entrusted to you?

- Have you set your affections on getting things that you think will make your life happier?

- Do you grieve or become bitter when your possessions are damaged or stolen?

- When damage comes to your life, possessions, or family, do you have the response of Job? "The LORD gave, and the LORD hath taken away; blessed be the name of the LORD" (Job 1:21).

- Do you rejoice in the wealth of things that money cannot buy—such as health, freedom, a good name, a clear conscience, and eternal salvation—more than temporal possessions?

- Do you believe that God has given you all you need?

The more I release earthly possessions, the more I can grasp eternal treasures.

"For we brought nothing into this world, and it is certain we can carry nothing out." —I Timothy 6:7

"Discontentment makes rich men poor while contentment makes poor men rich."

—Benjamin Franklin

The **deer mouse** displays contentment in its ability to make its home almost anywhere, making itself comfortable with whatever is available.

reativity comes by considering how to do an old task from an entirely new perspective.

Questions for a new Perspective

- What is the goal or purpose of this task?
- What steps are not absolutely necessary?
- How could necessary steps be carried out more efficiently?
- Could a machine be designed to do part or all of this job?
- Is there a parallel to this procedure in the world of nature?

reativity is the result of concentrating on a need and asking many questions about a solution.

"The more obstacles you have, the more opportunities there are for God to do something." —Clarence W. Jones

Creativity
vs. Underachievement

Creativity is cultivating wise thoughts, prudent words, and skillful actions to carry out God's will.

Definition

The Hebrew word for *create* is *bara*. It means "to shape; to form; to fashion." It was used to define God's creation of man in Genesis 1:27. A similar word— *yatsar*—was used in Genesis 2:7 when God *formed* man from the dust of the ground. Closely related to *yatsar* is *yetser*, which describes the action of a potter forming a vessel for a particular purpose. (See Isaiah 29:16.) The wisdom and understanding of the Creator is expressed and demonstrated in that which He creates.

Creativity is used for making not only *things* but also *plans*. Thus, the following two words amplify the quality of creativity:

- **Cunning**—This word combines skill, inventiveness, and cleverness with creativity. "Esau was a cunning hunter" (Genesis 25:27), David was "a cunning player on an harp" (I Samuel 16:16), and Daniel was "cunning in knowledge, and understanding science" (Daniel 1:4).

- **Subtilty**—Subtilty is the ability to strategize to accomplish a goal. It is using discretion and prudence in working out a plan. The Proverbs are written "to give subtilty to the simple, to the young man knowledge and discretion" (Proverbs 1:4).

Why Is Creativity Important?

Creativity determines the success we will achieve during our lifetime. Success is fulfilling the purposes for which God made us. To the degree that we are creative, we will fulfill those purposes. God the Creator made us in His own image and gave us the capacity to creatively carry out the good works He purposed to do through us. "For we are his workmanship, created in Christ Jesus unto good works, which God hath before ordained that we should walk in them" (Ephesians 2:10).

What Is the Purpose of Creativity?

The foundation of every character quality is genuine love, and one of the best ways to express love is through good works. Creativity is necessary to effectively carry out good works. The great importance of good works is indicated by the many Biblical references to them.

- "Be not overcome of evil, but overcome evil with **good**" (Romans 12:21).

- "And God is able to make all grace abound toward you; that ye, always having all sufficiency in all things, may abound to every **good work**" (II Corinthians 9:8).

- "As we have therefore opportunity, let us do **good** unto all men, especially unto them who are of the household of faith" (Galatians 6:10).

- "That ye might walk worthy of the Lord unto all pleasing, being fruitful in every **good work**, and increasing in the knowledge of God" (Colossians 1:10).

- A widow is to be supported by the Church if she is "well reported of for **good works**; if she have brought up children, if she have lodged strangers, if she have washed the saints' feet, if she have relieved the afflicted, if she have diligently followed every **good work**" (I Timothy 5:10).

- Rich believers are instructed to "do **good**, that they be rich in good works, ready to distribute, willing to communicate" (I Timothy 6:18).

- "If a man therefore purge himself from these, he shall be a vessel unto honour, sanctified, and meet for the master's use, and prepared unto every **good work**" (II Timothy 2:21).

- "In all things shewing thyself a pattern of **good works**" (Titus 2:7).

- "Who gave himself for us, that he might redeem us from all iniquity, and purify unto himself a peculiar people, zealous of **good works**" (Titus 2:14).

- "Put them in mind to be subject to principalities and powers, to obey magistrates, to be ready to every **good work**" (Titus 3:1).

- "This is a faithful saying, and these things I will that thou affirm constantly, that they which have believed in God might be careful to maintain **good works**" (Titus 3:8).

- "And let ours also learn to maintain **good works** for necessary uses, that they be not unfruitful" (Titus 3:14).

- "And let us consider one another to provoke unto love and to **good works**" (Hebrews 10:24).

- "Make you perfect in every **good work** to do his will, working in you that which is well-pleasing in his sight, through Jesus Christ; to whom be glory for ever and ever. Amen" (Hebrews 13:21).

- "Having your conversation honest among the Gentiles: that, whereas they speak against you as evildoers, they may by your **good works**, which they shall behold, glorify God in the day of visitation" (I Peter 2:12).

What Activates Creativity?

Creativity is activated by thoughts. Before God created the world, He determined in the counsel of His will that He would create man, provide a Redeemer, and establish good works for believers to follow. (See I Peter 1:19–20, Ephesians 1:4, Titus 2, and Ephesians 2:10.) If our thoughts are based on the Word of God, our creativity will be for good purposes. If our thoughts are not based on Scripture, our creativity will produce selfish or evil results.

Creativity is energized when thoughts are expressed in words. After God conceived creation in His mind, He spoke the words, and it came about. "God said, Let there be light," (Genesis 1:3) and "God said, Let us make man in our image" (Genesis 1:26). The power of words in the process of creativity explains why God warns that every word must be carefully chosen before spoken. "Death and life are in the power of the tongue: and they that love it shall eat the fruit thereof" (Proverbs 18:21).

The **raccoon** demonstrates creativity by opening locked doors and sealed containers.

*W*e are motivated to be creative when we are asked to carry out a task that is beyond our resources.

"When you do the common things of life in an uncommon way, you will command the attention of the world."
—George Washington Carver

*C*reativity can be used for good or bad—it is most often used to avoid unpleasant jobs.

Our ultimate source of creativity is God.

"How often do we attempt work for God to the limit of our incompetency rather than to the limit of God's omnipotency?" —J. Hudson Taylor

The Word of God that brought about creation can also produce creativity in us.

Creativity is the expression of wisdom that comes from a listening heart.

"I wisdom dwell with prudence, and find out knowledge of witty inventions." —Proverbs 8:12

How Does the Word of God Energize Creativity?

Jesus said, "The words that I speak unto you, they are spirit, and they are life" (John 6:63). He also said, "If ye abide in me, and my words abide in you, ye shall ask what ye will, and it shall be done unto you" (John 15:7). In both of these references, the Greek word *rhema* is used rather than *logos*. A *rhema* is a Biblical instruction given to an individual to carry out. For example, Peter was told by Jesus to cast the net on the other side of the boat. Peter explained, "Master, we have toiled all the night, and have taken nothing: nevertheless at thy word [*rhema*] I will let down the net" (Luke 5:5).

The *rhemas* God gives to us provide the direction for the good works He wants to accomplish in and through us. The Holy Spirit guides us in understanding God's Word and is actively involved in creativity. "Thou sendest forth thy spirit, they are created: and thou renewest the face of the earth" (Psalm 104:30).

How Can We Increase Our Creativity?

Creativity is an expression of wisdom. "I wisdom dwell with prudence, and find out knowledge of witty inventions" (Proverbs 8:12). Every believer has an opportunity to receive more wisdom by simply asking for it. "If any of you lack wisdom, let him ask of God, that giveth to all men liberally, and upbraideth not; and it shall be given him" (James 1:5). The conditions that God has established for wisdom are also important to follow. "But let him ask in faith, nothing wavering. For he that wavereth is like a wave of the sea driven with the wind and tossed" (James 1:6).

If we are serious about increasing our creativity, we should not only ask for wisdom but also cry out for it. "Yea, if thou criest after knowledge, and liftest up thy voice for understanding; If thou seekest her as silver, and searchest for her as for hid treasures; Then shalt thou understand the fear of the LORD, and find the knowledge of God. For the LORD giveth wisdom: out of his mouth cometh knowledge and understanding" (Proverbs 2:3–6). The ultimate source of wisdom is the Scriptures. The more we study, memorize, and meditate on them, the greater foundation we will have for true creativity.

Personal Evaluation

How creative are you?

- Do you cultivate wise thoughts by meditating on Scripture day and night?

- Do you find creative ways to encourage members of your family?

- Do you spend time in planning strategies to effectively present the Gospel?

- Do you seek to motivate others to carry out good works?

- Do you look at obstacles as hindrances or opportunities for creative solutions?

- Do you conquer boredom by finding new and challenging ways to do things?

- Does a lack of results motivate you to try a new and better method?

Decisiveness
vs. Double-Mindedness

Decisiveness is choosing to do what is right based on accurate facts, wise counsel, and clearly defined goals.

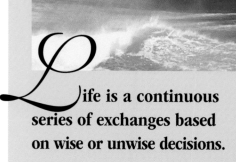

Definition

When Daniel faced a decision in Babylon about whether to obey the king's edict or God's commandment, it was not a difficult choice, because he had predetermined that he would obey only God, whatever the cost. "Daniel purposed in his heart that he would not defile himself with the portion of the king's meat, nor with the wine which he drank" (Daniel 1:8).

The Hebrew word for *purposed* means "to consider and determine." God wants each one of us to determine early in life that we will choose to do what is right, whatever the cost. He said, "I have set before you life and death, blessing and cursing: therefore choose life, that both thou and thy seed may live" (Deuteronomy 30:19).

The Foundation of Wise Decisions

The first step in decisiveness is choosing whom we are going to serve with our lives. Our natural inclination is to serve money with our time, energy, and creativity. We believe that by getting money, we can enjoy all the things that money can buy. We may realize, however, that it is wrong to serve money, and we may try to serve God along with money. However, Jesus warned, "No man can serve two masters:

for either he will hate the one, and love the other; or else he will hold to the one, and despise the other. Ye cannot serve God and mammon [money]" (Matthew 6:24).

Deciding to follow God means setting aside everything that competes with Him. "Now therefore fear the LORD, and serve him in sincerity and in truth: and put away the gods which your fathers served. . . . And if it seem evil unto you to serve the LORD, choose you this day whom ye will serve . . . but as for me and my house, we will serve the LORD" (Joshua 24:14–15).

The Cause of Foolish Decisions

The greatest hindrance to decisiveness is double-mindedness. "A double-minded man is unstable in all his ways" (James 1:8). He is like a wave of the sea which is driven by the wind and tossed to and fro.

The Greek word for *double-minded* is *dipsuchos*, which means "two-souled or vacillating." *Psuche* is the root for the English word *psychology*, and it involves the mind, will, and emotions. A double-minded person has divided desires. On the one hand, he wants to do what is right, but on the other hand, he wants to enjoy the pleasures of sin, which last only for a short season. (See Hebrews 11:25.)

---

*L*ife is a continuous series of exchanges based on wise or unwise decisions.

We exchange energy for money, money for food, and food for energy. The same is true on a spiritual level. We exchange temporal things for more of Christ or eternal riches for temporal things.

"Yea doubtless, and I count all things but loss for the excellency of the knowledge of Christ Jesus my Lord: for whom I have suffered the loss of all things, and do count them but dung, that I may win Christ."
—Philippians 3:8

"Difficulties are overcome when our hearts are ready to do the Lord's will, whatever it may be."
—George Müller

The Four *D*s of Decision Making

1. DON'T—If it is the responsibility of others, let them do it.

2. DELAY—If it should be done at a better time, wait.

3. DELEGATE—If others can do it better, let them.

4. DO IT—If none of the above apply, do it! —Dr. Glen Heck

*T*he little decisions we make now determine the big decisions we will make later.

Little choices determine character, which will dictate future responses.

*T*hose who avoid decision making thereby decide to let circumstances and others make decisions for them.

The **badger** is a quick decision maker when facing a predator. If it decides not to flee, it will expend all its energy in the fight.

Moses conquered double-mindedness by making a lifetime decision to identify with God and His people. "By faith Moses, when he was come to years, refused to be called the son of Pharaoh's daughter; Choosing rather to suffer affliction with the people of God, than to enjoy the pleasures of sin for a season" (Hebrews 11:24–25).

Decisiveness is based on wise and careful consideration of all available options. Moses considered and determined that the "reproach of Christ [was] greater riches than the treasures in Egypt: for he had respect unto the recompence of the reward" (Hebrews 11:26).

The Value of Seeking Out Wise Counsel

To have the confidence that our decisions are wise and correct, we must seek out wise counsel. In this, we should get experience as inexpensively as we can. Others have paid a high price for it through wrong decisions. They will usually give us the benefit of their experience just for the asking. They then gain some redemptive value for the pain and loss of past mistakes.

- "The way of a fool is right in his own eyes: but he that hearkeneth unto counsel is wise" (Proverbs 12:15).

- "Without counsel purposes are disappointed: but in the multitude of counsellors they are established" (Proverbs 15:22).

- "Hear counsel, and receive instruction, that thou mayest be wise in thy latter end" (Proverbs 19:20).

- "Where no counsel is, the people fall: but in the multitude of counsellors there is safety" (Proverbs 11:14).

How to Base Decisiveness on God's Word

Wise decision making must be based on God's will, not on our own natural inclinations, because "there is a way which seemeth right unto a man, but the end thereof are the ways of death" (Proverbs 14:12). Therefore, God warns: "He that trusteth in his own heart is a fool: but whoso walketh wisely, he shall be delivered" (Proverbs 28:26).

Every decision that Jesus made was based on His Heavenly Father's will. He stated, "I can of mine own self do nothing: as I hear, I judge: and my judgment is just; because I seek not mine own will, but the will of the Father which hath sent me" (John 5:30). God's will on a specific matter will be based on the universal, non-optional principles of life that He established throughout all His creation and which He explains and illustrates in the Bible. These principles can be summarized by asking the following questions when making a specific decision:

1. **Is my use of things consistent with the purposes for which God created them?** (money, food, clothes, marriage, family, time, friends, etc.)

2. **Whose jurisdiction am I under for this decision?** (parents, employer, government, or church) Decisiveness must never violate the overall jurisdiction of God and the moral principles of His Word.

3. **Can I make this decision with a clear conscience?** Any caution from conscience or the counsel of authorities must also be considered.

4. **Am I in harmony with all those involved in this decision?** Decisions based on bitterness or anger are sure to be wrong and costly.

5. **Have I yielded my rights on this matter?** George Müller was a great man of faith and learned to understand the will of God in specific decisions. He explained that the secret was getting his own heart in a state in which he had no will of his own. A practical way to accomplish this is to list all of the benefits of each choice and purpose to thank God for whatever choice He indicates is His will.

6. **Will it weaken or damage anyone else?** We are not to do anything that will cause a "weaker" brother to stumble, be offended, or be made weak. (See Romans 14:21.) Because of this, we are even to "abstain from all appearance of evil" (I Thessalonians 5:22).

7. **Is this fulfilling God's calling on my life?** God calls each believer to fulfill an important role in the advancement of His kingdom and the damage of Satan's kingdom. Every decision we make must be in harmony with these objectives. Our calling will involve praying for and serving all authorities with good works and assisting the fatherless and widows, as well as the poor and those from other nations.

Our primary calling is given in the Great Commission: "Go ye therefore, and teach all nations, baptizing them in the name of the Father, and of the Son, and of the Holy Ghost: Teaching them to observe all things whatsoever I have commanded you: and, lo, I am with you alway, even unto the end of the world" (Matthew 28:19–20).

How Fasting Enhances Decisiveness

For important decisions and to increase spiritual alertness for decision making, it is wise to set aside a day, or several days, for prayer and fasting. Jesus promises that if we fast secretly, He will reward us openly. (See Matthew 6:18.)

One of the many rewards of fasting is an increase in discernment and wise judgment. God promises that through fasting "thy light [shall] break forth as the morning . . . and thy darkness be as the noon day" (Isaiah 58:8, 10).

—Personal Evaluation—

How decisive are you?

- Have you made a foundational commitment to do what is right, whatever the cost?

- Have you decided to serve God rather than money, fame, or pleasure?

- Do you seek out wise counsel before making a decision?

- Have you purposed to discern God's will in every decision and then to do it?

- Do you fast and cry out to God for wisdom in decisions?

- Do you make decisions based on impulse or on *rhemas* from God's Word?

- Do you reject advice that is contrary to Scripture?

*D*ecisiveness is focusing on our destination, rather than focusing on distractions.

The more clearly we define our goals, the more skilled we can be in making wise decisions.

"I press toward the mark for the prize of the high calling of God in Christ Jesus." —*Philippians 3:14*

"I determined never to stop until I had come to the end and achieved my purpose."
—David Livingstone

*W*e build decisiveness when we refuse to reconsider a decision that we know is right.

Indulging in a pleasure may bring a moment of enjoyment but a lifetime of damage to others.

All deference should be based on the incredible sacrifice that Jesus made in order to bring people to salvation. (See Romans 14:20.) He asks us to consider what He did when we are called upon to show deference.

"For consider him that endured such contradiction of sinners against himself, lest ye be wearied and faint in your minds."

—Hebrews 12:3

Deference is protecting others in situations that would weaken or offend them.

Paul chose not to eat meat that was offered to idols, because to do so would offend other believers.

"Let not then your good be evil spoken of." —Romans 14:16

Deference
vs. Offensiveness

Deference is putting the welfare of others ahead of our own personal pleasures.

Definition

When Paul instructed believers to prefer one another in honor, he defined the essence of deference. The Greek word rendered *preferring* is *proegeomai*, meaning "to lead the way for others." It is a strong word that connotes "commanding with official authority, to be chief and have rule." Thus, as we defer to others, we experience the paradox spoken of by Jesus, "Whosoever of you will be the chiefest, shall be servant of all" (Mark 10:44).

Deference is making personal sacrifices to help others be successful and putting off words, attitudes, or actions that would cause others to be offended or weakened. We should defer whenever it will benefit the cause of Christ.

Deference and discretion work together. "The discretion of a man deferreth his anger; and it is his glory to pass over a transgression" (Proverbs 19:11).

The word *offense* adds further meaning to the concept of deference. "Giving no offense in any thing, that the ministry be not blamed" (II Corinthians 6:3). "Give none offense, neither to the Jews, nor to the Gentiles, nor to the church of God: Even as I please all men in all things, not seeking mine own profit, but the profit of many, that they may be saved" (I Corinthians 10:32–33).

Several Greek words are rendered *offense*. One is *proskomma*, which means "a stumbling block or an obstacle in the way, which if one strikes his foot against he stumbles or falls."

"Let us therefore follow after the things which make for peace, and things wherewith one may edify another. For meat destroy not the work of God. All things indeed are pure; but it is evil for that man who eateth with offense [*proskomma*]" (Romans 14:19–20).

In the following verse, the word *skandalizo* is rendered *offense*: "It is good neither to eat flesh, nor to drink wine, nor any thing whereby thy brother stumbleth, or is offended [*skandalizo*], or is made weak" (Romans 14:21).

The word *skandalizo* means "to entrap, to trip up, to entice to sin, to cause displeasure." It comes from the word *scandalon*, meaning much the same thing. "Wherefore, if meat [offered to idols] make my brother to offend [*skandalizo*], I will eat no flesh while the world standeth, lest I make my brother to offend [*skandalizo*]" (I Corinthians 8:13).

Examples of Deference

Scripture contains significant examples of those who demonstrated deference, and these testimonies provide precedents for parallel situations. Therefore, we are encouraged to meditate upon these testimonies so that we can accurately apply the precedents in new circumstances.

1. Deference to government

When a tax collector asked Peter if Jesus paid taxes, Peter said, "Yes!" However, Jesus asked Peter, "Of whom do the kings of the earth take custom or tribute? of their own children, or of strangers?" (Matthew 17:25).

Peter answered, "Of strangers. Jesus saith unto him, Then are the children free" (Matthew 17:26). Having established the fact that He had the right and freedom not to pay taxes, Jesus said, "lest we should offend [*skandalizo*] them . . . find a piece of money: that take, and give unto them for me and thee" (Matthew 17:27).

2. Deference to children

When the disciples asked Jesus, "Who is the greatest in the kingdom of heaven?" Jesus called a child to Him and set him in the middle of the disciples. Then He said, "Verily I say unto you, Except ye be converted, and become as little children, ye shall not enter into the kingdom of heaven" (Matthew 18:3).

Little children are expected to show deference to their parents and those around them. This humble deference is what Jesus praises: "Whosoever therefore shall humble himself as this little child, the same is greatest in the kingdom of heaven" (Matthew 18:4).

After praising the humility that prompts deference—in contrast to the carnal aspirations of the disciples—Jesus gives a fearful warning against offending such children.

"Whoso shall offend [*skandalizo*] one of these little ones which believe in me, it were better for him that a millstone were hanged about his neck, and that he were drowned in the depth of the sea" (Matthew 18:6).

The conscience of a child is very sensitive. Vulgar words and actions to which adults may have grown callous can be very hurtful and offensive to children. All must show deference to children.

Following His warning, Jesus offers detailed instruction about offending children with impurity.

"Woe unto the world because of offenses [*skandalon*]! for it must needs be that offenses come; but woe to that man by whom the offense cometh! Wherefore if thy hand or thy foot offend thee, cut them off, and cast them from thee: it is better for thee to enter into life halt or maimed, rather than having two hands or two feet to be cast into everlasting fire.

"And if thine eye offend thee, pluck it out, and cast it from thee: it is better for thee to enter into life with one eye, rather than having two eyes to be cast into hell fire.

"Take heed that ye despise not one of these little ones; for I say unto you, That in heaven their

Good manners are daily displays of deference.

"There is no such thing as being a gentleman at important moments; it is at unimportant moments that a man is a gentleman. . . . If once his mind is possessed in any strong degree with the knowledge that he is a gentleman, he will soon cease to be one."

—G. K. Chesterton

The very life of a **timber wolf** depends upon its ability to show deference to the leader of the pack. If a wolf asserts itself, the leader will attack it in fury until the offending wolf offers its neck as an acknowledgment that it offended by putting itself first.

The "father of faith" showed deference and thereby avoided destruction.

When conflict erupted between the herdsmen of Abraham and his nephew Lot over limited grazing areas, Abraham divided the land and allowed Lot to make the first choice. Lot chose the most attractive property, but with his choice came the destruction of what took place in Sodom and Gomorrah. (See Genesis 13.)

How a man won a crown of life by showing deference in the face of death.

John Harper and his little daughter were passengers on the *Titanic*. When he realized the ship was sinking, he made sure his daughter was safe and then gave his life preserver to another. Fighting the frigid water, he used his last bit of strength to lead others to eternal life.

"Be thou faithful unto death, and I will give thee a crown of life."
—*Revelation 2:10*

angels do always behold the face of my Father which is in heaven" (Matthew 18:7–10).

3. Deference to believers

Frugal shoppers are always looking for bargains, and first-century believers were no exception. Thus, when they saw the best meat in town on sale for the cheapest price, they bought it.

This meat was on the bargain counter for a reason—it had been dedicated to the temple gods, and the priests wanted to get their money from it.

When new believers who had renounced temple worship saw older believers buying this meat they became offended, and a major controversy erupted in the young church. This disagreement was strong enough to warrant a ruling by the Jerusalem Council and a lengthy exhortation from the inspired pen of Paul.

In this delicate matter, Paul appeals for deference by those on both sides of the controversy. He appealed especially to those who thought it was right to eat the meat. "Let us not therefore judge one another any more: but judge this rather, that no man put a stumblingblock or an occasion to fall in his brother's way" (Romans 14:13). This statement is a precise description of the word *skandalon*.

The great importance of deference can be seen in this narrative. Paul agrees with those who say that there is nothing wrong with the meat itself. However, eating the meat becomes wrong if another believer is offended by it or if it is eaten with any inward caution given by the Holy Spirit.

"I know, and am persuaded by the Lord Jesus, that there is nothing unclean of itself: but to him that esteemeth any thing to be unclean, to him it is unclean. But if thy brother be grieved with thy meat, now walkest thou not charitably. Destroy not him with thy meat, for whom Christ died" (Romans 14:14–15).

Paul's admonition was further confirmed by the Jerusalem Council, which declared that Gentile believers were not subject to the Mosaic laws but were to observe four "necessary things."

"That ye abstain from meats offered to idols, and from blood, and from things strangled, and from fornication: from which if ye keep yourselves, ye shall do well" (Acts 15:29).

The final confirmation on the vital importance of deference in this matter comes from the message of the Holy Spirit to two of the seven churches in Asia:

To the church of Pergamos: "I have a few things against thee, because thou hast there them that hold the doctrine of Balaam, who taught Balac to cast a stumblingblock before the children of Israel, to eat things sacrificed unto idols, and to commit fornication" (Revelation 2:14).

To the church of Thyatira: "I have a few things against thee, because thou sufferest that woman Jezebel, which calleth herself a prophetess, to teach and to seduce my servants to commit fornication, and to eat things sacrificed unto idols" (Revelation 2:20).

4. Deference to the Word

After Paul affirmed the need to "give none offense, neither to the Jews, nor to the Gentiles, nor to the church of God" (I Corinthians 10:32), he states his own commitment to deference: "Even as I please all men in all things, not seeking mine own profit, but the profit of many, that they may be saved" (I Corinthians 10:33).

In the previous chapter, Paul explains how he demonstrated deference. "Though I be free from all men, yet have I made myself servant unto all, that I might gain the more.

"And unto the Jews I became as a Jew, that I might gain the Jews; to them that are under the law, as under the law, that I might gain them that are under the law; To them that are without law, as without law, (being not without law to God, but under the law to Christ,) that I might gain them that are without law.

"To the weak became I as weak, that I might gain the weak: I am made all things to all men, that I might by all means save some. And this I do for the gospel's sake" (I Corinthians 9:19–23).

God's Mandate for Deference

Deference requires more than choosing to do things that are good. Deference requires that we choose things that are excellent, that we in no way hinder our own walk or the walks of others.

"That your love may abound yet more and more in knowledge and in all judgment; That ye may approve things that are excellent; that ye may be sincere and without offense till the day of Christ" (Philippians 1:9–10).

Results of Failing to Show Deference

Our lack of deference can be a major contributing factor to the failures of those who are weaker in their faith or more sensitive than we are. Because of a lack of deference by those who claim to be God's followers, many have turned against Him in bitterness. Therefore, if we are aware of anyone who has been offended by our lack of deference, we should go to that person, humble ourselves, ask for forgiveness, and then renew our commitment to show deference.

Personal Evaluation

How much deference do you show to others?

- Do you place stumbling blocks in the way of others by the things that you say, do, or wear?

- Do you have modesty and privacy in your home to protect children from stirring up wrong desires?

- Do you protect children from evil?

- Do you keep your home free from things that offend your children or cause them to struggle?

- Do you justify music or activities that offend or weaken fellow Christians?

- Do you offend people of other cultures, races, or ethnic groups by the words you use to describe them?

- Do you adjust as much as you can to accommodate those from other backgrounds and philosophies?

- Do you understand and follow protocol when visiting another country?

- Do you pay questionable taxes in order not to bring offense to the Gospel?

Deference is exchanging my rights for the permanent joy of another's spiritual growth.

One of the most effective missionaries of all time was J. Hudson Taylor. He won the hearts of the people of inland China and drew multitudes to the Lord by deferring to them and adjusting to their customs and style of clothing.

Deference is leading the way in showing others the true meaning of self-denial.

"Be kindly affectioned one to another with brotherly love; in honour preferring one another."

—Romans 12:10

Refusing to show deference is saying, "My momentary interests are more important than your eternal welfare."

Dependability
vs. Inconsistency

Dependability is purposing in our hearts to do the will of God whatever the cost.

*D*ependability in small assignments is the prerequisite for big responsibilities.

"He that is faithful in that which is least is faithful also in much."

—Luke 16:10

"Great occasions for serving God come seldom, but little ones surround us daily."

—St. Francis de Sales

*T*he standards for our weights and measures are based on the dependability of God's creation and the laws that govern it.

Definition

A dependable person is defined in Scripture as one who is faithful. The Greek word for *faithful* is *pistos* and means "trustworthy; true; reliable; and sure." Paul was instructed to teach the Gospel to faithful men who would be able to teach others.

The Hebrew word for *faithful* is *aman*. It means "to build up or support; to foster as a parent; to nurse; to be steadfast."

The Importance of Dependability

This is the one quality that all believers should want their lives characterized by. It is the one quality Jesus will use to evaluate our work for Him: "Well done, thou good and faithful servant" (Matthew 25:21).

It is also the one quality that is required for God to entrust resources to us and the quality that will win a crown for eternity: "It is required in stewards, that a man be found faithful" (I Corinthians 4:2). "Be thou faithful unto death, and I will give thee a crown of life" (Revelation 2:10).

Characteristics of Dependability

- **A dependable person will be in harmony with the heart and mind of God.** "I will raise me up a **faithful** priest, that shall do according to that which is in mine heart and in my mind" (I Samuel 2:35). "For my thoughts are not your thoughts, neither are your ways my ways, saith the LORD. For as the heavens are higher than the earth, so are my ways higher than your ways, and my thoughts than your thoughts" (Isaiah 55:8–9). "Delight thyself also in the LORD; and he shall give thee the desires of thine heart" (Psalm 37:4).

- **A dependable person has a great reverence for God.** "I gave my brother Hanani, and Hananiah the ruler of the palace, charge over Jerusalem for he was a **faithful** man and feared God above many" (Nehemiah 7:2).

- **A dependable person is faithful in little things as well as big things.** "He that is **faithful** in that which is least is faithful also in much" (Luke 16:10).

- **A dependable person has a heart attitude of faithfulness.** "[Thou] foundest his [Abraham's] heart **faithful** before thee, and madest a covenant with him" (Nehemiah 9:8).

- **A dependable person keeps confidential information private.** "A talebearer revealeth secrets: but he that is of a **faithful** spirit concealeth the matter" (Proverbs 11:13).

- **A dependable person communicates energy and health.** "A wicked messenger falleth into mischief: but a **faithful** ambassador is health" (Proverbs 13:17).

- **A dependable person is truthful in all that he says.** "A **faithful** witness will not lie, but a false witness will utter lies" (Proverbs 14:5).

- **A dependable person will not tell people how good he is.** "Most men will proclaim every one his own goodness: but a **faithful** man who can find?" (Proverbs 20:6).

- **A dependable person encourages those whom he serves.** "As the cold of snow in the time of harvest, so is a **faithful** messenger to them that send him: for he refresheth the soul of his masters" (Proverbs 25:13).

- **A dependable person is faultless in his work.** "Then the presidents and princes sought to find occasion against Daniel concerning the kingdom; but they could find none occasion nor fault; forasmuch as he was **faithful**, neither was there any error or fault found in him" (Daniel 6:4).

- **A dependable person deals wisely with resources and relationships.** (see Luke 16:1–15).

Rewards of Dependability

- **A dependable person will raise up a spiritual lineage of faithful descendants.** "And I will raise me up a **faithful** priest, that shall do according to that which is in mine heart and in my mind: and I will build him a sure house; and he shall walk before mine anointed for ever" (I Samuel 2:35).

- **A dependable person will be given greater responsibilities.**

Nehemiah gave Hanani and Hananiah, the ruler of the palace, "charge over Jerusalem: for he was a faithful man, and feared God above many" (Nehemiah 7:2).

- **A dependable person will receive special praise and honor from the Lord.** "Well done, good and **faithful** servant; thou hast been **faithful** over a few things, I will make thee ruler over many things: enter thou into the joy of thy lord" (Matthew 25:23).

- **A dependable person will be protected by the Lord.** "O love the LORD, all ye his saints: for the LORD preserveth [guards; protects] the **faithful**" (Psalm 31:23).

- **A dependable person will abound with God's blessings.** "A **faithful** man shall abound with blessings: but he that maketh haste to be rich shall not be innocent" (Proverbs 28:20).

- **A dependable person will be given a crown of life.** "Be thou faithful unto death, and I will give thee a crown of life" (Revelation 2:10).

The Motivation for Dependability

Dependability is not letting down the people who are counting on us. There are several factors that should motivate us to such dependability. The first and greatest motivation should be realizing that what we do to benefit others, we are actually doing for the Lord Jesus Christ. Jesus explained this by saying, "Inasmuch as ye have done it unto one of the least of these my brethren, ye have done it unto me" (Matthew 25:40).

Timothy was a man of dependability, and Paul said of him, "For I have no man likeminded,

Can others count on you?

To keep your word?

To stay on schedule?

To be alert to details?

To make wise decisions?

To use your time wisely?

To complete assignments?

"If Jesus Christ died and died for me, then no sacrifice can be too great for me to make for Him." —C.T. Studd

In order to survive the harshness of the Arctic, **musk oxen** depend on each other to overcome fierce predators and frigid winters. Herds of musk oxen encircle their young to protect them from enemies.

*O*ur dependability is directly related to our dependence on God's ability.

"I can do all things through Christ which strengtheneth me."

—Philippians 4:13

*T*he test of faithfulness is a job that requires more than what was anticipated.

"He that sweareth to his own hurt, and changeth not. . . . shall never be moved." —Psalm 15:4–5

"Excellence is to do a common thing in an uncommon way."

—Booker T. Washington

who will naturally care for your state. For all seek their own, not the things which are Jesus Christ's" (Philippians 2:20–21).

The second motivation should be realizing that our service for others will be evaluated by the Lord when we stand before Him. "We must all appear before the judgment seat of Christ; that every one may receive the things done in his body, according to that he hath done, whether it be good or bad" (II Corinthians 5:10).

A third motivation should be the awareness of Christ's imminent return. Jesus gave a parable to emphasize this point.

"The Lord said, Who then is that **faithful** and wise steward, whom his lord shall make ruler over his household, to give them their portion of meat in due season? Blessed is that servant, whom his lord when he cometh shall find so doing" (Luke 12:42–43).

The Source of Power for Dependability

Even though God and others expect us to be dependable, God knows that our ability to demonstrate such a quality does not reside within us—our strength must come from Him. It is through His faithfulness to us that we can be faithful to others. But how do we "tap in" to His faithfulness?

Paul explains the process in his letters to the first-century Church. He discovered that the power of Christ is available only to those who acknowledge their weakness before Him. The first expression of weakness is crying out to Him for salvation. Next, it is crying out to Him in daily dependence upon Him. Paul learned how to translate trials

and tribulations into reminders of his own weakness and of Christ's sufficiency.

These reminders were so important to Paul that he gloried in them by thanking God for them and seeing potential benefits in and through them. Paul was dependable to the end of his ministry and explained the secret to his faithfulness. "Therefore I take pleasure in infirmities, in reproaches, in necessities, in persecutions, in distresses for Christ's sake: for when I am weak, then am I strong" (II Corinthians 12:10).

Personal Evaluation

How dependable are you?

- When you give your word to do something, can others always count on you to do it, even if it is more difficult than you expected?

- If you experience unexpected difficulties, do you use them as excuses for not finishing a task?

- Do you picture the things you do for others as actually serving Jesus Christ?

- Can your service providers depend on you to pay your bills promptly?

- Can members of your family count on you to turn down other opportunities in order to be with them for special events?

- Can the Lord depend on you to make the wisest use of the resources He has entrusted to you?

- Do you graciously but firmly decline invitations that will distract you from carrying out your responsibilities?

Determination

vs. Faintheartedness

Determination is looking at insurmountable obstacles as opportunities to cry out for God's supernatural intervention.

Definition

One Hebrew word translated *determined* is *amar*, which means "to say in one's heart; to think; to command; to promise; to intend." Another Biblical term that helps define determination is the verb *purpose*. One Hebrew word for *purpose* is *yatsar*, meaning "predetermine." God used this word when He said, "I have purposed it, I will also do it" (Isaiah 46:11).

Determination deals with a mind-set prior to a task, while endurance involves the carrying out of the task. Determination presupposes careful consideration of the cost and requirements of a task and a decision that the task is worth whatever expenses are necessary to achieve it.

Who Demonstrated Determination in Scripture?

- Solomon "determined to build an house for the name of the LORD, and an house for his kingdom" (II Chronicles 2:1).

- "Daniel purposed in his heart that he would not defile himself with the portion of the king's meat, nor with the wine which he drank: therefore he requested of the prince of the eunuchs that he might not defile himself" (Daniel 1:8).

- David determined to mourn over Abner's death with fasting until the evening. "When all the people came to cause David to eat meat while it was yet day, David sware, saying, So do God to me, and more also, if I taste bread, or aught else, till the sun be down" (II Samuel 3:35).

- The disciples "determined to send relief unto the brethren which dwelt in Judaea" (Acts 11:29).

- Paul "determined not to know any thing among you, save Jesus Christ, and him crucified" (I Corinthians 2:2).

Why Is Determination Important?

Life consists of choices. If we make the right choices, we experience the blessings of God. If we make the wrong choices, we experience destruction and death. After wise choices are made, determination is needed to carry them out. Wise choices will usually be challenged by difficulties and temptations.

Moses demonstrated determination when he chose to suffer affliction with the children of Israel rather than to enjoy the pleasures of sin that last for only a season. On the other hand, Esau did not determine to protect his birthright and therefore sold it for a bowl of pottage. Years later, when he realized

*N*ever give up!

"At first the task looks difficult, then it is impossible; then it is done." —J. Hudson Taylor

Reaching a goal requires more than skill—it requires determination. This means rejecting distractions, such as discouragement and doubt. Often, failure is due not to a lack of talent or ability but to a lack of persistence during difficult times.

"When God is about to do something great, He starts with a difficulty. When He is about to do something truly magnificent, he starts with an impossibility."

—Armin Gesswein

Swimming against swift river currents and waterfalls, **king salmon** determine each year to travel hundreds of miles from the sea to their spawning grounds upstream.

*D*etermination is purposing to exert as much energy as needed to reach a goal.

"When I say 'I can't,' it means 'I won't.'"

—Oswald Chambers

Determination is like a bomber pilot passing the point of no return, thereby cutting off the option of retreat.

"I press toward the mark for the prize of the high calling of God in Christ Jesus." —*Philippians 3:14*

"To have failed once is not so much a pity as is to not try again."

—John Wanamaker

his mistake, he desperately sought to recover it, but was unable to, even after many tears (See Hebrews 11:25; 12:16–17).

How Do We Develop Determination?

We develop determination by recognizing the losses or gains resulting from a particular choice. Moses chose to suffer with the children of Israel. He recognized that "the reproach of Christ [brought] greater riches than the treasures in Egypt: for he had respect unto the recompence of the reward" (Hebrews 11:26).

What Hinders Determination?

The fear of man is a strong hindrance to determination, because it does not allow us to decide with the Lord what is the best choice. Instead, we try to guess what other people think is the right choice and what they will think of us if we make a different decision than they would. Fear brings torment (see I John 4:18), and this torment brings bondage. "The fear of man bringeth a snare" (Proverbs 29:25).

A double mind is another hindrance to determination. A double-minded person is like a wave of the sea driven backward and forward with every passing wind. This makes determination impossible. "A double-minded man is unstable in all his ways" (James 1:8).

What Are We to Be Determined About?

1. Keeping vows

"When thou vowest a vow unto God, defer not to pay it; for he hath no pleasure in fools: pay that which thou hast vowed. Better is it that thou shouldest not vow, than that thou shouldest vow and not pay. Suffer not thy mouth to cause thy flesh to sin; neither say thou before the angel, that it was an error: wherefore should God be angry at thy voice, and destroy the work of thine hands?" (Ecclesiastes 5:4–6).

2. Seeking the Lord with the whole heart

David was a man after God's own heart. His determination to seek the face of the Lord was a constant motivation during his life. "As the hart panteth after the water brooks, so panteth my soul after thee, O God" (Psalm 42:1). God promises a special reward for those who promise to seek Him with the whole heart. "Blessed are they that keep his testimonies, and that seek him with the whole heart" (Psalm 119:2).

3. Maintaining a clear conscience

Paul told Timothy that he was sending him out with faith and a clear conscience and that if he laid these weapons aside, he would make shipwreck of his soul. Regarding himself, Paul said, "And herein do I exercise myself, to have always a conscience void of offense toward God, and toward men" (Acts 24:16).

Personal Evaluation

How determined are you?

- Do you determine to follow Christ, no matter what the cost?
- Do you have Biblical commitments that will direct your decisions in life?
- Do you commit to reach a goal and overcome any obstacles you encounter along the way?
- Do you have a motivating purpose in life?
- Do you persevere on tasks that are more difficult than what you expected?
- Do you allow problems or failures to keep you from trying again?

Diligence
vs. Slothfulness

Diligence is accepting each task as a special assignment from the Lord and using all my energies to do it quickly and skillfully.

Definition

Several Hebrew and Greek words are translated *diligence* in the Bible. They communicate such concepts as rising early; searching out with painstaking effort; being earnest, eager, and determined; working swiftly, skillfully, and efficiently; and pursuing a task promptly and energetically. One of the richest word pictures for diligence is found in the Hebrew word *charuwts*. It means "a trench that is dug, or gold that is mined."

The California Gold Rush of 1849 provides a powerful illustration of diligence. Men living on the East Coast dropped everything and rushed out to the West Coast to dig for gold.

They worked swiftly and thoroughly without regard for personal weariness or sacrifice. They were motivated to work because they visualized what they could do with the gold they discovered. If this same energy and motivation were invested in every project that we undertake, the quality of diligence would be seen and honored.

The Great Rewards of Diligence

Valuable rewards are promised to those who are diligent. For example, diligent workers will receive riches, leadership, favor, a standing before rulers, an understanding of the meaning of life, and honor from God.

- "Seest thou a man diligent in his business? he shall stand before kings; he shall not stand before mean men" (Proverbs 22:29).

- "The hand of the diligent shall bear rule" (Proverbs 12:24).

- "The hand of the diligent maketh rich" (Proverbs 10:4).

The Biblical Encouragement to Be Diligent

God encourages us to have diligence in the following areas:

- Resolving legal disputes (See Luke 12:58.)

- Carrying out leadership responsibilities (See Romans 12:8.)

- Doing good works (See I Timothy 5:10.)

- Seeking the Lord. (See Hebrews 11:6.)

- Watching over fellow believers (See Hebrews 12:15.)

- Making your calling and election sure (See II Peter 1:10.)

- Developing Godly character. (See II Peter 1:5–7.)

- Working for personal peace and purity. (See II Peter 3:14.)

*H*old back nothing!

The diligent man gives himself completely to a task in order to accomplish it. He is rewarded with an audience before great men and rulers.

"Seest thou a man diligent in his business? he shall stand before kings; he shall not stand before mean men."
—Proverbs 22:29

"Absence of occupation is not rest; A mind quite vacant is a mind distressed."
—William Cowper

*W*hen we are motivated by love, our labor becomes rest.

"Whoever loves much does much."
—Thomas á Kempis

*D*iligence is doing a task with the motivation of love and an attitude of joy.

"Whatsoever ye do, do it heartily, as to the Lord, and not unto men."

—Colossians 3:23

"The lazy Christian hath his mouth full of complaints, when the active Christian hath his heart full of comforts."
—Thomas Brooks

"Learn to tell the difference between activity and work."
—John Wanamaker

Rarely is the beaver inactive. It constantly builds, maintains, works ahead, and cares for its family. Even after its own dam and lodge are established, the beaver keeps busy building additional dams and lodges for future generations.

The Key to Developing Diligence

True diligence requires an expenditure of energy that is opposite to our human nature. We naturally tend to make soft choices and let others do the hard work. Whenever we are asked to carry out a difficult task, we usually ask ourselves two questions: "What will I gain if I do it?" or "What will I lose if I do not do it?" God provides answers to these questions in the following passage of Scripture.

"Whatsoever ye do, do it heartily, as to the Lord, and not unto men; Knowing that of the Lord ye shall receive the reward of the inheritance: for ye serve the Lord Christ" (Colossians 3:23).

Therefore, our motivation for diligence is to realize that we are not simply working for an earthly employer but that we are actually employed by the Lord Jesus Christ. He will make a thorough inspection of all that we do and reward us for diligence, not only in this life but throughout all of eternity.

Because Jesus Christ is our employer, we do not need to worry if we are not recognized for extra effort that we invest in quality work, nor do we need to wonder whether He will see if we overlooked or avoided details that might not be noticed by others. With this understanding, we should be motivated to fulfill the instruction of Ecclesiastes 9:10:

"Whatsoever thy hand findeth to do, do it with thy might."

If you have failed to demonstrate diligence in all your projects, then you have not adequately represented the Lord Jesus Christ Whom you serve. You have also disappointed those who were expecting more diligence and productivity from you. It would be wise for you to ask forgiveness of the Lord and those whom you have disappointed and to purpose now to develop true diligence in every task that is set before you.

—*Personal Evaluation*—

How diligent are you?

- Do you complete an assigned task quickly and enthusiastically, or do you reluctantly fit it into your schedule?

- Do you plan ahead on a job to do it the quickest and most efficient way?

- Do you redeem valuable minutes by moving quickly on the job, or do you walk slowly?

- Do you look forward to going on to a new job or to resting after a job?

- Do you complete chores so thoroughly that your parents consider you a diligent worker?

- Do you do a job to first please the Lord and then your employer?

- Do you go the extra mile, working wholeheartedly to complete each job?

- Do you use every minute of company time to make your employer successful?

Discernment

vs. Judgment

Discernment is the ability to distinguish between what is good and what is evil, in order to make wise decisions.

Definition

The concept of discernment is defined by several Hebrew words. *Shama* means "to hear, to consider, to perceive," *yada* "to know, to understand, to recognize," and *biyn*, "to separate mentally, to distinguish." A fourth word, *mishpat*, is used to refer to good judgment and means "to give a verdict based on God's law."

The Greek word translated *discern* is *diakrino* and means "to separate thoroughly and withdraw from, to make a difference, to be partial to what is good, to discern and decide."

What Are We to Discern?

When God told Solomon to ask for anything he wanted, Solomon asked for discernment. "Give therefore thy servant an understanding heart . . . that I may discern between good and bad" (I Kings 3:9).

God commanded the priests of Israel to "teach my people the difference between the holy and profane, and cause them to discern between the unclean and the clean" (Ezekiel 44:23). Mature believers are defined as those "who by reason of use have their senses exercised to discern both good and evil" (Hebrews 5:14). The word *senses* refers to our organs of perception: the eyes, ears, nose, tongue, hands, mind, and heart. We are to increase their ability to make fine distinctions between good and evil by constant exercise.

The Importance of Discerning Between Good and Evil

In Scripture, the opposite of holiness is uncleanness, as indicated by the following passages:

- "God hath not called us unto uncleanness, but unto holiness" (I Thessalonians 4:7).

- "As ye have yielded your members servants to uncleanness and to iniquity unto iniquity; even so now yield your members servants to righteousness unto holiness" (Romans 6:19).

The apostle Peter links New Testament holiness with the Old Testament instruction on holiness: "As obedient children, not fashioning yourselves according to the former lusts in your ignorance: But as he which hath called you is holy, so be ye holy in all manner of conversation; Because it is written, Be ye holy; for I am holy" (I Peter 1:14–16).

In this passage, Peter quotes directly from Leviticus, which describes approximately ten different

Discernment is spiritual sight that is not dimmed by lack of faith, virtue, knowledge, self-control, patience, godliness, brotherly kindness, or love.

"He that lacketh these things is blind, and cannot see afar off, and hath forgotten that he was purged from his old sins." —II Peter 1:9

"Discernment is the power to interpret what we see and hear." —Oswald Chambers

Discernment is the ability to see the hand of God in every circumstance and to understand His intentions through each one.

"All things work together for good to them that love God, to them who are the called according to his purpose." —Romans 8:28

The **bobcat** is an effective hunter. It is able to discern the intentions of its prey by evaluating every movement.

Discernment vs. JUDGMENT

1. One who discerns examines his own life. One who judges overlooks similar faults in himself.

2. One who discerns checks out all the facts. One who judges forms opinions and then looks for supporting evidence.

3. One who discerns deals privately with another person's failures. One who judges condemns publicly.

"As thine eye observeth others, so again are the eyes of others upon thee."

—Thomas á Kempis

categories of uncleanness. These include uncleanness in physical and moral areas. This one book contains over seventy references to the word *holy*.

"I am the LORD your God: ye shall therefore sanctify yourselves, and ye shall be holy; for I am holy: neither shall ye defile yourselves" (Leviticus 11:44). "Ye shall be holy: for I the LORD your God am holy" (Leviticus 19:2). "Sanctify yourselves therefore, and be ye holy: for I am the LORD your God" (Leviticus 20:7).

What Are the Consequences of Uncleanness?

Regulations against uncleanness govern the proper care of the body of a believer, which is the temple of the Holy Spirit. Defiling the temple brings the judgment of God. "Know ye not that ye are the temple of God, and that the Spirit of God dwelleth in you? If any man defile the temple of God, him shall God destroy; for the temple of God is holy, which temple ye are" (I Corinthians 3:16–17).

An even greater consequence comes when a believer defiles his body with moral uncleanness. He causes every other member of the body of Christ to be affected. Every believer is a member of the spiritual body of Christ. "So we, being many, are one body in Christ, and every one members one of another" (Romans 12:5). God has "set the members every one of them in the body, as it hath pleased him" (I Corinthians 12:18).

The interrelationship between the members of the body of Christ

is compared to the oneness of marriage. "So ought men to love their wives as their own bodies. He that loveth his wife loveth himself. . . . They two shall be one flesh. This is a great mystery: but I speak concerning Christ and the church" (Ephesians 5:28, 31–32).

The awesome result of this corporate union is that when one member commits a sin, the entire body of believers is damaged. "Whether one member suffer, all the members suffer with it" (I Corinthians 12:26).

This truth explains the warning in I Corinthians 6:15–19: "Know ye not that your bodies are the members of Christ? shall I then take the members of Christ, and make them the members of an harlot? God forbid. What? know ye not that he which is joined to an harlot is one body? for two, saith he, shall be one flesh. But he that is joined unto the Lord is one spirit."

The same truth is given to the Israelites. "The children of Israel committed a trespass in the accursed thing: for Achan . . . took of the accursed thing: and the anger of the LORD was kindled against the children of Israel" (Joshua 7:1). A discerning believer will understand that every thought, word, and action must be authorized by the Word of God and guarded by the Holy Spirit. Any violation must be repented of and confessed.

The Lord ordained the communion table as a time for thorough self-examination, with the awareness that confession of sin and asking forgiveness of the local body of Christ must be made before communion is taken. Failure to discern the true purpose of Christ's death and our responsibility to the body of believers is the cause of weakness, sickness, and premature death.

"Wherefore whosoever shall eat this bread, and drink this cup of the Lord, unworthily, shall be guilty of the body and blood of the Lord. But let a man examine himself, and so let him eat of that bread, and drink of that cup. For he that eateth and drinketh unworthily, eateth and drinketh damnation to himself, not discerning the Lord's body. For this cause many are weak and sickly among you, and many sleep" (I Corinthians 11:27–30).

How Do We Gain Discernment?

The answer is contained in Solomon's request of the Lord. "Give therefore thy servant an understanding heart . . . that I may discern between good and bad" (I Kings 3:9). An understanding heart is a "hearing heart." It listens to the voice of conscience, the words of Scripture, and the prompting of the Holy Spirit.

In James 1:5, we are urged to ask for wisdom and are assured that God will give it to all who ask for it in faith. We can, therefore, expect that as Solomon was granted his request, so we will be granted a similar one. As we exercise our senses in making each decision, our discernment will increase.

The tragic experience of those who reject the truth is that they are deceived. "They received not the love of the truth, that they might be saved. And for this cause God shall send them strong delusion, that they should believe a lie" (II Thessalonians 2:10–11).

What Are the Indicators of a Judgmental Spirit?

If the failures of others decrease our concern for the faults we know we have and instead improve our opinion of ourselves, then we are being judgmental.

We are judging when we share the failures of another with those who are not part of the solution. Bitterness, the mention of past failures, and a desire for vengeance are also signs of a judgmental spirit.

─ Personal Evaluation ─

How much discernment do you have?

- Do you ask God for an understanding heart to discern between good and bad?

- Do you follow holiness by rejecting all forms of uncleanness?

- Do you dedicate your body to God as a temple of the Holy Spirit?

- Do you ask God to remove anything in your life that would hinder you from hearing the voice of the Holy Spirit?

- Do you listen to both sides of a story before making conclusions?

- Do you evaluate the benefits for God's letting something happen?

- Do you consider a person's life and background before making a judgment?

- When you see someone making a wrong decision, do you desire to help?

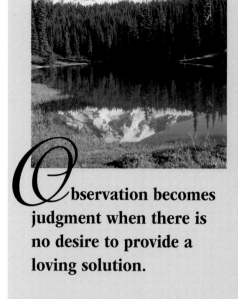

*O*bservation becomes judgment when there is no desire to provide a loving solution.

"Discernment is God's call to intercession, never to fault-finding." —Oswald Chambers

*T*ruth and love must always be combined with discernment.

- Truth without love is harshness.

- Love without truth is compromise.

"Beware of allowing the discernment of wrong in another blind you to the fact that you are what you are by the grace of God." —Oswald Chambers

Discretion is knowing when it is best to say nothing at all.

When you figure out an answer, learn to wait for someone to request it. A simple man opens his mouth and confirms his foolishness, but a discreet man keeps silent and is considered wise.

"Even a fool, when he holdeth his peace, is counted wise: and he that shutteth his lips is esteemed a man of understanding." —Proverbs 17:28

"Tis better to be silent and be thought a fool, than to speak and remove all doubt." —Abraham Lincoln

Discretion is knowing how to describe unpleasant things in a pleasant way.

"A word fitly spoken is like apples of gold in pictures of silver." —Proverbs 25:11

Discretion
vs. Simple-Mindedness

Discretion is using wisdom to avoid damaging attitudes, words, and actions and to give insightful counsel.

Definition

A close synonym to *discretion* in Scripture is the word *prudent*. Just as discreet behavior avoids damaging situations, so a prudent person understands cause-and-effect-sequences and acts accordingly. "A prudent man foreseeth the evil, and hideth himself: but the simple pass on, and are punished" (Proverbs 22:3).

There are several Hebrew words that are translated *prudent*. A primary word is *aruwm* which denotes cleverness. When combined with the proper motives and knowledge, a prudent person is able to avoid problems and think out insightful achievements. "Every prudent man dealeth with knowledge: but a fool layeth open his folly" (Proverbs 13:16). "The wisdom of the prudent is to understand his way: but the folly of fools is deceit" (Proverbs 14:8).

Some of the further characteristics of prudent behavior are:

- **Creative skill**—"I wisdom dwell with prudence, and find out knowledge of witty inventions." —Proverbs 8:12

- **Good judgment**—"A prudent man covereth shame."— Proverbs 12:16

- **Caution in speaking**—"A prudent man concealeth knowledge: but the heart of fools proclaimeth foolishness."—Proverbs 12:23

- **Initiative in learning**—"The heart of the prudent getteth knowledge; and the ear of the wise seeketh knowledge."—Proverbs 18:15

- **Checking out information**—"The simple believeth every word: but the prudent man looketh well to his going."—Proverbs 14:15

- **Openness to reproof**—"He that regardeth reproof is prudent." —Proverbs 15:5

The Importance of Discretion

Discretion, when properly used, will protect a man's health, wealth, and wisdom. "Discretion shall preserve thee, understanding shall keep thee" (Proverbs 2:11). There are several different Hebrew words that are translated *discretion* or *discreet*. The words, together with the context in which they are used, describe the meaning and application of discretion.

1. Discretion is developing and exercising an understanding heart.

An understanding heart is also a listening and obedient heart. "My son, attend unto my wisdom, and bow thine ear to my understanding: That thou mayest regard discretion [*mezimmah*], and that thy lips may keep knowledge. For the lips of a strange woman drop as an honeycomb, and her mouth is smoother than oil: But her end is bitter as wormwood, sharp as a two-edged sword" (Proverbs 5:1–4). The Hebrew word *mezimmah* conveys the idea of devising plans that are innovative, witty, and insightful.

2. Discretion is distinguishing right from wrong and choosing right.

Discretion knows what attitudes, words, and actions are right, honorable, and just and acts upon them. "A good man sheweth favour, and lendeth: he will guide his affairs with discretion. Surely he shall not be moved for ever: the righteous shall be in everlasting remembrance. He hath dispersed, he hath given to the poor; his righteousness endureth for ever; his horn shall be exalted with honour" (Psalm 112:5–6, 9). The Hebrew word for *discretion* in this verse is *mishpat.* It means "giving a judgment and making a verdict."

3. Discretion is treasuring and using wisdom.

To treasure something is to guard it, to cherish it, and to delight in it. "My son, let not them depart from thine eyes: keep sound wisdom and discretion: So shall they be life unto thy soul, and grace to thy neck. Then shalt thou walk in thy way safely, and thy foot shall not stumble. When thou liest down, thou shalt not be afraid: yea, thou shalt lie down, and thy sleep shall be sweet. (Proverbs 3:21–24).

The Hebrew word for *discretion* in this passage is *mezimmah* (depicting inventiveness). The use of such innovation and insight will

produce treasures. One treasuring money rather than wisdom may get riches but will not be able to sleep well at night because of his worry over business and fear of losing money.

4. Discretion is recognizing and responding to the motives of people.

Those who have wicked and deceptive motives should be avoided. Solomon became successful and famous because he had wisdom, understanding, and discretion. However, near the end of his life, he lost his discretion, and his heart was drawn away by immoral women. "Discretion shall preserve thee, understanding shall keep thee . . . To deliver thee from the strange woman, even from the stranger which flattereth with her words" (Proverbs 2:11, 16).

5. Discretion is turning knowledge into wise counsel.

Proverbs was written "to know wisdom and instruction; to perceive the words of understanding; To receive the instruction of wisdom, justice, and judgment, and equity; To give subtilty to the simple, to the young man knowledge and discretion [*mezimmah*]" (Proverbs 1:2–4). *Mezimmah* emphasizes the subtlety and insight of the counsel that is given.

6. Discretion is having the spirit of wisdom and walking in it.

Joseph is one of the most outstanding role models of discretion in the Scripture. He had a listening and obedient ear to his father, he used discretion in responding to the wicked and lustful motives of Potiphar's wife,

Realizing that its every step is vital in avoiding its enemies, the discreet **red fox** avoids its pursuers by making quick changes in direction and covering its tracks.

*A*n indiscreet word or action takes a moment to do but results in a lifetime of regret.

"*A prudent man foreseeth the evil, and hideth himself; but the simple pass on, and are punished.*"
—*Proverbs 27:12*

"*Wherefore, my beloved brethren, let every man be swift to hear, slow to speak, slow to wrath*" —*James 1:19*

Discretion is looking past problems and discussing the potential of a person or project.

When we learn how to see and communicate to others the solution for a blemish or weakness, new life is given. When we learn how to describe potential because of a blemish or weakness, hope is given.

"The mouth of a righteous man is a well of life. . . . The lips of the righteous know what is acceptable."

—*Proverbs 10:11, 32*

"He that keepeth his mouth keepeth his life: but he that openeth wide his lips shall have destruction."

—*Proverbs 13:3*

"Sometimes our best statements are made by saying nothing at all."

—Oswald Chambers

and he demonstrated discretion when he gave the following wise counsel to Pharaoh:

"Now therefore let Pharaoh look out a man discreet and wise, and set him over the land of Egypt. Let Pharaoh do this, and let him appoint officers over the land, and take up the fifth part of the land of Egypt in the seven plenteous years. And let them gather all the food of those good years that come, and lay up corn under the hand of Pharaoh, and let them keep food in the cities. And that food shall be for store to the land against the seven years of famine, which shall be in the land of Egypt; that the land perish not through the famine" (Genesis 41:33–36).

"Pharaoh said unto Joseph, Forasmuch as God hath shewed thee all this, there is none so discreet and wise as thou art: Thou shalt be over my house, and according unto thy word shall all my people be ruled: only in the throne will I be greater than thou" (Genesis 41:39).

7. Discretion is controlling destructive emotions.

A person may have wisdom in giving counsel to others but lack the ability to control his own emotions of fear, frustration, and anger. However, "the discretion of a man deferreth his anger; and it is his glory to pass over a transgression" (Proverbs 19:11). The Hebrew word for *discretion* in this verse is *sekel*. It means "intelligence, understanding, and prudence." The word *transgression* means "to revolt morally, spiritually, or legally."

Discretion in this case would be to discern whose jurisdiction these "rebels" are under and to let their authorities deal with

them. "He that passeth by, and meddleth with strife belonging not to him, is like one that taketh a dog by the ears" (Proverbs 26:17). Such action will cause the meddler to be injured.

Similarly, we are not to fret ourselves because of evildoers or to get angry with their evil deeds, because God will soon deal with them. "Fret not thyself because of evildoers, neither be thou envious against the workers of iniquity. . . . Rest in the LORD, and wait patiently for him: fret not thyself because of him who prospereth in his way, because of the man who bringeth wicked devices to pass. Cease from anger, and forsake wrath: fret not thyself in any wise to do evil" (Psalm 37:1, 7–8). (See also Amos 5:12–15.)

┌ *Personal Evaluation* ┐

How discreet are you?

- Do you know how to determine the value of an activity?

- Do you say what is on your mind without first evaluating its effect on others?

- Do you welcome reproof from those who see you do or say wrong things?

- Do you learn from others' mistakes so that you do not repeat them?

- Do you stand alone for doing right and avoid all appearance of evil?

- Do you choose your friends on the basis of their wisdom rather than their popularity?

- Do you refrain from spreading gossip, slander, and damaging reports?

Endurance

vs. Discouragement

Endurance is experiencing the power of God's love by rejoicing in trials and tribulations.

Definition

Endurance is associated with the physical stamina required for a race. However, the character quality of endurance is much deeper than physical stamina. It includes the strength that comes by rejoicing in the reproaches of following the ways of God.

Kakopatheo, "to suffer trouble, to be afflicted, to undergo hardship"; and *anechomai*, "to hold oneself up against, to put up with, to bear and forbear"; are translated in the New Testament as *endure*. *Hupomeno*, also rendered *endure*, means "to stay under, to undergo, to have fortitude, to persevere, to suffer, to take patiently, and to remain."

To endure is to tenaciously hold on until a goal is accomplished. Jacob clung to the angel and declared, "I will not let you go until you bless me!" God not only blessed him but affirmed, "Thy name shall be called no more Jacob, but Israel: for as a prince hast thou power with God and with men, and hast prevailed" (Genesis 32:28).

What Are We to Endure?

The following passages explain the types of trials we are to endure:

1. **Endure hardness**—"As a good soldier of Jesus Christ" (II Timothy 2:3).

2. **Endure afflictions**—"When they will not endure sound doctrine" (II Timothy 4:3).

3. **Endure persecutions**—"That ye may be counted worthy of the kingdom of God, for which ye also suffer" (II Thessalonians 1:5).

4. **Endure tribulations**—"Which is a manifest token of the righteous judgment of God" (II Thessalonians 1:5).

5. **Endure grief**—"For this is thankworthy, if a man for conscience toward God endure grief, suffering wrongfully" (I Peter 2:19).

6. **Endure chastening**—So that "God dealeth with you as with sons" (Hebrews 12:7).

7. **Endure temptations**—So you can "receive the crown of life, which the Lord hath promised to them that love him" (James 1:12).

8. **Endure all things**—"For the elect's sakes" (II Timothy 2:10).

How Do We Endure?

Endurance is based on hope. A runner will endure rigorous and painful training for the hope that he will win the race. Jesus endured the cross and despised the shame for the joy of knowing that His death would conquer Satan and

---

*E*ndurance is focusing on a goal greater than distractions along the way.

When we realize that we have limited strength, we will reject unnecessary demands in order to conserve our energy resources.

"Let us lay aside every weight, and the sin which doth so easily beset us, and let us run with patience the race that is set before us."
—Hebrews 12:1

"No rock is so hard but that a little wave may beat admission in a thousand years."
—Alfred, Lord Tennyson

*O*bedience leads us to inexhaustible resources of strength.

We must recognize and acknowledge our weaknesses in order to draw upon the strength of Christ. We can have confidence that God will provide what is necessary to accomplish an impossible task. God always enables us to do what He calls us to do.

"He giveth power to the faint; and to them that have no might he increaseth strength." —Isaiah 40:29

*F*ollow champions. They set the pace for winning the race.

"If thou hast run with the footmen, and they have wearied thee, then how canst thou contend with horses? and if in the land of peace, wherein thou trustedst, they wearied thee, then how wilt thou do in the swelling of Jordan?" —Jeremiah 12:5

*R*unner
Two Fears of a

1. Running out of strength before reaching the goal

2. Reaching the finish line with energy left over.

"I press toward the mark for the prize of the high calling of God in Christ Jesus." —Philippians 3:14

*E*ndurance comes by knowing we will win the prize unless we give up on the race.

As a seed must die before bearing fruit, so God brings "death of a vision" to test our endurance and then rewards us with supernatural fulfillment.

"And let us not be weary in well-doing: for in due season we shall reap, if we faint not." —Galatians 6:9

bring redemption to the redeemed for all eternity. The believer's hope is that by enduring trials, he will experience a greater measure of spiritual power in this life as well as rewards in Heaven.

This power includes the fruit of the Spirit—love, joy, and peace. This threefold sequence of the Holy Spirit in us, followed by tests resulting in the power of the Holy Spirit upon us, is repeated throughout Scripture. The Christian life begins with faith, then hope is needed during times of testing and tribulation. The result is genuine love. (See chart below.)

Biblical Examples of Endurance

- Elijah stood against the evil of his day and was hunted down, but he was faithful to the end (I Kings 19).
- John the Baptist was imprisoned for his stand on divorce and remarriage, yet he remained faithful to his death (Matthew 11:11).
- Daniel maintained Godly standards during the reign of four kings. He was tested when others attempted to take his life, but he endured to the end (Daniel 1:21).

The Filling of the Spirit	The Testing of the Spirit	The Power of the Spirit
1. Jesus Christ was filled by the Spirit at His baptism (Luke 4:1).	He was led by the Spirit into the wilderness for testing.	Jesus returned in the power of the Spirit (Luke 4:14).
2. The disciples were filled with the Spirit when Jesus breathed on them.	They were to wait in Jerusalem until they received power.	The Holy Spirit came upon them in power, and multitudes believed (Acts 1–3).
3. Paul was "filled with the Holy Ghost" at his conversion (Acts 9:17–18).	He gloried in infirmities, reproaches, necessities, persecutions, and distresses.	"I glory in my infirmities, that the power of Christ may rest upon me" (II Corinthians 12:9).
4. The Thessalonian believers received the Holy Spirit through Paul's preaching.	They had patience and faith in all the persecutions and tribulations they endured (II Thessalonians 1:3–5).	Their faith grew exceedingly, and their love toward each other abounded (I Thessalonians 1:3).
5. All believers receive the Holy Spirit into their spirits at salvation (Romans 8:9–16) and can ask God to fill their souls with His Holy Spirit (Luke 11:13).	The Spirit leads all believers into fiery trials, temptations, and reproaches (I Peter 4:12–14; James 1:1–3; Matthew 5:11–12).	"If ye be reproached for the name of Christ, happy are ye; for the spirit of glory and of God resteth upon you" (I Peter 4:14).

- Luke endured with Paul to the end (II Timothy 4:11).
- Demas failed the endurance test. Rather than serve Paul in prison, he left to enjoy the pleasures of this world (II Timothy 4:10).

How Does Truth Motivate Endurance?

Truth sets us free from the destructive attitudes and influences that diminish endurance.

When trials and temptations come, we are to meet and endure them with the following four responses:

1. Thank God for each trial.

We can be thankful for all things, because all things come from the hand of God. They are for our benefit and can teach us character. They also "work together for good to them that love God." Job endured a great affliction of trial, because he understood this point, "the LORD gave, and the LORD hath taken away; blessed be the name of the LORD" (Job 1:21).

2. Rejoice in all things.

Once we recognize the benefits that God intends through our trials, we can rejoice in them. If we lack wisdom to discern these benefits, we can simply ask God for it and He will give it to us.

3. Cry out when necessary.

Some situations should not be endured, and God will bring relief when we cry out to Him. "Call upon me in the day of trouble: I will deliver thee, and thou shalt glorify me" (Psalm 50:15).

4. Overcome by doing good.

"Be not overcome of evil, but overcome evil with good" (Romans 12:21).

Personal Evaluation

How strong is your endurance?

- Do you live as a soldier who is in the most critical spiritual war ever waged, or as a civilian in a time of peace, prosperity, and pleasure?

- Do you rejoice when rejected by those who do not follow the ways of God, or do you complain that you have to suffer for the beliefs and standards of true discipleship?

- Do you rejoice in being falsely accused and blamed for things you did not do, or do you become reactionary, defensive, and bitter toward those who question your integrity?

- Do you accept God's chastening for things you have done wrong, or do you become discouraged and want to give up on the Christian life?

- Do you resist temptation and bring every thought into captivity, or do you easily surrender to the lusts of the flesh and the lusts of the mind?

- Do you look forward to trials and persecutions so you can experience more of the power of Christ's love, or do you have a fear of man and suffering?

The palm tree endures abuse that would kill other trees, because it is not harmed by surface wounds.

The source of life in a palm tree is at its center rather than just beneath the outward surface, as in other trees. Its roots go deep into the ground and draw nourishment during times of drought. The longer it endures, the sweeter its fruit becomes.

"The righteous shall flourish like the palm tree: he shall grow like a cedar in Lebanon." —Psalm 92:12

"Do not pray for tasks equal to your strength, but for strength equal to your tasks."
—Phillips Brooks

The **camel** illustrates the secret of endurance by maintaining the inward reserves to withstand "desert experiences."

Enthusiasm
vs. Apathy

Enthusiasm is God's energy in my spirit expressing itself through my mind, will, and emotions.

*T*he flame of a candle is like enthusiasm in our souls—self consuming. The flame of an oil lamp is like enthusiasm of our spirit—continuous when properly filled.

"Be filled with the Spirit," and "Let the word of Christ dwell in you richly in all wisdom."

—*Ephesians 5:18* and *Colossians 3:16*

*M*aintaining enthusiasm requires continuous fellowship with the Word of God and the Spirit of God.

"Quench not the Spirit."

—*I Thessalonians 5:19*

Definition

The word *enthusiasm* is made up of two Greek words, *en* meaning "in" and *theos*, which means "God." To be enthusiastic is to be energized and inspired by God. A Biblical counterpart to this word is *fervent*. To be fervent in spirit is to "boil with heat; to be hot, as in boiling with genuine love for God and others."

Another Biblical term for enthusiasm is *zeal*, from the Greek word *zelos* meaning "excitement of mind, ardor, or fervor of spirit." *Zelos* is ardor in pursuing, embracing, or defending someone or something. Another Biblical word for enthusiasm is *earnest*. The Hebrew word *charah*, translated *earnestly*, means "to be hot, to act furiously, or to burn." A Biblical expression for enthusiasm is to "leap for joy,"and is expressed by the Greek word *stirato*, meaning "to jump, to leap with joy."

Commands to Be Enthusiastic

Every believer is instructed to be enthusiastic in the basic matters of Christian living. "Let love be without dissimulation. Abhor that which is evil; cleave to that which is good. Be kindly affectioned one to another with brotherly love; in honour prefer-ring one another; Not slothful in business; **fervent in spirit**; serving the Lord" (Romans 12:9–11).

Scripture identifies specific areas in which to be enthusiastic and then adds further instruction on how to do it. "But it is good to be zealously affected always in a good thing" (Galatians 4:18).

What Are We to Be Enthusiastic About?

• Be Enthusiastic About God.

Paul was "**zealous** toward God" even before his conversion (see Acts 22:3). However, it was "zeal without knowledge." He was "zealous of the religious traditions of his forefathers" (Galatians 1:14). When he became a believer, however, he transferred that same zeal to advancing the kingdom of God.

Webster's 1828 dictionary describes this transformation of zeal as the maturing of enthusiasm. It defines enthusiasm as a "violent passion or excitement of the mind, in pursuit of some object, inspiring confidence of success. [It is] the same heat of imagination, chastised by reason or experience, [that] becomes a noble passion [and] an ardent zeal. [It] forms sublime ideas and prompts to the ardent pursuit of laudable objects. . . . Such is the enthusiasm of the patriot, the hero, and the Christian."

- **Be Enthusiastic About Loving Others.**

"Above all things have fervent charity among yourselves: for charity shall cover the multitude of sins" (I Peter 4:8). The Corinthian believers exercised fervent love toward Paul. Titus "told us your earnest desire, your mourning, your **fervent** mind toward me; so that I rejoiced the more" (II Corinthians 7:7).

Fervent love is possible only if we first purify our souls by obeying God's truth. Otherwise we will have a mixture of affection with wrong motives and desires: "Seeing ye have purified your souls in obeying the truth through the Spirit unto unfeigned love of the brethren, see that ye love one another with a pure heart **fervently**" (I Peter 1:22).

- **Be Enthusiastic About Prayer.**

"The effectual fervent prayer of a righteous man availeth much [makes much power available]" (James 5:16). One of Paul's co-laborers joined him in having this mind of prayer for other believers: "Epaphras, who is one of you, a servant of Christ, saluteth you, always labouring **fervently** for you in prayers, that ye may stand perfect and complete in all the will of God. For I bear him record, that he hath a great **zeal** for you, and them that are in Laodicea, and them in Hierapolis" (Colossians 4:12–13).

- **Be Enthusiastic About Good Works.**

All believers are to be enthusiastic about doing sacrificial work that will benefit others. These works must be done without any motive of personal reward or glory. They should be carried out so that others get the credit and God gets the

The humpback whale shows its enthusiasm for life by energetically leaping into midair and singing songs that reverberate for hundreds of miles through the ocean waters.

glory. Jesus Christ "gave himself for us, that he might redeem us from all iniquity, and purify unto himself a peculiar people, **zealous** of good works" (Titus 2:14). Based on this, we are able to "provoke [one another] unto love and to good works" (Hebrews 10:24).

The enthusiasm of the Corinthian believers in giving an offering for needy believers motivated others to follow their example. Paul wrote, "Your **zeal** [in giving] hath provoked very many" (II Corinthians 9:2).

- **Be Enthusiastic About Repentance.**

The same zeal we are to have in serving God and others, we are to have in maintaining a good conscience toward God and man. The Laodicean believers, for whom Epaphras earnestly prayed, lacked enthusiasm. They were not "hot" for their Lord; they were "lukewarm." God reproved them for this condition and warned them to repent.

"I know thy works, that thou art neither cold nor hot: I would thou wert cold or hot. So then because thou art lukewarm, and neither cold nor hot, I will spue thee out of my mouth. . . . As many as I love, I rebuke and chasten: be **zealous** therefore, and repent" (Revelation 3:15–16, 19).

- **Be Enthusiastic About Trials and Reproaches.**

Jesus taught us to "rejoice, and be **exceeding glad**" when men speak evil of us (see Matthew 5:12). Paul took "pleasure in infirmities,

*E*nthusiasm is passionate devotion to the work of God.

"Every man is at his best when he adds enthusiasm to . . . his undertakings."

—John Wanamaker

*E*nthusiasm is the by-product of having a life purpose that is worth dying for.

"It is good to be zealously affected always in a good thing."

—*Galatians 4:18*

*E*nthusiasm turns ordinary actions into extraordinary achievements.

"Not by might, nor by power, but by my spirit, saith the LORD of hosts."
—Zechariah 4:6

*E*nthusiasm is the secret energy of those who are truly successful.

"Wherever you are, be all there. Live to the hilt every situation you believe to be the will of God."
—Jim Elliot

*E*nthusiasm is expressing to those around me the power of God's working in me.

in reproaches, in necessities, in persecutions, in distresses" (II Corinthians 12:10).

How Do We Generate Enthusiasm?

Genuine enthusiasm is not something we activate by our own energy. It is the harmonious interaction with the Holy Spirit of God that produces enthusiasm. For this reason, we are to "quench not the spirit," nor grieve Him with things in our lives that displease Him (I Thessalonians 5:19; see also Ephesians 4:30).

It is important to distinguish the enthusiasm of our spirits from the excitement of our souls. Those who try to stir up enthusiasm in their mind, will, or emotions will eventually experience depression and burnout.

Enthusiasm in our souls is like a candle. It gives light, but it is self-consuming. On the other hand, enthusiasm generated in our spirits is like the flame of an oil lamp. As long as we are filled by the Spirit of God and the Word of God, enthusiasm, like an oil-filled lamp, will burn indefinitely.

The Psalmist describes the way in which the spirit encourages the soul in enthusiasm, because it is possible for the soul to be sorrowful and the spirit to be enthusiastic at the same time. "Why art thou cast down, O my soul? and why art thou disquieted within me? hope thou in God: for I shall yet praise him, who is the health of my countenance, and my God" (Psalm 42:11).

Who Demonstrated Enthusiasm?

- Paul was a champion of enthusiasm. His fervency and zeal for

the Lord caused him to pour out his life on the altar of sacrifice for believers. (See Philippians 2:17.)

- Apollos was "an eloquent man, and mighty in the scriptures. . . . Being fervent in the spirit, he spake and taught diligently the things of the Lord" (Acts 18:24–25).

- Regarding the household of Stephanas, Scripture states "That they have addicted themselves to the ministry of the saints" (I Corinthians 16:15).

Personal Evaluation

How enthusiastic are you?

- Do you give energy to all those around you by being enthusiastic?

- Have you experienced the indwelling of the Holy Spirit through salvation in Christ?

- As a believer, have you asked your Heavenly Father to fill your life with the Holy Spirit?

- Do you experience emotional drain or depression by trying to act enthusiastic with your emotions rather than through God's Spirit?

- Do you fill the "lamp" of your spirit with daily fellowship with God through His Spirit and His Word?

- Do you give everyone a warm, enthusiastic smile, or only those who are your close friends?

- Do you get more excited about sports than the challenge of the Christian life?

- Do you read novels more fervently than you study the Scriptures?

Faith
vs. Unbelief

**Faith is recognizing God's will
in a given matter and acting upon it.**

Definition

The Greek word for *faith* is *pistis*. It comes from the root word *peitho,* which means "to be persuaded, to convince by reason, to agree with evidence, to rely with inward certainty, to be confident." Faith is based on the promises of God, which are so certain that waiting for them is not discouraging and acting upon them is natural. "Faith is the substance of things hoped for, the evidence of things not seen" (Hebrews 11:1).

Why Is Faith So Important?

"Without faith it is impossible to please him; for he that cometh to God must believe that he is, and that he is a rewarder of them that diligently seek him" (Hebrews 11:6).

- We are justified by faith (made perfect in God's sight). (See Romans 3:28.)

- We are saved from our sins by faith. (See Ephesians 2:8–9.)

- We are sanctified and cleansed by faith. (See Acts 26:18.)

- Our hearts are purified by faith. (See Acts 15:9.)

- We have access by faith into God's grace. (See Romans 5:2.)

- We can "move mountains" by faith. (See Matthew 17:20.)

How Do We Get Faith?

An initial measure of faith to believe in God is given to every person in the world. Jesus commended the faith of little children by stating, "Whosoever shall not receive the kingdom of God as a little child, he shall not enter therein" (Mark 10:15).

Faith for salvation comes by hearing the Word of God. "So then faith cometh by hearing, and hearing by the word of God" (Romans 10:17). After salvation, faith is acquired as we receive messages through Scripture and act upon them.

Before Scripture was written, the great men and women of faith often heard directly from God. Noah was warned of God to build the ark, and Abraham was called by God to go out of his country. (See Hebrews 11:7–8.)

How Does the Word of God Activate Faith?

Two primary Greek terms are translated *word* in the New Testament. The first, *logos,* refers to the total inspired Word of God. Jesus is called the living *logos* of God. (See John 1:1.)

The second term is *rhema.* A *rhema* is a passage from Scripture given to specific individuals for their personal application. When

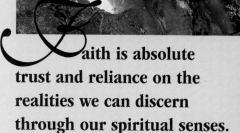

aith is absolute trust and reliance on the realities we can discern through our spiritual senses.

"For we walk by faith, not by sight."
—II Corinthians 5:7

"Faith never means gullibility. The man who believes everything is as far from God as the man who refuses to believe anything."
—A. W. Tozer

aith and obedience are so closely intertwined that you cannot have one without the other.

"Faith and obedience are bound up in the same bundle; he that obeys God trusts God; and he that trusts God obeys God."
—C. H. Spurgeon

> "Faith by its nature must be tried. . . . Faith untried has no character value for the individual."
>
> —Oswald Chambers

Although not equipped with wings, the **flying squirrel** takes a "leap of faith" each time it glides from branch to branch.

Jesus told Peter to cast the fishing nets on the other side of the boat, Peter answered, "Master, we have toiled all the night, and have taken nothing: nevertheless at thy word [*rhema*] I will let down the net" (Luke 5:5).

Further passages that explain the *rhemas* of God are as follows.

- "But he answered and said, It is written, Man shall not live by bread alone, but by every word [*rhema*] that proceedeth out of the mouth of God" (Matthew 4:4).

- "So then faith cometh by hearing, and hearing by the word [*rhema*] of God" (Romans 10:17).

- "And take the helmet of salvation, and the sword of the Spirit, which is the word [*rhema*] of God" (Ephesians 6:17).

- "Husbands, love your wives, even as Christ also loved the church, and gave himself for it; That he might sanctify and cleanse it with the washing of water by the word [*rhema*]" (Ephesians 5:25–26).

- "If ye abide in me, and my words [*rhemas*] abide in you, ye shall ask what ye will, and it shall be done unto you" (John 15:7).

The Quality of Faith Varies in Individuals

- We can have weak faith or strong faith—Romans 4:19–20
- We can have faith that is tested or untested—I Peter 1:7
- We can have little faith or great faith—Matthew 8:10, 26
- We can be lacking in faith or abounding in faith—I Thessalonians 3:10, II Thessalonians 1:3

Faith Must Be Expressed in Actions

"Even so faith, if it hath not works, is dead, being alone. Yea, a man may say, Thou hast faith, and I have works: shew me thy faith without thy works, and I will shew thee my faith by my works" (James 2:17–18). In God's hall of fame, those who had faith acted upon it. By faith Noah built an ark. By faith Abraham went out from his homeland. By faith Moses rejected the treasures of Egypt and chose to suffer affliction with the children of Israel (see Hebrews 11).

Faith Can Be Exercised for the Benefit of Others

When a man who was suffering from palsy was brought to Jesus by four of his friends, we are not told about the faith of the man. Rather, we are informed that the faith of his four friends actually caused him to be restored. "And, behold, they brought to him a man sick of the palsy, lying on a bed: and Jesus seeing their faith said unto the sick of the palsy; Son, be of good cheer; thy sins be forgiven thee" (Matthew 9:2).

Personal Evaluation

How strong is your faith?

- Do you watch for *rhemas* as you read through Scripture?
- Do you memorize and meditate upon the *rhemas* God gives you?
- Do you believe that God is living and that He rewards those who diligently seek Him?
- Do you pray in generalities or make specific requests to the Lord?
- Do you wait for God's provision or do you borrow money for the things you think you should have?
- Do you have examples in your life of God working supernaturally through your faith?

Flexibility
vs. Resistance

Flexibility is not setting my affections on plans or places that could be changed by those whom I am serving.

Definition

Flexibility is a very important and necessary character quality, yet the word *flexibility* is not used in the Bible. Thus, a search for the concept of flexibility must be carried out. One must understand that in order to be flexible, change must occur, and that change produces tension. According to studies, one of the most stressful events in life is uprooting the family and moving it to a new location—especially one that is unknown.

With this in mind, we discover that flexibility is one of the first qualities that God teaches His followers. He called Abraham to leave his country and kindred and move to a land that God would show him. He called the nation of Israel out of Egypt and throughout their wilderness journey had them watch the cloud over the Tabernacle. When the cloud moved, they were to move. Therefore, they had to be in a constant state of flexibility.

When Jesus called His disciples, He asked them to leave their homes and vocations and follow after Him.

Peter described the essence of flexibility when he wrote, "I beseech you as strangers and pilgrims . . . ," (I Peter 2:11). A stranger is a visitor from another country who is just passing through, and a pilgrim is one who is traveling to a sacred destination. The necessity for such an outlook is underscored by our need to be in the world but not of the world.

God begs us to "love not the world, neither the things that are in the world. If any man love the world, the love of the Father is not in him. For all that is in the world, the lust of the flesh, and the lust of the eyes, and the pride of life, is not of the Father, but is of the world. And the world passeth away, and the lust thereof: but he that doeth the will of God abideth for ever" (I John 2:15–17).

Additionally, in I Peter 2:11, a flexible attitude is related to conquering the lusts that war against the soul. "Dearly beloved, I beseech you as strangers and pilgrims, abstain from fleshly lusts, which war against the soul."

Biblical Examples of Flexibility

Abraham is the father of faith. (See Galatians 3:6–9.) In the very call of God upon Abraham's life, he was required to have flexibility. "Now the Lord had said unto Abram, Get thee out of thy country, and from thy kindred, and from thy father's house, unto a land that I will shew thee" (Genesis 12:1).

In the Scriptures, the land of Egypt is a type of the world, and

---

The deeper our roots go into the love of Christ, the greater our capacity for flexibility.

"That ye, being rooted and grounded in love, May be able to comprehend with all saints what is the breadth, and length, and depth, and height; And to know the love of Christ, which passeth knowledge, that ye might be filled with all the fulness of God."
—Ephesians 3:17–19

A person who is inflexible to God's ways will usually be very flexible to false ideas.

"And for this cause God shall send them strong delusion, that they should believe a lie." —II Thessalonians 2:11

"That we henceforth be no more children, tossed to and fro, and carried about with every wind of doctrine, by the sleight of men, and cunning craftiness, whereby they lie in wait to deceive." —Ephesians 4:14

It takes the wisdom of God to know when to be flexible and when to be firm.

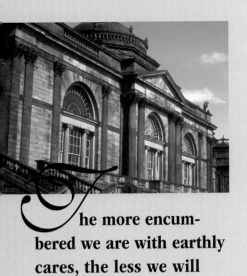

The more encumbered we are with earthly cares, the less we will understand flexibility.

"No man that warreth entangleth himself with the affairs of this life; that he may please him who hath chosen him to be a soldier."

—II Timothy 2:4

"For where your treasure is, there will your heart be also." —Luke 12:34

Flexibility is being ready and willing to move when God says "move" and to stay when He says "stay."

"One life yielded to God at all costs is worth thousands only touched by God."

—Oswald Chambers

There is a natural tendency to resist flexibility by viewing this world as our final destination.

"Their inward thought is, that their houses shall continue for ever, and their dwelling places to all generations; they call their lands after their own names." —Psalm 49:11

the nation of Israel is a type of all believers whom God wants to lead out of the bondage of worldly lusts into a land of promise.

During their travels from Egypt to the Promised Land, the people were to watch the cloud of God. If it moved, they were to move with it. "When the cloud was taken up from over the tabernacle, the children of Israel went onward in all their journeys: But if the cloud were not taken up, then they journeyed not till the day that it was taken up. For the cloud of the Lord was upon the tabernacle by day, and fire was on it by night, in the sight of all the house of Israel, throughout all their journeys" (Exodus 40:36–38).

David was a man after God's own heart. (See Acts 13:22.) God taught him flexibility by stirring up the heart of King Saul to be jealous of David and to try to kill him. David had to flee from place to place for his life. Flexibility training was an important part of his preparation for national leadership. It forced him to focus on God and His ways rather than his own earthly surroundings.

Jesus taught all His disciples the same quality when He told them to forsake all and follow Him. "Whosoever doth not bear his cross, and come after me, cannot be my disciple" (Luke 14:27).

On one occasion, three disciples wanted to "settle in." "Then answered Peter, and said unto Jesus, Lord, it is good for us to be here: if thou wilt, let us make here three tabernacles." It is significant that "while he yet spake, behold, a bright cloud overshadowed them." (See Matthew 17:4–5.)

Who Failed the Test of Flexibility?

While Lot was with Abraham, he moved from place to place in a tent, but then he "pitched his tent" toward the cities of Sodom and Gomorrah and soon was in the city of Sodom with all its sin and wickedness. When two angels came to bring Lot and his family out of the city, before its destruction, Lot's wife resisted.

When she left, she disobeyed God's instruction by looking back at the burning city and was immediately turned into a pillar of salt. (See Genesis 19.) This account is important because when Jesus taught His disciples not to grasp after their own lives and goals, He said, "Remember Lot's wife" (Luke 17:32).

Both Mary and Martha followed the Lord and ministered to His needs. When Martha needed Mary's help in preparing a meal, she accused Mary of being inflexible. However, Jesus explained to Martha that true flexibility is waiting on the Lord rather than worrying about the details of serving Him.

"Now it came to pass, as they went, that he entered into a certain village: and a certain woman named Martha received him into her house. And she had a sister called Mary, which also sat at Jesus' feet, and heard his word. But Martha was cumbered about much serving, and came to him, and said, Lord, dost thou not care that my sister hath left me to serve alone? bid her therefore that she help me. And Jesus answered and said unto her, Martha, Martha, thou art careful and troubled about many things: But one thing is needful: and Mary hath chosen that good part, which shall not be taken away from her" (Luke 10:38–42).

How Does Flexibility Relate to Serving?

The ultimate example of flexibility in serving is referred to in the following passage: "Behold, as the eyes of servants look unto the hand of their masters, and as the eyes of a maiden unto the hand of her mistress; so our eyes wait upon the LORD our God" (Psalm 123:2).

In Biblical times, the heads of households would have hand signals for different instructions, which their servants understood and quickly carried out. In order to know what to do, the servants had to keep their eyes on the hands of their masters at all times. Their own plans and agendas were always subject to the hand signals of their masters.

Flexibility is the willingness to change plans or ideas according to the direction of our authorities. The less we become emotionally involved in plans or ideas, the easier it will be to change them. Therefore, we are to guard our "heart with all diligence; for out of it are the issues of life" (Proverbs 4:23).

Martha was attentive to the details of serving, but Mary was attentive to the personal teaching and direction of the Lord.

Ultimately, flexibility is based on the desire and delight to do the will of God, and an inflexible attitude reveals a persistence to do our own will. David was flexible because he delighted to do the will of God (see Psalm 40:8).

─ *Personal Evaluation* ─

How flexible are you?

- When plans are changed, do you get discouraged, or do you immediately look for reasons why the new plans are better?

- Do you quickly adjust to a change of direction, or does it require time for you to mentally and emotionally adjust?

- When you learn that you must move, does it cause anxiety in you, or do you rejoice in it as a further reminder that you are a stranger and a pilgrim?

- Do your parents or employers have to explain instructions twice, or do you understand what they mean the first time?

- When God calls you to a ministry or work, do you resist and make yourself busy with other activities?

- When others suggest a better way to do something, do you try it or do you keep doing it the way you had been doing it?

- Do you misuse flexibility by having no daily plans or life goals?

- Is your life so encumbered with possessions and debt that it would be impractical or impossible to exercise flexibility at the leading of the Lord?

- Are the thoughts of your heart in harmony with the will of God so that changes are easy transitions?

The **ruby-throated hummingbird** is a picture of flexibility as it uses whatever position or direction necessary to carry out its work. It can fly backward, forward, up, down, sideways, or just hover in one place.

The degree of pain we experience when required to be flexible reveals the extent to which our affections are set on things of this world.

When did two dreams require instant flexibility and thereby save the life of a king? (See Matthew 2:12–13.)

vs. Bitterness

Forgiveness is responding to offenders so that the power of God's love through me can heal them.

God's formula for forgiveness: seventy times seven equals zero.

"Lord, how oft shall my brother sin against me, and I forgive him? till seven times? Jesus saith unto him, I say not unto thee, Until seven times: but, Until seventy times seven." —Matthew 18:21–22

"If he trespass against thee seven times in a day, and seven times in a day turn again to thee, saying, I repent; thou shalt forgive him." —Luke 17:4

Giving forgiveness to a believer is a gift to yourself, because we are all members of one Body.

Definition

Forgiveness is clearing the record of an offender and choosing to bear any continuing consequences of the offense.

The primary word used in Scripture to define forgiveness is *aphiemi*. It means "to send away." The implication is to send away a debtor with his debt paid.

This is the word used by Jesus when He said, "And forgive us our debts, as we forgive our debtors" (Matthew 6:12).

A Greek word for *forgiving* is *charizomai*. It means "to do something pleasant or agreeable, to do a favour to, to give graciously, to give freely." This is the word used by Paul when he wrote, "Be ye kind one to another, tenderhearted, forgiving one another even as God for Christ's sake hath forgiven you" (Ephesians 4:32).

Why Forgiveness Is Important

There are serious consequences to one who refuses to forgive an offender. Listed below are serious physical, mental, emotional, and spiritual consequences to anyone who refuses to forgive an offender.

• We are not forgiven.

Jesus said, "If ye forgive men their trespasses, your heavenly Father will also forgive you: But if ye forgive not men their trespasses, neither will your Father forgive your trespasses" (Matthew 6:14–15).

• We are tormented.

When a servant who was forgiven of a great debt refused to forgive a fellow servant who owed him a small debt, the Lord said, "O thou wicked servant, I forgave thee all that debt, because thou desiredst me: Shouldest not thou also have had compassion on thy fellowservant, even as I had pity on thee? And his lord was wroth, and delivered him to the tormentors, till he should pay all that was due unto him. So likewise shall my heavenly Father do also unto you, if ye from your hearts forgive not every one his brother their trespasses" (Matthew 18:32–35).

• We are defiled.

When we are offended, God gives us the grace to forgive our offenders. Therefore, we are to "follow peace with all men, and holiness, without which no man shall see the Lord: Looking diligently lest any man fail of the grace of God; lest any root of bitterness springing up trouble you, and thereby many be defiled" (Hebrews 12:14–15).

• We damage our health.

If we refuse to forgive our offenders, we will not be able to properly observe the Lord's table. "For this cause many are weak and sickly among you, and many sleep [die prematurely]" (I Corinthians 11:30).

How Forgiveness Relates to Pardon

If someone kills a member of our family, we are to forgive that person. However, we do not have the authority to grant a pardon because we do not have the jurisdiction over that crime. Therefore, even with our forgiveness, that person will suffer the continuing consequences of the offense. Forgiveness is clearing the record of an offender and restoring fellowship. However, the seeds of destruction may continue to have serious consequences.

After David committed adultery with Bathsheba and arranged the murder of her husband, he repented. "Nathan said unto David, The Lord also hath put away thy sin; thou shalt not die" (II Samuel 12:13). David's sin was forgiven, but there were further consequences. "Thus saith the Lord, Behold, I will raise up evil against thee out of thine own house, and I will take thy wives before thine eyes, and give them unto thy neighbour" (II Samuel 12:11).

How We Learn to Forgive

When people are asked if they can recall someone who deeply hurt or offended them, they usually respond immediately by saying, "Yes!" The question must then be asked, have these offenders been fully forgiven?

A lack of forgiveness creates bitterness, and bitterness is like the disease of leprosy. Those who have leprosy lose any sensation of pain; therefore, they are unaware of when they are hurting themselves or others. Similarly, those who are bitter are often unaware of how they hurt other people with their words, attitudes, and actions. In order to motivate people to forgive, God uses commands, contrasts, and concepts.

Commands to Forgive

- "And be ye kind one to another, tenderhearted, forgiving one another, even as God for Christ's sake hath forgiven you" (Ephesians 4:32).

- "Forbearing one another, and forgiving one another, if any man have a quarrel against any: even as Christ forgave you, so also do ye" (Colossians 3:13).

- "Judge not, and ye shall not be judged: condemn not, and ye shall not be condemned: forgive, and ye shall be forgiven" (Luke 6:37).

- "Take heed to yourselves: If thy brother trespass against thee, rebuke him; and if he repent, forgive him" (Luke 17:3).

Concepts to Understand Forgiveness

- **Pleading for mercy vs. pleading for more time**

The servant who refused to forgive a small debt after being released from a huge debt was not able to give mercy, because he did not ask for it. He asked instead for an extension of time: "Have patience with me, and I will pay thee all" (Matthew 18:26). The wise master put him in prison with tormentors to cause him to realize

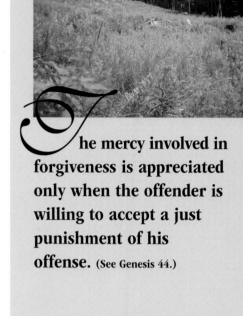

*T*he mercy involved in forgiveness is appreciated only when the offender is willing to accept a just punishment of his offense. **(See Genesis 44.)**

"If you are suffering from a bad man's injustice, forgive him lest there be two bad men."
—St. Augustine

A **sheep** quickly rebounds from hardship. It will take suffering and affliction without retaliating or uttering a sound.

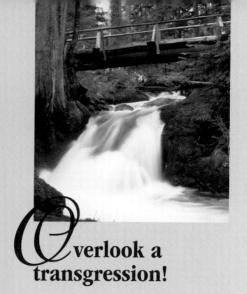

Overlook a transgression!

"The discretion of a man deferreth his anger; and it is his glory to pass over a transgression."

—*Proverbs 19:11*

"I will permit no man to narrow and degrade my soul by making me hate him."

—Booker T. Washington

True forgiveness disregards any thoughts of retaliation or revenge.

An offense is an indication of a violation of God's principles. We can be sure that our offender will suffer consequences from God.

"Dearly beloved, avenge not yourselves, but rather give place unto wrath: for it is written, Vengeance is mine; I will repay, saith the Lord."

—*Romans 12:19*

that he could never pay it all back. Only then would he plead for mercy and be able to give it to others. (See Luke 7:41–48.)

- **Clearing the conscience vs. responding with harshness**

When David tried the case of the man who stole his neighbor's pet sheep, he became angry and demanded an extreme punishment. The law required only four sheep for the stolen one. However, David was unable to give justice or mercy, because he was guilty of the same offense. When we harshly judge others, we condemn ourselves because we do the same things. (See Romans 2:1–3.)

- **Having the goal of love vs. retaliation**

There are three steps to receiving the power of God's Spirit. The first is being filled with the Holy Spirit. This takes place by the indwelling of the Spirit at salvation (see Romans 8:15) and the filling of the Spirit when we ask our Heavenly Father for it. (See Luke 11:13 and Ephesians 5:18.)

The second step is the testing of the Holy Spirit. Paul lists some of these tests in II Corinthians 12:10: "Therefore I take pleasure in infirmities, in reproaches, in necessities, in persecutions, in distresses for Christ's sake: for when I am weak, then am I strong." We pass the test of the Holy Spirit by giving thanks in every test (see I Thessalonians 5:18), rejoicing in every test (see Philippians 4:4), and when necessary, crying out to God for deliverance (see Psalm 50:15).

To the degree that we pass the test of a trial, we experience the power of the Holy Spirit, which begins with love, joy, and

peace. This pattern is illustrated in the life of Jesus. He was filled with the Spirit and led by the Spirit into the wilderness, and then He returned in the power of the Spirit. (See Luke 4:1–14.)

This sequence is also explained in our calling. First, we are called to be holy and to dedicate ourselves to the Lord. (See Romans 12:1–2.) Then, we are called to suffer. (See I Peter 2:21.) Third, we are called to the glory of God's power upon us. (See I Peter 5:10.) Glory follows suffering. For example, "If ye be reproached for the name of Christ, happy are ye; for the spirit of glory and of God resteth upon you: on their part he is evil spoken of, but on your part he is glorified" (I Peter 4:14).

If the suffering God brings to our lives is not recognized as a test from His hand to produce the power of love and God's glory, Satan will turn it into bitterness, which will bring a lack of forgiveness and destruction.

- **Edifying the Body of Christ vs. cutting off**

Paul explains that every believer is a member of the Body of Christ, and we are all connected one with another. Therefore, if we refuse to forgive a fellow believer, we are actually refusing to forgive ourselves.

This recognition of fellow believers as members of the Body of Christ is referred to in the passage on the Lord's Table. Those who violate this concept are not discerning the Lord's body. "Wherefore whosoever shall eat this bread, and drink this cup of the Lord, unworthily, shall be guilty of the body and blood of the Lord. But let a man examine himself, and so let him eat of that bread, and drink of that cup. For he that eateth and drinketh unworthily, eateth and drinketh damnation to himself, not discerning the Lord's body. For this cause many are weak and sickly among you, and many sleep" (I Corinthians 11:27–30).

- **Having fellowship through suffering vs. weakness**

Paul spoke of resurrection power that was available to every Christian who was willing to go through suffering. "That I may know him, and the power of his resurrection, and the fellowship of his sufferings, being made conformable unto his death" (Philippians 3:10). Every believer is called to the death of self-indulgences so that we can experience more of the power of Christ.

This is the same power that is given to those who victoriously pass the tests of suffering. Such suffering is also explained by Peter to those who return good for evil. "Not rendering evil for evil, or railing for railing: but contrariwise blessing; knowing that ye are thereunto called, that ye should inherit a blessing" (I Peter 3:9).

Developing a Forgiving Spirit

1. View an offender as an "instrument" in God's hands.

2. Thank God for the benefits He plans from an offense.

3. Determine what character qualities God wants to develop in you through the offense.

4. Realize that suffering is a normal part of the Christian life.

Two Rewards for Forgiveness

The first reward of being offended is an extra measure of God's grace. (See Hebrews 12:15.)

The second reward of an offense is discovering how God meant it for good. "But as for you, ye thought evil against me; but God meant it unto good, to bring to pass, as it is this day, to save much people alive" (Genesis 50:20).

Personal Evaluation

How forgiving are you toward offenders?

- Is it your goal in life to gain the power of genuine love?

- Are there people whom you have not forgiven?

- Do you see offenses as tests to rejoice and thank God?

- Are you fearful that if you forgive an offender he will not learn from his mistakes?

- Do you believe that it is your responsibility to make sure your offenders are punished?

- Do you fear that forgiving an offender will encourage him to offend again?

- Does the thought of certain offenders bring pain and hurt to you?

- Do you compare offenses against you to your greater offense to Christ?

- Have you looked for ways to return good to those who have done you evil?

- Do you picture offenders who are believers as related to you in the Body of Christ?

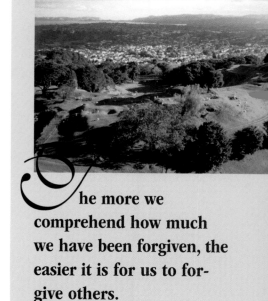

The more we comprehend how much we have been forgiven, the easier it is for us to forgive others.

"Forgiving one another, even as God for Christ's sake hath forgiven you."
—Ephesians 4:32

"He that cannot forgive others breaks the bridge over which he must pass himself; for every man has need to be forgiven."
—Thomas Fuller

By focusing on an offender, he then becomes our standard, and in condemning his actions, we unknowingly take on his attitudes.

The same attitudes we react to in others will therefore soon be seen in us.

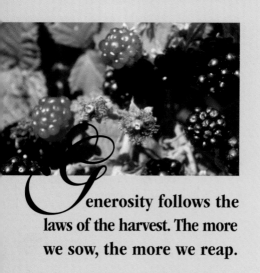

Generosity

vs. Stinginess

Generosity is demonstrating the nature of God by wisely reinvesting the resources that He has entrusted to us.

*G*enerosity follows the laws of the harvest. The more we sow, the more we reap.

"He which soweth sparingly shall reap also sparingly; and he which soweth bountifully shall reap also bountifully." —II Corinthians 9:6

*T*he hand that gives, gathers.

To give out of desire for praise is vain.

To give out of necessity is pain.

To give out of love joyfully is great gain.

"Give, and it shall be given unto you; good measure, pressed down, and shaken together, and running over, shall men give into your bosom. For with the same measure that ye mete withal it shall be measured to you again." —Luke 6:38

*G*enerosity begins with the seeds of faith, increases with the trials of hope, and blossoms with the fruit of genuine love.

"A man there was, and they called him mad; The more he gave, the more he had." —John Bunyan

Definition

Loving

Several Biblical words describe the concepts that make up generosity. First and most important is that of love. The Biblical word for love is *charity*, which embodies giving to the poor and needy. John points out that love without giving is hypocrisy. "But whoso hath this world's good, and seeth his brother have need, and shutteth up his bowels of compassion from him, how dwelleth the love of God in him?" (I John 3:17).

It is not possible to have love without generosity, but it is possible to have generosity without love. "Though I bestow all my goods to feed the poor, and though I give my body to be burned, and have not charity, it profiteth me nothing" (I Corinthians 13:3).

Sowing

The second Biblical word is *sowing*, because generosity follows the laws of the harvest. The more generous we are in sowing, the greater will be our harvest in true riches. "He which soweth sparingly shall reap also sparingly; and he which soweth bountifully shall reap also bountifully" (II Corinthians 9:6).

Honoring

A further word describing generosity is *honor*. The Greek word for *honor* is *timao*—it means "to place value upon." We are instructed: "Honour thy father and mother; which is the first commandment with promise (Ephesians 6:12). We honor aging parents by giving to their needs. We honor civil authorities by paying taxes. When we give to the poor, we honor the Lord and He promises to repay. "He that hath pity upon the poor lendeth unto the LORD; and that which he hath given will he pay him again" (Proverbs 19:17). Generosity is not just giving, it is giving abundantly or joyfully.

Distributing

Another word describing generosity is *distributing*. One Greek word for *distribute* is *koinoneo*, which has the rich meaning of fellowship among believers. We are to distribute (*koinoneo*) to the necessity of the saints. (See Romans 12:13.) All believers are members of one body. Therefore, when we give to other members we are actually benefiting ourselves. Paul explains that as we meet their needs now, our needs will be met in the future. "By an equality, that now at this time your abundance may be a supply for their want, that their abundance also may be a supply for your want: that there may be equality" (II Corinthians 8:14).

Grace

The word *grace* is also related to generosity. Paul used this word in praising the Gentile believers for their liberal distribution of gifts to the saints in Jerusalem and to all men. He went on to explain that it was through God's grace that they had the means to give and that their giving was an expression of that grace. "God is able to make all grace abound toward you; that ye, always having all sufficiency in all things, may abound to every good work" (II Corinthians 9:8). Those who received the gifts praised God for the grace that prompted them. They prayed for the givers and desired "the exceeding grace of God" which the givers possessed (see II Corinthians 9:14).

Stewardship

The concept of stewardship is also involved in generosity. A steward is one who is entrusted with the assets of the master and is responsible to make wise investments with them. A wise steward understands that the assets he has under his control do not belong to him and should be returned to the master with increase.

Jesus gave a parable of wise stewards who doubled the resources entrusted to them. They were praised. A third steward returned what he was given and was condemned.

The Rewards of Generosity

Many people refuse to be generous because they falsely believe that what they give, they lose. Yet the opposite is true. Those who are generous receive far more than they give and in a wide range of areas.

1. A bright countenance

Generosity is at the very heart of the nature of God, and because God is light, those who are generous share in His brightness.

When Jesus spoke of giving, he related it to the eyes. A good eye is a generous eye, and a stingy eye is an evil eye. "The light of the body is the eye: if therefore thine eye be single, thy whole body shall be full of light. But if thine eye be evil, thy whole body shall be full of darkness" (Matthew 6:22–23). (See also Proverbs 28:22.)

A further reference to light and giving is in Matthew 5:16: "Let your light so shine before men, that they may see your good works, and glorify your Father which is in heaven."

2. A special love from the Lord

"God loveth a cheerful giver" (II Corinthians 9:7). The qualities and motivations of a cheerful giver are described in this passage: One who purposes in his heart to give, not "grudgingly, or of necessity."

The love that God has for a generous giver is an *agapao* love, which is a giving love. Thus, when we give to others cheerfully, God gives back to us. The Greek word for *cheerful* is *hilaros* and means "prompt, willing, joyful, and hilarious."

3. The fear of the Lord

The fear of the Lord is the continual awareness that we are in His presence and that He watches over all that we think, say, and do.

There are three levels of the fear of the Lord. The first level is

With its large bill, the **pelican** generously provides fish for its young as well as other pelicans unable to feed themselves.

*T*he test of generosity is not how much we give, but how much we have left.

*W*ho gave more than everyone yet less than anyone? (See Mark 12:42–44.)

"Take my silver and my gold, not a mite would I withhold."
—Frances Ridley Havergal

$\mathcal{L}$acking money is God's "school" to teach us the importance of being generous when we abound. (See II Corinthians 8:14.)

$\mathcal{I}$n this world, it is not what we take up, but what we *give up* that makes us rich.

There is that maketh himself rich, yet hath nothing: there is that maketh himself poor, yet hath great riches. —Proverbs 13:7

"We make a living by what we get; we make a life by what we give."
—Sir Winston Churchill

---

a fear of punishment for wrong-doing in His presence. The second level is a fear of damaging His reputation. The third and highest level is a fear of endangering an intimate relationship with Him.

The great reward of this third level is described in Proverbs 22:4: "By humility and the fear of the Lord are riches, and honor, and life."

The fear of the Lord is learned by generosity. "Thou shalt truly tithe all the increase of thy seed. . . . That thou mayest learn to fear the LORD thy God always" (Deuteronomy 14:22–23).

4. Treasures in Heaven

We are not to lay up treasures on earth where moth and rust corrupt and where thieves break through and steal, but rather we are to lay up for ourselves "treasures in heaven, where neither moth nor rust doth corrupt, and where thieves do not break through nor steal" (Matthew 6:20).

The promise of treasures in Heaven was given to the Rich Young Ruler if he would exercise generosity. "Go thy way, sell whatsoever thou hast, and give to the poor, and thou shalt have treasure in heaven: and come, take up the cross, and follow me" (Mark 10:21).

5. Victory over the "root of evil"

Generosity breaks the bondage of greed and overcomes the love and worship of money. The love of money gives us the illusion that our life is made up of the things that we possess. It also makes us idolaters when we expect from money what only God can provide, such as security, peace, and joy.

6. Escape from lusts and sorrows

Those who desire to be rich "fall into temptation and a snare, and into many foolish and hurtful lusts, which drown men in destruction and perdition. For the love of money is the root of all evil: which while some coveted after, they have erred from the faith, and pierced themselves through with many sorrows" (I Timothy 6:9–10).

The Motivation of Generosity

In addition to the rewards of generosity, we should be motivated by the realization that whatever wealth we have is not the result of our ingenuity but of God's generosity. We are not to say in our hearts, "My power and the might of mine hand hath gotten me this wealth. But thou shalt remember the LORD thy God: for it is he that giveth thee power to get wealth" (Deuteronomy 8:17–18).

Because God gives us our wealth, He also has the authority and power to take it back. Job acknowledged this when he stated, "The LORD gave, and the LORD hath taken away; blessed be the name of the LORD" (Job 1:21).

If we are generous in giving back to God, He protects and increases our wealth. However, if we do not honor God with our increase, we are actually taking what rightfully belongs to God, thus robbing Him. He then allows our wealth to be devoured by situations and circumstances beyond our control. "Will a man rob God? Yet ye have robbed me. But ye say, Wherein have we robbed thee? In tithes and offerings. Ye are cursed with a curse: for ye have robbed me, even this whole nation. Bring ye all the tithes into the storehouse, that there may be meat in mine house, and prove me now herewith, saith the LORD of hosts, if I will not open you the windows of heaven, and pour you out a blessing, that there shall not be room enough to receive it. And I will rebuke the devourer for your sakes, and he shall not destroy the fruits of your ground; neither shall your vine cast her fruit before the time in the field, saith the LORD of hosts" (Malachi 3:8–11).

An even greater motivation for generosity should be to gain more of Jesus Christ and to experience more of His power. It was for these goals that Paul "suffered the loss of all things." (Philippians 3:8).

Steps for Generosity

Dedicate all resources to God.

The first step toward generosity is to dedicate all our resources to God, which will include our money, time, possessions, and strength.

Practice personal frugality.

Based on the requirements of stewardship, we must spend as little as we can on ourselves so that we can have as much as possible available to reinvest in ways that will bring multiplied returns.

Give as God directs.

The goal of generosity is to demonstrate the love of God so that others will be drawn to Him. When a person in need receives an anonymous gift that meets the need, God is glorified and the giver is in line for eternal rewards. But

if we give for the purpose of public praise, we receive the praise of people, but lose out on the greater rewards that come from God.

"But when thou doest alms, let not thy left hand know what thy right hand doeth: That thine alms may be in secret: and thy Father which seeth in secret himself shall reward thee openly" (Matthew 6:3–4).

Personal Evaluation

How generous are you?

- Do you see God as the Provider of all wealth?

- Do you view yourself as a steward of God's resources?

- Have you dedicated all your resources back to God?

- Do you honor God with a generous portion of all your (His) increase?

- Are you living as frugally as you can so you have more to reinvest?

- Do you distribute to the needs of fellow believers when you know about them?

- When you give, do you base it on what you can afford or on what God can provide though you?

- Have you rejected the goal of being rich in money, but made it your goal to be rich in good works?

- How often have you sacrificed things you wanted in order to give to the needs of others?

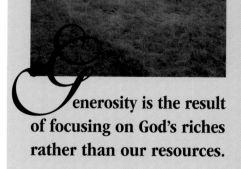

Generosity is the result of focusing on God's riches rather than our resources.

"For every beast of the forest is mine, and the cattle upon a thousand hills." —Psalm 50:10

Spare or share?

If we give grudgingly, wondering how much we can spare, we will never have the joy of discovering how much we can share. *(See II Corinthians 9:7.)*

Generosity is God's highway to prosperity. Stinginess is our pathway to poverty.

Generosity is paying on the debt of love that every believer owes to the Lord. (See Romans 13:8.)

"I do not believe one can settle how much we ought to give. I am afraid the only safe rule is to give more than we can spare." —C. S. Lewis

Gentleness
vs. Harshness

Gentleness is supporting others during their times of weakness so that they can achieve their full potential in the Lord.

Gentleness is looking past the hardness of a face and seeing a delicate spirit on the inside.

Often, the outward gruffness of a person is a self-made shield to protect a wounded and hurting spirit. It is also a cry for understanding.

Gentleness comes as we humble ourselves and do to others as we would have them do to us.

*"The wisdom that is from above is first pure, then peaceable, **gentle**, and easy to be entreated, full of mercy and good fruits, without partiality, and without hypocrisy."* —James 3:17

Definition

One Hebrew word for *gentleness* is *anah*. It is a root word with a wide range of meanings: "to humble and abase oneself in order to pay attention to and respond to others, to condescend, to look down, to keep an eye on, to listen, to sing, to cry out for, to testify, to lift up."

The Practical Expression of Gentleness

Gentleness is demonstrated in our responses to others, especially those who are under our care. We are to discipline ourselves in order to recognize the weaknesses and limitations of others and respond to them with a soft answer and patient encouragement. We are to nurture them with joyful singing, wise answers, crying out to God on their behalf, and lifting them up when they falter.

The Biblical Models of Gentleness

1. A shepherd caring for sheep

The very life and health of the sheep depend on the gentleness of the shepherd. The understanding of a gentle shepherd is expressed in Jacob's reply to his brother, who wanted the sheep to travel with his four hundred men. "And he said unto him, My lord knoweth that the children are tender, and the flocks and herds with young are with me: and if men should overdrive them one day, all the flock will die. Let my lord, I pray thee, pass over before his servant: and I will lead on **softly [gently]**, according as the cattle that goeth before me and the children be able to endure" (Genesis 33:13–14).

The Lord compares Himself to a gentle shepherd in the following passage: "Behold, the Lord GOD will come with strong hand, and his arm shall rule for him: behold, his reward is with him, and his work before him. He shall feed his flock like a shepherd: he shall gather the lambs with his arm, and carry them in his bosom, and shall **gently** lead those that are with young" (Isaiah 40:10–11). The Hebrew word for *gently lead* in this passage is *nahal*. It means "to carry, to lead, to protect, to sustain."

Jesus describes Himself as the Good Shepherd who lays down His life for His sheep. "I am the good shepherd: the good shepherd giveth his life for the sheep" (John 10:11).

2. A mother with her infant

Paul uses the concept of gentleness when describing his love and care for those whom he led to Christ: "We were gentle among you, even as a nurse cherisheth her children" (I Thessalonians 2:7).

The Greek word for *cherisheth* is *thalpo*. It means "to keep warm; to foster with tender care." It carries with it the picture of a mother hen covering her young with her feathers.

A nursing mother knows that her infants are very vulnerable and easily damaged by harsh treatment or neglect. She knows that they are dependent on her for loving care, nourishment, and protection. In I Thessalonians 2:7, the word Paul used for *gentle* means "to be kind, mild, and affable."

How a Gentle Spirit Is Developed

We learn gentleness at the hands of those who are gentle with us. One of the reasons God allows suffering is to provide us with opportunities to express gentleness to others. This concept is reflected in the definition of the Hebrew word *gentleness* (*anah*): "to abase oneself, to afflict oneself, to chasten self, to deal hardly with oneself."

The concept of gentleness through self-abasement was taught by Jesus to His disciples when He said, "If any man will come after me, let him deny himself, and take up his cross, and follow me" (Matthew 16:24). "Come unto me," Jesus said, "all ye that labour and are heavy laden, and I will give you rest. Take my yoke upon you, and learn of me; for I am meek and lowly in heart: and ye shall find rest unto your souls" (Matthew 11:28–29). The word *lowly* means "cast down, humiliated, of low degree."

In order to teach us how to be lowly, God carefully takes us through trials. In them, He gives us comfort and counsel so that we will be prepared to share with others who are going through similar trials. "Blessed be God, even the Father of our Lord Jesus Christ, the Father of mercies, and the God of all comfort; Who comforteth us in all our tribulation, that we may be able to comfort them which are in any trouble, by the comfort wherewith we ourselves are comforted of God" (II Corinthians 1:3–4).

How Gentleness Makes Us Great

Twice in Scripture, David testifies, "Thy gentleness hath made me great" (II Samuel 22:36; Psalm 18:35). In these passages, the Hebrew word for *great* is *rabah*. It means "to increase in abundance, to excel exceedingly, to enlarge in every way, to gather much, to multiply."

Gentleness begins with pain and sorrow and ends in an abundant increase. This is the way of God. If we die to ourselves, we will live; if we give bountifully, we will receive bountifully; if we sow in tears, we will reap in joy.

The life of Jabez is a beautiful picture of the meaning and potential of gentleness. *Jabez* means "sorrow." His mother gave him this name because she "bare him with sorrow." Names in the days of Jabez were very important. Often they were predictors of a person's future. However, Jabez wanted to change the focus and goal of his life, so he called on the God of Israel, saying, "Oh that thou wouldest bless me indeed, and enlarge my coast, and that thine

Because the **Eastern bluebird** feeds six to ten times an hour, hatchlings achieve independence in as little as two weeks.

The quality of gentleness cannot be evaluated by the one giving it, only by the one receiving it.

"A righteous man regardeth the life of his beast: but the tender mercies of the wicked are cruel."
—*Proverbs 12:10*

"The Lord makes us more like Him in our dealings with souls. The servants are often hard on one another, but is the Master hard?"
—Amy Carmichael

*T*he fires of adversity that burn hurtful thistles and thorns in a person's life give opportunity for a new growth of gentleness.

"Beloved, think it not strange concerning the fiery trial which is to try you, as though some strange thing happened unto you: But rejoice, inasmuch as ye are partakers of Christ's sufferings; that, when his glory shall be revealed, ye may be glad also with exceeding joy."
—I Peter 4:12–13

*A*ccepting God's comfort and grace during trials develops an attitude of kindness and gentleness toward others.

"To speak evil of no man, to be no brawlers, but gentle, shewing all meekness unto all men." —Titus 3:2

"Few of us will ever have the opportunity to perform great deeds of heroism, but to every one of us there is given the chance day by day to be sweet and gracious and winsome." —Margaret Sangster

hand might be with me, and that thou wouldest keep me from evil, that it may not grieve me! And God granted him that which he requested" (I Chronicles 4:10).

How Gentleness Is Basic to Wisdom

When James describes the qualities of wisdom, he includes gentleness: "But the wisdom that is from above is first pure, then peaceable, gentle, and easy to be entreated, full of mercy and good fruits, without partiality, and without hypocrisy" (James 3:17).

The gentleness that comes from true wisdom is the result of an understanding heart. That is exactly what Solomon requested from the Lord: "Give therefore thy servant an understanding heart to judge thy people" (I Kings 3:9). The Hebrew word for *understanding* in this passage is *shama*. *Shama* is used in the following passage for the word *hearing*: "Hear [*shama*], O Israel, the statutes and judgments which I speak in your ears this day, that ye may learn them, and keep, and do them" (Deuteronomy 5:1). Thus, gentleness is the result of a hearing heart.

The word *shama* is also translated *obey* in Scripture. As we listen to the Word of God and follow the leading of the Holy Spirit, we will escape the harshness and corruption of the lusts of the flesh and experience the fruit of the Spirit, which is "love, joy, peace, longsuffering, gentleness, goodness, faith, Meekness, temperance" (Galatians 5:22–23). The word *gentleness* in this passage is *chrestotes*, which refers to moral excellence in character and attitude.

A practical expression of wisdom and gentleness is to speak evil of no one and to seek peace and harmony with everyone. "Put them [all believers] in mind to . . . speak evil of no man, to be no brawlers, but **gentle**, shewing all meekness unto all men" (Titus 3:1–2). "The servant of the Lord must not strive; but be **gentle** unto all men, apt to teach, patient" (II Timothy 2:24).

Personal Evaluation

How gentle are you?

- Have you developed self-discipline and abasement in order to be attentive to the hurts and needs of others?

- When you give instructions or responses to others, do you take into consideration their weaknesses and limitations?

- Do you have a shepherd's mind-set toward those who are looking to you for spiritual leadership or example?

- Have you translated past pain and suffering in your life into reminders to protect others and prepare them to have a right response to any offenders?

- Are you irritable and reactionary when people with needs intrude upon your time or energy?

- Do you speak evil of someone you dislike?

- Do you look for ways to teach those who are not as spiritually mature as they should be?

- Do you give a soft answer so that you do not offend or discourage others?

- Do you see potential in others and purpose to help them grow in the Lord?

Gratefulness
vs. Murmuring

Gratefulness is expressing sincere appreciation to God and to others for the ways that they have benefited my life.

Definition

True gratefulness springs from an awareness of our total unworthiness and inadequacy before a holy and just God. If we received what we deserved, we would all be destroyed in an eternal hell. "It is of the LORD's mercies that we are not consumed" (Lamentations 3:22).

In light of our condition before God, Jesus instructs us to be "poor in spirit." This attitude is like that of a beggar along the side of the road hoping for his daily needs to be met and being grateful for anything that anyone does for him.

The Greek word *eucharistos*, translated *thankful*, is in harmony with this attitude. It means "mindful of favors; grateful." Expectations of others, based on a false assumption of our personal importance, destroy a spirit of gratefulness and instead produce presumption and murmuring.

The Importance of Gratefulness

Gratefulness is the foundation of a believer's walk with God and of God's daily will for our lives. "In every thing give thanks: for this is the will of God in Christ Jesus concerning you" (I Thessalonians 5:18).

By giving thanks for all things, including unexpected trials, physical infirmities, people who reproach or persecute us, mundane necessities of life, and distressing situations, we will pass the test of the Holy Spirit and receive the power of genuine love, joy, and peace. It is for this reason that we are to have grateful spirits.

Reasons to Thank God for All Things

It is easy to thank God for the things that obviously benefit us. However, to be grateful for trials and tribulations requires faith and obedience. The following points should provide further understanding for being grateful:

1. Because all things come from God's hand

It is easy to understand that "Every good gift and every perfect gift is from above, and cometh down from the Father of lights" (James 1:17), but what about the attacks of Satan? Job had the wisdom to understand that all his sufferings, ultimately, came from God. After losing everything he had, he worshiped God by saying, "Naked came I out of my mother's womb, and naked shall I return thither: the LORD gave, and the LORD [not Satan] hath taken away; blessed be the name of the LORD" (Job 1:21).

---

*G*ratefulness is receiving all things from the sovereign hand of God and finding the benefits in each one.

"Every good gift and every perfect gift is from above, and cometh down from the Father of lights."
—James 1:17

"When it comes to life, the critical thing is whether you take things for granted or take them with gratitude."
—G. K. Chesterton

*G*ratefulness depends on the ability to see or anticipate the benefits in God's bigger program.

If a neighbor burned down an expensive garage you had just built, how would you feel? Would your feelings change if you learned that your father had taken out an insurance policy on the garage, in your name, for one million dollars?

$\mathcal{N}$othing holds back a heart from gratitude so much as holding on to expectations.

"My soul, wait thou only upon God; for my expectation is from him."
—Psalm 62:5

"A proud man is seldom a grateful man; he never thinks he gets as much as he deserves." —Henry Ward Beecher

$\mathcal{T}$hank God for what you *do* have instead of murmuring about what you *don't* have.

"So much has been given to me, I have no time to ponder over that which has been denied." —Helen Keller

Paul had the same discernment when he spoke of the messenger of Satan that came to buffet him. "There was given to me a thorn in the flesh, the messenger of Satan to buffet me, lest I should be exalted above measure. For this thing I besought the Lord thrice, that it might depart from me. And he said unto me, My grace is sufficient for thee: for my strength is made perfect in weakness" (II Corinthians 12:7–9).

God rewarded Job's gratefulness by giving him back double what he had lost. Paul was rewarded with the power of Christ and the glory of eternal riches.

2. Because all things are for our good

The statement is true that "all things work together for good to them that love God" (Romans 8:28). Even the sufferings that we go through are for our benefit. Paul wrote, "For I reckon that the sufferings of this present time are not worthy to be compared with the glory which shall be revealed in us" (Romans 8:18).

God reasons that because the chastenings of a father are good for his children, how much more His disciplines should benefit us. "Furthermore we have had fathers of our flesh which corrected us, and we gave them reverence: shall we not much rather be in subjection unto the Father of spirits, and live?" (Hebrews 12:9).

The prophet Jeremiah also observed, "It is good for a man that he bear the yoke in his youth. He sitteth alone and keepeth silence, because he hath borne it upon him. He putteth his mouth in the dust; if so be there may be hope. He giveth his cheek to him that smiteth him: he is filled full with reproach. For the Lord will not cast off for ever: But though he cause grief, yet will he have compassion according to the multitude of his mercies" (Lamentations 3:27–32).

3. Because all things can produce Godly character

The verse following Romans 8:28 explains how all things work together for good. "For whom he did foreknow, he also did predestinate to be conformed to the image of his Son, that he might be the firstborn among many brethren" (Romans 8:29). It is for the goal of character training that we are not to resent trials or tribulations but instead welcome them as friends, because they are given to develop one's character.

"My brethren, count it all joy when ye fall into divers temptations; Knowing this, that the trying of your faith worketh patience. But let patience have her perfect work, that ye may be perfect and entire, wanting nothing" (James 1:2–4).

4. Because a right response will produce genuine love

After being filled with the Spirit, we will be led by the Spirit into a time of testing. If we thank God for and rejoice in every test, we will then experience the power of the Spirit, which begins with love, joy, and peace. This sequence is explained in the fifth chapter of Romans:

"We glory in tribulations also: knowing that tribulation worketh patience; And patience, experience; and experience, hope: And hope maketh not ashamed; because the love of God is shed abroad in our hearts by the Holy Ghost which is given unto us" (Romans 5:3–5).

Love is the greatest power on the face of the earth. Through love, God is able to accomplish supernatural work in our lives and the lives of others that will bring about eternal achievement.

5. Because all things, including trials, can bring us closer to God

When things go well with us, we tend to forget God. David testified, "In the day of my trouble I sought the Lord" (Psalm 77:2). He further stated, "Before I was afflicted I went astray: but now have I kept thy word. . . . It is good for me that I have been afflicted; that I might learn thy statutes. . . . I know, O LORD, that thy judgments are right, and that thou in faithfulness hast afflicted me" (Psalm 119:67, 71, 75).

Even when God removes the pressure of a difficult circumstance, we tend to forget and neglect to be grateful. When ten lepers were healed, only one returned to thank the Lord. Because of this tendency, God will often put us in "impossible" situations so we can experience His deliverance and glorify Him. "Call upon me in the day of trouble: I will deliver thee, and thou shalt glorify me" (Psalm 50:15).

When Should We Be Motivated to Be Thankful?

1. **When we remember His name**—"It is a good thing to give thanks unto the LORD, and to sing praises unto thy name, O most High" (Psalm 92:1). "By him therefore let us offer the sacrifice of praise to God continually, that is, the fruit of our lips giving thanks to his name" (Hebrews 13:15).

2. **When we remember His holiness**—"Sing unto the LORD, O ye saints of his, and give thanks at the remembrance of his holiness" (Psalm 30:4).

3. **In a special time of worship during the night**—"At midnight I will rise to give thanks unto thee because of thy righteous judgments" (Psalm 119:62).

4. **During gatherings with other believers**—"I will give thee thanks in the great congregation: I will praise thee among much people" (Psalm 35:18). "Let the word of Christ dwell in you richly in all wisdom; teaching and admonishing one another in psalms and hymns and spiritual songs, singing with grace in your hearts to the Lord. And whatsoever ye do in word or deed, do all in the name of the Lord Jesus, giving thanks to God and the Father by him" (Colossians 3:16–17).

5. **When surrounded by evil**—"Therefore I will give thanks unto thee, O LORD, among the heathen, and I will sing praises unto thy name" (II Samuel 22:50).

6. **When your faith is put to the test**—"Now when Daniel knew that the writing was signed, he went into his house; and his windows being open in his chamber toward Jerusalem, he kneeled upon his knees three times a day, and prayed, and gave thanks before his God, as he did aforetime" (Daniel 6:10).

People are motivated to improve the areas of their lives in which they receive praise.

"To say 'well done' to any bit of good work is to take hold of the powers which have made the effort and strengthen them beyond our knowledge." —Phillips Brooks

Grateful people appreciate what they have; murmurers don't want what they are given.

An ungrateful spirit is a rebuke to those who are providing for you and a complaint against God.

"The LORD heareth your murmurings which ye murmur against him: and what are we? your murmurings are not against us, but against the LORD." —Exodus 16:8

The **porcupine** displays gratefulness through its satisfaction with the food and shelter it has been given.

*G*ratefulness is defined by God as a sacrifice because it means surrendering our natural tendency to murmur.

"I will offer to thee the sacrifice of thanksgiving, and will call upon the name of the LORD." —Psalm 116:17

"Think not on what you lack as much as on what you have."

—Greek Proverb

7. **When in need of a miracle**—Jesus "took the seven loaves and the fishes, and gave thanks, and brake them, and gave to his disciples, and the disciples to the multitude" (Matthew 15:36).

8. **When eating a meal**—"And when he had thus spoken, he took bread, and gave thanks to God in presence of them all: and when he had broken it, he began to eat" (Acts 27:35).

9. **When we see growth in another believer**—"Thanks be to God, which put the same earnest care into the heart of Titus for you" (II Corinthians 8:16).

10. **When remembering the saints in prayer**—"We give thanks to God always for you all, making mention of you in our prayers" (I Thessalonians 1:2).

Practical Ways to Thank Others

A genuine spirit of thankfulness to God will also produce a practical gratefulness to others. Here are some ways in which true gratefulness can be expressed.

1. **By telling them**—Thank others for what they have done and for the qualities demonstrated through their actions.

2. **By writing to them**—Letters should be prompt, neatly written, and well thought out.

3. **By public recognition**—Tell others of the kind deeds done by specific individuals and how your life has been benefited by those deeds.

4. **By giving gifts to them**—These gifts should be appropriate and of value to the ones receiving them. The personal thoughtfulness behind the gift is of greater

importance than the actual gift.

5. **By spending time with them**—For the lonely or discouraged, quality time or a special outing would mean more than a letter or gift.

6. **By informing them of your prayers for them**—Paul routinely began his letters by explaining how he thanked God for the believers to whom he wrote. (See Ephesians 1:16, Colossians 1:3, I Thessalonians 1:2, and II Thessalonians 2:13.)

Personal Evaluation

How grateful are you?

- Do you begin each morning by thanking God for a new day?

- Do you look for things you usually take for granted and thank God for them?

- Do you thank God for your health and strength?

- Do you quickly express thanks to other people?

- Do you rejoice in trials and tribulations?

- Do you think of creative ways to express gratefulness to God and others?

- Do you look for benefits in the things that normally cause murmuring?

- Do you give public recognition to individuals who have helped you?

- Do you pray for those who have benefited you?

- Do you thank God for your human authorities and pray for them?

Honor

vs. Disrespect

Honor is humbling myself in the presence of a God-given authority and expressing my devotion with an appropriate gift.

Definition

The first aspect of honor is a spirit of reverence. A primary Hebrew word for *reverence* is *shachah*. It means "to depress oneself, to prostrate oneself in order to pay homage to one in authority, to bow down, to crouch, to fall down and do obeisance."

Jonathan's lame son, Mephibosheth, "fell on his face, and did reverence [*shachah*]" (II Samuel 9:6). "Bathsheba bowed with her face to the earth, and did reverence to the king" (I Kings 1:31).

Shachah is translated *worship* in Joshua 5:14: "Joshua fell on his face to the earth, and did worship [*shachah*]" the captain of the host of the Lord. It is also translated worship in Psalm 95:6: "O come, let us worship and bow down: let us kneel before the LORD our maker."

True reverence and the fear of the Lord are closely associated. The Hebrew word *yare* is translated as both *fear* and *reverence*: "Ye shall reverence my sanctuary: I am the LORD" (Leviticus 19:30). "I am a companion of all them that fear thee, and of them that keep thy precepts" (Psalm 119:63). Reverence also involves honor. The Greek word for *honor* is *timao*. It means "to prize, to fix a valuation, to value someone at a price, to esteem, to revere." Scripture provides a significant listing of those whom we are to reverence and honor.

Honor and Respect

In addition to reverence, worship, and honor, the concept of respect must be considered. The Greek word for *respect* is *apoblepo*, which means "to look away from all else to the person or object being reverenced, to look steadfastly." This word is used to describe how Moses looked steadfastly (*apoblepo*) at the "recompense of reward" and therefore was able to accept the reproaches of Christ as of greater value than all the treasures of Egypt. (See Hebrews 11:26.)

In contrast, Esau failed to reverence his birthright and therefore sold it for a bowl of pottage. Afterward, when he would have inherited the blessing, he was unable to obtain it, though he "sought it carefully with tears" (Hebrews 12:16–17).

The Key to Reverence

Sincere reverence for people grows out of a proper fear of the Lord, since He is the One who created all men and established structures of authority. There are actually three levels of the fear of the Lord, as indicated by three Hebrew and Greek words. Each level involves a progressive understanding and reverence for the ways of God and His dealings with mankind.

To reverence a ruler is to be reminded that God gave him his authority and will work through it to accomplish His will.

"The king's heart is in the hand of the LORD, as the rivers of water: he turneth it whithersoever he will."
—Proverbs 21:1

"God is the judge: he putteth down one, and setteth up another."
—Psalm 75:7

A fool reacts to the personality of a ruler. A wise man respects the position of a ruler.

Our ultimate appeal is not to the ruler on the throne, but to God Who placed him there.

"There is no power but of God: the powers that be are ordained of God."
—Romans 13:1

*M*onuments are built for men and women who regard honor as more valuable than their lives.

A Single Phrase More Powerful Than Torture

During the Vietnam War, a group of soldiers was captured and held in a concentration camp. Routinely, they would be taken from their crude barracks and told to sign certain false documents or be tortured.

When a guard would come to the barracks door and call out a prisoner's name, his fellow prisoners would whisper one phrase to him as he walked by. That phrase gave him the courage to maintain his integrity through excruciating torture.

Each survivor continues to be challenged by this phrase. One of those prisoners was Sam Johnson, who is now a United States congressman. The phrase that challenged them all was:

*H*onor! **Return with**

First Level:
Fear of punishment

All people should have this level of fear. (Hebrew [3372] *yare*; Greek [2126] *eulabes*.)

- Because God sent wild lions among them in Samaria, the king appointed a priest to teach the people to fear (*yare*) the Lord, but still they did not turn from their idols. (II Kings 17:28–32)

- Daniel prayed to the great and dreadful (*yare*) God Who kept His word. (Daniel 9:2–4)

- The people of Israel feared God (*yare*) when they saw the Egyptian army destroyed in the Red Sea. (Exodus 14:31)

- Devout (*eulabes*) men of every nation reverenced God. (Acts 2:5)

Second Level:
Fear of causing shame

This is fear that motivates Godly action. (Hebrew [3373] *yare*; Greek [2125] *eulabeomai*. Morally reverent and circumspect)

- Abraham offered Isaac on the altar: "Now I know that thou fearest [*yare*] God" (Genesis 22:12).

- Joseph told his brothers he feared (*yare*) God and sent them home to his father. (Genesis 42:18)

- Pharaoh's servants who feared (*yare*) God sought protection from the hail. (Exodus 9:20)

- Men who feared (*yare*) the Lord were to be appointed rulers in Israel. (Exodus 18:21)

- Obadiah hid 100 prophets from Jezebel's wrath because he feared (*yare*) the Lord. (I Kings 18:3–4)

- Job was "a perfect and an upright man, one that feareth [*yare*] God, and escheweth evil" (Job 1:8).

- Hezekiah feared (*yare*) the Lord and sought Him. (Jeremiah 26:19)

- Jonah told the sailors to throw him overboard to calm the storm because Jonah feared (*yare*) God. (Jonah 1:9, 12)

- Noah prepared an ark, being moved with fear (*eulabeomai*) and saved his household. (Hebrews 11:7)

Rewards for those with this fear:

- God will teach you in the right way. (Psalm 25:12)

- God will show you His covenant. (Psalm 25:14)

- God's eye of protection will be upon you. (Psalm 33:18)

- Angels will surround and deliver you. (Psalm 34:7)

- You will not lack anything. (Psalm 34:9)

- God pities you as His children. (Psalm 103:13)

- God will show mercy to your grandchildren. (Psalm 103:17)

- God will take pleasure in you. (Psalm 147:11)

- The Sun of righteousness shall arise unto you. (Malachi 4:2)

Third Level:
Fear of losing intimacy

A dread of losing an intimate relationship with God. (Hebrew [3374] *yirah*; Greek [2124] *eulabeia*.)

- "I will put my fear [*yirah*] in their hearts, that they shall not depart from me" (Jeremiah 32:40).

- Whereby we may serve God acceptably with reverence and godly fear [*eulabeia*]" (Hebrews 12:28).

- David stated, "He that ruleth over men must be just, ruling in the fear [*yirah*] of God" (II Samuel 23:3).

- David said to God, "I will come into thy house in the multitude of thy mercy and in thy fear [*yirah*] will I worship" (Psalm 5:7).

- "And the spirit of the LORD shall rest upon him, the spirit of wisdom and understanding, the spirit of counsel and might, the spirit of knowledge and of the fear [*yirah*] of the LORD; And shall make him of quick understanding in the fear [*yirah*] of the LORD" (Isaiah 11:2–3).

Rewards for those with this fear:

- True wisdom begins on this level. (Psalm 111:10)

- It is also the beginning of knowledge. (Proverbs 1:7)

- Your days will be prolonged. (Proverbs 10:27)

- You will have strong confidence. (Proverbs 14:26)

- You will enjoy a fountain of life. (Proverbs 14:27)

- You will be satisfied and will not be visited with evil. (Proverbs 19:23)

- You will have riches, honor, and life. (Proverbs 22:4)

How to Find the Fear of the Lord

Understanding the fear of the Lord is one of the most important and valuable discoveries we can make—especially its third level. When we realize its importance, we will be able to expend the spiritual effort that is required to achieve it.

"If thou criest after knowledge, and liftest up thy voice for understanding; If thou seekest her as silver, and searchest for her as for hid treasures; Then shalt thou understand the fear of the LORD, and find the knowledge of God" (Proverbs 2:3–5).

Personal Evaluation

How much honor do you give?

- Do you have a continual awareness that God is watching all that you think, say, and do?

- Do you bow before the Lord in honor of His holiness?

- Have you bowed the knee to Jesus Christ and proclaimed that He is your Lord?

- As the temple of the Holy Spirit, do you treat your body with respect?

- Do you honor the name of the Lord by living according to each aspect of His name?

- Would your parents say that you fully and sincerely honor and obey them?

- Do you honor the Lord with generous giving from all your increase?

- Do you respect government authorities as ministers of God for your good?

- Do you pay your accurate share of taxes and fees punctually?

- Do you view your employer as an instrument through whom God is working on you?

- Do you spend the Lord's Day delighting in Him rather than in your own pursuits?

- When an elderly person enters the room, do you stand up in respect?

- Do you look for ways to praise others and to deflect praise when you receive it?

It is a paradox that throngs will wait for hours to catch just a glimpse of a passing dignitary, while those who see him often tend to ignore him.

Leadership is a lonely road, and leaders long for fellowship with those who understand their pressures.

"We beseech you, brethren, to know them which labour among you, and are over you in the Lord, and admonish you; And to esteem them very highly in love for their work's sake." —I Thessalonians 5:12–13

When we honor a leader, we actually honor ourselves, because the leader represents us.

"Obey them that have the rule over you, and submit yourselves: for they watch for your souls, as they that must give account, that they may do it with joy, and not with grief: for that is unprofitable for you." —Hebrews 13:17

Leaders tend to gauge their responses by the level of honor that is given to them.

"For rulers are not a terror to good works, but to the evil. Wilt thou then not be afraid of the power? do that which is good, and thou shalt have praise of the same."

—Romans 13:3

"An evil man seeketh only rebellion: therefore a cruel messenger shall be sent against him."

—Proverbs 17:11

The **Great Plains bison** show honor to the elder bison by following him as he leads the herd to new areas for grazing.

Whom to Honor

1. The Lord Jesus Christ
"All things were made by him; and without him was not any thing made that was made" (John 1:3).

2. God the Father
"Now unto the King eternal, immortal, invisible, the only wise God, be honour and glory for ever and ever" (I Timothy 1:17).

3. The Holy Spirit
"He will reprove the world of sin, and of righteousness, and of judgment" (John 16:8). "The Spirit itself beareth witness with our spirit, that we are the children of God" (Romans 8:16).

4. The Name of the Lord
"O LORD our Lord, how excellent is thy name in all the earth!" (Psalm 8:9). "There is none other name under heaven given among men, whereby we must be saved" (Acts 4:12). "Glory ye in his holy name" (Psalm 105:3). "Thou shalt not take the name of the LORD thy God in vain" (Exodus 20:7).

5. Your Father and Mother
"Honour thy father and thy mother: that thy days may be long upon the land" (Exodus 20:12). "Whoso curseth his father or his mother, his lamp shall be put out in obscure darkness" (Proverbs 20:20).

6. Marriage Partner
"Therefore shall a man leave his father and his mother, and shall cleave unto his wife: and they shall be one flesh" (Genesis 2:24).

7. Spiritual Leaders
"And he gave some . . . pastors and teachers; For the perfecting of the saints, for the work of the ministry, for the edifying of the body of Christ" (Ephesians 4:11–12).

How to Honor

Bow and Confess—"That at the name of Jesus every knee should bow . . . And that every tongue should confess that Jesus Christ is Lord, to the glory of God the Father" (Philippians 2:10–11).

Present Our Bodies—"A living sacrifice, holy, acceptable unto God" (Romans 12:1). "Honour the LORD with thy substance, and with the firstfruits of all thine increase" (Proverbs 3:9).

Sanctify and Yield—"Your body is the temple of the Holy Ghost" (I Corinthians 6:19). "Yield your members servants to righteousness" (Romans 6:19). "Grieve not the holy Spirit of God, whereby ye are sealed unto the day of redemption" (Ephesians 4:30).

Know, Exalt, and Use—He is the Alpha and Omega, the Beginning and the Ending. The Creator of Heaven and earth. He is the Deliverer, the Eternal God, and Father of our Lord Jesus Christ. He is the Great Physician, the High and Lofty One, and the Immortal. He is the Judge of All the Earth, the King of Kings, and Lord of Lords, the Mighty God, the Never-Failing Friend. The Omnipotent and Omnipresent Prince of Peace, the Ruler of Nations. He is the Supreme and Triune God. He is the Victorious and Only Wise God.

Obey and Assist—"Children, obey your parents in the Lord: for this is right. Honour thy father and mother . . . That it may be well with thee" (Ephesians 6:1–3). "My son, keep thy father's commandment, and forsake not the law of thy mother" (Proverbs 6:20). Care for parents in their old age. (See Matthew 15:1–11 and I Timothy 5:8.)

Reverence and Respect—"The wife see that she reverence her husband" (Ephesians 5:33). "Likewise, ye husbands, dwell with them according to knowledge, giving honour unto the wife, as unto the weaker [more delicate] vessel, and as being heirs together of the grace of life" (I Peter 3:7).

Submit and Support—"Let the elders that rule well be counted worthy of double honour" (I Timothy 5:17). "Remember them which have the rule over you, who have spoken unto you the word of God. . . . Obey them that have the rule over you, and submit yourselves" (Hebrews 13:7, 17).

8. Government Leaders

"For rulers are not a terror to good works, but to the evil. Wilt thou then not be afraid of the power? . . . For he is the minister of God to thee for good" (Romans 13:3–4).

9. Employers

"Servants, be obedient to them that are your masters according to the flesh, with fear and trembling, in singleness of your heart, as unto Christ; . . . With good will doing service, as to the Lord, and not to men" (Ephesians 6:5, 7).

10. The Lord's Day

"Remember the sabbath day, to keep it holy. Six days shalt thou labour, and do all thy work: But the seventh day is the sabbath of the LORD thy God: in it thou shalt not do any work . . . wherefore the LORD blessed the sabbath day, and hallowed it" (Exodus 20:8–11).

11. The Elderly

"With the ancient is wisdom; and in length of days understanding" (Job 12:12).

12. Widows Without Family

"Pure religion and undefiled before God and the Father is this, To visit the fatherless and widows in their affliction, and to keep himself unspotted from the world" (James 1:27).

13. All Believers

"So we, being many, are one body in Christ, and every one members one of another" (Romans 12:5).

14. All People

"Honour all [people]. Love the brotherhood" (I Peter 2:17). "Let each esteem other better than themselves" (Philippians 2:3).

Submit and Pay Tribute—"Let every soul be subject unto the higher powers. For there is no power but of God: the powers that be are ordained of God" (Romans 13:1). "Render therefore to all their dues: tribute to whom tribute is due; custom to whom custom; fear to whom fear; honour to whom honour" (Romans 13:7).

Serve Faithfully—"Let as many servants as are under the yoke count their own masters worthy of all honour, that the name of God and his doctrine be not blasphemed. . . . Rather do them service, because they are faithful and beloved, partakers of the benefit. These things teach and exhort" (I Timothy 6:1–2).

Delight in His Day—"If thou turn away thy foot from the sabbath, from doing thy pleasure on my holy day; and call the sabbath a delight, the holy of the LORD, honourable; and shalt honour him, not doing thine own ways, nor finding thine own pleasure, nor speaking thine own words: Then shalt thou delight thyself in the LORD; and I will cause thee to ride upon the high places of the earth, and feed thee with the heritage of Jacob thy father" (Isaiah 58:13–14).

Stand When They Enter—"Thou shalt rise up before the hoary head, and honour the face of the old man, and fear thy God: I am the LORD" (Leviticus 19:32).

Support and Encourage—"Honour widows that are widows indeed. But if any widow have children or nephews, let them learn first to shew piety at home, and to requite their parents: for that is good and acceptable before God" (I Timothy 5:3–4).

Honor All Alike—"And those members of the body, which we think to be less honourable, upon these we bestow more abundant honour" (I Corinthians 12:23). "Whether . . . one member be honoured, all the members rejoice with it" (I Corinthians 12:26).

Give and Deflect Praise—"Let us do good unto all men, especially unto them who are of the household of faith" (Galatians 6:10). "In honour preferring one another" (Romans 12:10).

God never wastes parents on teenagers. He chooses just the right ones to carry out His bigger plans.

The primary goal of parents should not be to trust their children, but to understand them. The more parents understand their children, the more children will trust their parents.

One of the best credentials for success is the honor that God gives those who honor their parents.

"Honour thy father and mother; which is the first commandment with promise; That it may be well with thee, and thou mayest live long on the earth."
—Ephesians 6:2–3

Hospitality

vs. Unfriendliness

Hospitality is using what God has given to us to demonstrate His love for others.

*T*rue hospitality is bringing guests to a home in which the character of Christ is being lived out on a daily basis.

Hospitality begins with an inventory of the physical and spiritual resources we can share with our guests.

"A good man out of the good treasure of the heart bringeth forth good things." —Matthew 12:35

*H*ospitality is sharing the love and light of Christ with those who are attracted to it.

"If we walk in the light, as he is in the light, we have fellowship one with another." —I John 1:7

Definition

The Greek word for *hospitality* is *philoxenos*. *Philos* means "close friend" and *xenos* means "strangers or guests." Hospitality is a concern for the welfare of those who are in need of food, clothing, or shelter. In Scripture, *philoxeos* could be appropriately translated "caring for strangers as if they were close friends or loved ones."

What Is Hospitality?

Jesus taught the principle of hospitality by saying, "When thou makest a dinner or a supper, call not thy friends, nor thy brethren, neither thy kinsmen, nor thy rich neighbours; lest they also bid thee again, and a recompence be made thee. But when thou makest a feast, call the poor, the maimed, the lame, the blind: And thou shalt be blessed; for they cannot recompense thee: for thou shalt be recompensed at the resurrection of the just" (Luke 14:12–14).

Commands to Do It

1. "Use hospitality one to another without grudging" (I Peter 4:9).

2. "Distributing to the necessity of saints; given to hospitality" (Romans 12:13). Note: The word *given* means "to pursue, to press forward, and to follow after."

3. "Be not forgetful to entertain strangers: for thereby some have entertained angels unawares" (Hebrews 13:2).

4. A bishop must be "given to hospitality" and "a lover of hospitality," because hospitality is to be a ministry of the Church. (See I Timothy 3:2 and Titus 1:8.)

The Scope of Hospitality

Hospitality should be a natural response of those who practice the teachings of Jesus, because it demonstrates the love and light of God. Love and light do not choose their recipients; they are available to all who need them.

"Ye have heard that it hath been said, Thou shalt love thy neighbour, and hate thine enemy. But I say unto you, Love your enemies, bless them that curse you, do good to them that hate you, and pray for them which despitefully use you, and persecute you; That ye may be the children of your Father which is in heaven: for he maketh his sun to rise on the evil and on the good, and sendeth rain on the just and on the unjust. For if ye love them which love you, what reward have ye? do not even the publicans the same? And if ye salute your brethren only, what do ye more than others?

do not even the publicans so? Be ye therefore perfect, even as your Father which is in heaven is perfect" (Matthew 5:43–48).

The same message is given in James. "If a brother or sister be naked, and destitute of daily food, And one of you say unto them, Depart in peace, be ye warmed and filled; notwithstanding ye give them not those things which are needful to the body; what doth it profit?" (James 2:15–16).

Guidelines for Hospitality

Even though believers are to have the spirit of hospitality and demonstrate hospitality to all who need it, there are specific restrictions about the type of people who are to be brought into a person's home.

1. A believer is not to eat a meal with another believer who persists in immoral behavior. "But now I have written unto you not to keep company, if any man that is called a brother be a fornicator, or covetous, or an idolater, or a railer, or a drunkard, or an extortioner; with such an one no not to eat" (I Corinthians 5:11).

2. One who promotes false doctrine is not to be brought into the home. "If there come any unto you, and bring not this doctrine, receive him not into your house, neither bid him God speed" (II John 10).

3. A believer is not to have fellowship with an openly immoral or angry person. "And have no fellowship with the unfruitful works of darkness, but rather reprove them. For it is a shame even to speak of those things which are done of them in secret" (Ephesians 5:11–12). "Make no

friendship with an angry man; and with a furious man thou shalt not go" (Proverbs 22:24).

4. A deceitful person or a liar should not be brought into the home. "He that worketh deceit shall not dwell within my house: he that telleth lies shall not tarry in my sight" (Psalm 101:7).

Rewards of Hospitality

Believers are urged to show hospitality to strangers; the one you serve may be far more important than you realize. "Be not forgetful to entertain strangers: for thereby some have entertained angels unawares" (Hebrews 13:2).

Examples of rewards:

• Abraham showed hospitality to two strangers who were angels. They informed him of the coming judgment upon Sodom and Gomorrah. This gave Abraham an opportunity to intercede for the people and to save Lot and his daughters (Genesis 18).

• Lot was a man of hospitality and demonstrated it by providing housing and protection to the same two angels who appeared to Abraham. He was aware of the dangers that would face these visitors if they were to stay in the streets overnight. His commitment to their protection was incredible. Through his hospitality, he and his daughters escaped the destruction that came upon Sodom and Gomorrah (Genesis 19).

• The widow of Zarephath provided hospitality for Elijah. At his request, she used her last bit of meal and oil to bake him bread. God rewarded her hospitality

Bighorn sheep show hospitality by looking after each other and sharing resources in their rugged mountain environment.

*W*hen there is room in the heart, there is room in the house. **—Dutch Proverb**

One who practices hospitality takes on the work of Jesus Christ and becomes a channel of His love to others.

"Inasmuch as ye have done it unto one of the least of these my brethren, ye have done it unto me."
—Matthew 25:40

*O*ur guests will feel as comfortable in our house as we are with the preparations we made for them.

The time to be concerned about how your house looks is not when guests arrive, but when guests are invited.

Four Levels of Friendship

1. Acquaintance Level

Those whom we meet along the way, about whom we know general information

2. Casual Level

Those who are involved with us in activities and with whom we can discuss common interests, concerns, ideas, and opinions

3. Close Level

Those with whom we have common life goals and the ability to motivate each other to reach them

4. Intimate Level

Those with whom we share a mutual commitment to character goals and a freedom to point out blind spots in one another

by providing food for her and her son, along with Elijah, as long as the famine lasted (I Kings 17:8–16).

- The Shunammite woman took initiative and provided a furnished chamber for Elisha on his regular trips through the city. God rewarded her hospitality by giving her a son and later bringing him back to life when he died (II Kings 4:8–37).

- Peter brought Jesus to his home. His mother-in-law was sick, and because of Peter's hospitality, Jesus raised her up to good health (Matthew 8:14–15).

The Key to Developing Hospitality

The ultimate reward of showing hospitality is knowing that whenever we provide food, clothing, or shelter for one of the least in God's kingdom, we are doing it unto Christ.

"For I was an hungered, and ye gave me meat: I was thirsty, and ye gave me drink: I was a stranger, and ye took me in: Naked, and ye clothed me: I was sick, and ye visited me: I was in prison, and ye came unto me.

"Then shall the righteous answer him, saying, Lord, when saw we thee an hungered, and fed thee? or thirsty, and gave thee drink? When saw we thee a stranger, and took thee in? or naked, and clothed thee? Or when saw we thee sick, or in prison, and came unto thee?

"And the King shall answer and say unto them, Verily I say unto you, Inasmuch as ye have done it unto one of the least of these my brethren, ye have done it unto me" (Matthew 25:35–40).

Personal Evaluation

How hospitable are you?

- Have you purposed to develop a spirit of hospitality and to use your home to demonstrate it?

- Have you removed clutter in your home that would be a distraction to visitors?

- Have you taught each member of your family to practice proper etiquette whether or not there are visitors in the home?

- Have you learned specific questions to ask in order to develop friendships with your guests?

- When you invite others into your home, is your goal their comfort, or to impress them with the lavishness of your home?

- Do you have items in your home that illustrate answers to prayer or are testimonies of God's power?

- During conversation, do you focus on the interests of your guests or on the things you and your family have done?

- Have you prepared family activities, such as quoting a passage of Scripture or playing music, that would encourage your guests?

- Do you have a peaceful atmosphere in your home, with appropriate music and a spirit of harmony among family members?

- Do you have anything in your home that would offend a visitor?

Humility
vs. Pride

Humility is recognizing and acknowledging my total dependence upon the Lord and seeking His will for every decision.

Definition

Several Hebrew words are translated *humble*. One is *anah*, which means "to look down, to abase oneself, to afflict and chasten, to deal harshly, and to weaken." King David expressed humility of soul by wearing sackcloth and by fasting: "My clothing was sackcloth: I humbled my soul with fasting" (Psalm 35:13).

Another Hebrew word for *humble* is *kana*, which means "to bend the knee, bring into subordination, to subdue." God used this word in II Chronicles 7:14: "If my people, which are called by my name, shall humble themselves, and pray, and seek my face . . . then will I hear from heaven."

Rewards of Humility

The greatest reward of humility is becoming like the Lord Jesus Christ. He identifies His character as that of being "meek and lowly in heart." The word *lowly* means "not rising far from the ground, brought low with grief, low in spirit, of low degree."

Other rewards of humility are what every person longs for—true riches, high honor, and abundant life. "By humility and the fear of the Lord are riches, and honour, and life" (Proverbs 22:4).

The Swift and Severe Punishment for Pride

Pride is believing that we have achieved what God and others have done for us and through us. Pride is reserving for myself the right to make final decisions. Pride is building all of life around me and my wants.

God's swift punishment on pride is illustrated in the lives of King Herod and King Nebuchadnezzar. God did not immediately punish Herod for slaughtering babies or killing the Apostle James, but when Herod gave a great oration to the people of Tyre and Sidon, and they fell down and worshiped him as a god, "immediately the angel of the Lord smote him, because he gave not God the glory" (Acts 12:23).

When King Nebuchadnezzar boasted, "Is not this great Babylon, that I have built for the house of the kingdom by the might of my power, and for the honour of my majesty?" God immediately punished him. While the word was in the king's mouth, God struck him with a mental breakdown and took away his kingdom until he worshiped the King of Heaven. (See Daniel 4:30–37.)

The reason for God's startling swiftness of punishment on pride may very well be the fact that it

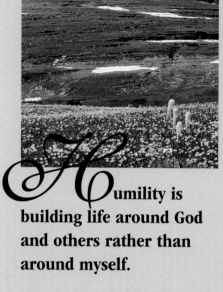

*H*umility is building life around God and others rather than around myself.

"Yea, all of you be subject one to another, and be clothed with humility: for God resisteth the proud, and giveth grace to the humble."
—I Peter 5:5

"All God's giants have been weak men who did great things for God, because they reckoned on God being with them."
—J. Hudson Taylor

*I*f we refuse to humble ourselves, there are many others who are eager to help us do it.

Thinking too little of yourself is false humility and is just as wrong as thinking too much of yourself.

The **turkey vulture** has repulsive features, yet it plays a vital role in maintaining the health of nature by devouring carcasses that would otherwise spread disease and death.

*H*umility is realizing that we ourselves are nothing, but we are everything in Christ.

"For I know that in me (that is, in my flesh,) dwelleth no good thing."
—Romans 7:18

"The higher a man is in grace, the lower he will be in his own esteem."
— C. H. Spurgeon

"The greatest of all faults is to be conscious of none."
—Thomas Carlyle

was the sin that caused Satan and a third of the angels to be cast out of Heaven. Satan said in his heart, "I will ascend into heaven, I will exalt my throne above the stars of God . . . I will be like the most High" (Isaiah 14:13–14).

Pride was the same sin that caused Adam and Eve to fall. Satan tempted them to violate God's command so that they, through their own efforts, could be on an equal level with God. Satan said, "God doth know that in the day ye eat thereof, then your eyes shall be opened, and ye shall be as gods" (Genesis 3:5).

Pride is putting ourselves on an equal level with God-given authority. Humility is abasing ourselves and submitting to the righteous rule of God and His authorities.

Our Choice: Humble Ourselves—or Be Humbled by God

God appeals to all of us to take the initiative to humble ourselves. If we fail to do this, He will humble us through circumstances, opposition, infirmities, or weaknesses.

- "Humble yourselves in the sight of the Lord, and he shall lift you up" (James 4:10).
- "Humble yourselves therefore under the mighty hand of God, that he may exalt you in due time" (I Peter 5:6).

Notice that we are to first and foremost humble ourselves in the eyes of the Lord, not necessarily in the eyes of others. He can see the true condition of our hearts, whether we are flattering ourselves with compliments or

sincerely abasing ourselves and exalting Him.

King Nebuchadnezzar learned what happens when a man fails to humble himself. However, after being humbled by God, he gave proper glory to the Lord, "At the end of the days I Nebuchadnezzar lifted up mine eyes unto heaven, and mine understanding returned unto me, and I blessed the most High, and I praised and honoured him that liveth for ever, whose dominion is an everlasting dominion, and his kingdom is from generation to generation" (Daniel 4:34).

Humility Begins in Our Spirits; Pride Begins in Our Hearts.

When our spirits are in full fellowship with the Spirit of God, we will have humble hearts.

- "For thus saith the high and lofty One that inhabiteth eternity, whose name is Holy; I dwell in the high and holy place, with him also that is of a contrite and humble spirit, to revive the spirit of the humble, and to revive the heart of the contrite ones" (Isaiah 57:15).
- "Better it is to be of an humble spirit with the lowly, than to divide the spoil with the proud" (Proverbs 16:19).
- "A man's pride shall bring him low: but honour shall uphold the humble in spirit" (Proverbs 29:23).

Pride Is Taking Credit for What God Gave Us.

If we fail to recognize that everything we have and do is because of the mercy and grace of God, we will tend to think that we are responsible for our achievements. Thus, we will lift up our hearts in pride.

- When King Uzziah became strong, "his heart was lifted up to his destruction" (II Chronicles 26:16).
- When Nebuchadnezzar's "heart was lifted up, and his mind hardened in pride, he was deposed from his kingly throne" (Daniel 5:20).
- When the prince of Tyrus became prosperous, God observed, "By thy great wisdom and by thy traffic hast thou increased thy riches, and thine heart is lifted up because of thy riches . . . and thou hast said, I am a God, I sit in the seat of God" (Ezekiel 28:5).

God's Checklist for Humility

The clearest guidance we could receive on how to humble ourselves is to follow Biblical instruction on how to do it and to learn from God's biographies what others did to humble themselves. Humility must begin with a contrite spirit, as explained in Colossians 3:12: "Put on therefore, as the elect of God, holy and beloved, bowels of mercies, kindness, humbleness of mind."

James 4:6–10 speaks of humility and gives a checklist for achieving it. "God resisteth the proud, but giveth grace unto the humble. . . . Humble yourselves in the sight of the Lord, and he shall lift you up."

1. Submit yourselves to God with total, unconditional surrender to His will.
2. Resist the devil, allowing no secret sin or hindering weight.
3. Draw nigh to God by seeking His face through the Scriptures.
4. Cleanse your hands by confessing all sin and making restitution.
5. Purify your hearts, making sure there is no secret desire to continue sinning.
6. Be afflicted and mourn and weep. Grieve over the awfulness of sin.
7. Let your laughter be turned to mourning and your joy to heaviness.
8. Do all this in the sight of the Lord, and He will lift you up.

God Hears Those Who Come to Him in Humility.

A passage parallel to that of James 4 on humbling ourselves is given in II Chronicles 7:14, **"If my people, which are called by my name, shall humble themselves, and . . .**

1. **Pray**—Acknowledging our sins and God's holiness.
2. **Seek My face**—Set aside every distraction that competes with Christ.
3. **Turn from their wicked ways**— Have a change of life as well as a change of heart.

"Then will I hear from heaven. . . ."

True inward repentance and contriteness will have outward evidences. God notes the following expressions of humility and how He responded to them.

- Ahab—"It came to pass, when Ahab heard those words, that he rent his clothes, and put sackcloth upon his flesh, and fasted, and lay in sackcloth, and went softly" (I Kings 21:27). Then God responded, "Seest thou how Ahab humbleth himself before

*H*umility is the natural response of being in the presence of God.

The fear of the Lord is the awareness that we are continually in the presence of the Lord. Thus, humility and the fear of the Lord are interdependent.

"By humility and the fear of the LORD are riches, and honour, and life."
—*Proverbs 22:4*

"A man who clings to his own righteousness is like a man who grasps a millstone to prevent himself from sinking in a flood."
—C. H. Spurgeon

"Those who think too much of themselves don't think enough."
—Amy Carmichael

*I*f you are holding others back so you can get ahead, you will never go anywhere.

Those who look down on others miss the joy of looking upon the face of Jesus.

We must become nothing before we can become something.

*H*umility is expressed by a servant's spirit that is excited about making others successful.

The best test of whether or not we view ourselves as servants is how we respond when treated like one.

Christ "made himself of no reputation, and took upon him the form of a servant, and was made in the likeness of men." —Philippians 2:7

me? because he humbleth himself before me, I will not bring the evil in his days" (I Kings 21:29).

- Josiah—"It came to pass, when the king had heard the words of the law, that he rent his clothes." He also acknowledged the iniquities of his fathers: "Because our fathers have not kept the word of the Lord, to do after all that is written in this book." The Lord responded, "Because thine heart was tender, and thou didst humble thyself before God, when thou heardest his words against this place, and against the inhabitants thereof, and humbledst thyself before me, and didst rend thy clothes, and weep before me; I have even heard thee also, saith the LORD" (II Chronicles 34:19, 21, 27).

Specific Ways to Humble Ourselves

1. Welcome critics—bless those who curse you.
2. Volunteer for menial tasks.
3. Ask others about blind spots.
4. Express gratefulness.
5. Listen to others instead of talking about yourself.
6. Kneel in prayer.
7. Let authorities make final decisions.
8. Ask forgiveness for wrongs you have done.
9. Praise and honor others.
10. Take time for prayer and fasting.
11. Give sacrificially.
12. Give testimony of God's grace.
13. Deflect praise.
14. Be a servant.

How humble are you?

- When people disagree with you, do you argue for your position?
- Do you tend to cut off those who ignore you?
- Are you hurt when those whom you dislike are honored?
- Do you find it difficult to admit you are wrong?
- Do you inwardly react when people criticize you?
- Do you give your opinions before being asked for them?
- Do you enjoy sharing about your accomplishments?
- Do you talk more than you listen?
- Are you more concerned about your reputation or God's?
- Do you give the impression that you have no problems?
- Do you seek ways to humble yourself?
- Do you do things for praise and compliments?
- Do you accept praise rather than deflecting it?
- Are you quick to correct others when they make mistakes?
- Do you react when you do not receive credit you are due?
- Do you feel important?
- Do you compare yourself to others rather than God?

Initiative
vs. Idleness

Initiative is acting on the *rhemas* that God gives to us in His Word.

Definition

Initiative is expressed in two ways: by thoughts and by deeds. The Hebrew word *chashab* (translated *think*) defines the thinking phase of initiative. It means to plan, calculate, invent, and imagine.

The most frequently used Greek word for *doing, poieo*, describes the action phase of initiative, meaning "to make, to produce, to execute, and to institute."

Initiative is based on the faith of knowing God's will through the *rhemas* of God's Word and the works of carrying them out. Initiative that does not spring from faith is iniquity.

Why Is Initiative Important?

Initiative is foundational to all other qualities. It is the first quality that God used to demonstrate His love to us and the first quality that we must use in responding to His love. Initiative is seeing and doing what needs to be done before being asked to do it. Initiative is using the energy of God (grace) to achieve the will of God, as directed by the Spirit of God.

God took initiative before the world was founded to provide redemption for us. (See I Peter 1:18–20.) He also demonstrated initiative by creating the heaven and the earth. (See Genesis 1:1.)

Initiative is required to carry out every other character quality, including gratefulness, forgiveness, punctuality, diligence, and joyfulness. It is also essential to fulfilling the commands of Scripture such as "pray without ceasing," "lay up treasures in heaven," "do good unto all," "maintain good works," and "go ye into all the world."

How Is Initiative Activated?

Initiative is activated by thoughts and words. Scripture teaches us that power for good or for evil is in our thoughts and words. "For as he thinketh in his heart, so is he" (Proverbs 23:7). "Bringing into captivity every thought to the obedience of Christ" (II Corinthians 10:5). "Death and life are in the power of the tongue: and they that love it shall eat the fruit thereof" (Proverbs 18:21). With our words, we can do the will of God or the work of Satan. Therefore, "by thy words thou shalt be justified, and by thy words thou shalt be condemned" (Matthew 12:37).

When God formed the world, He generated creative energy by words. "The worlds were framed by the word of God, so

Initiative is carrying out the will of God by being in tune with the heart of God.

"I delight to do thy will, O my God: yea, thy law is within my heart." —Psalm 40:8

Great leaders learn discernment for wise initiatives on the back side of the desert.

Idleness is the ground in which every form of evil takes root.

The hour of idleness is the hour of temptation.

"Satan is much more in earnest than we are—he buys up the opportunity while we are wondering how much it will cost."

—Amy Carmichael

When Initiative Inspired the World

On February 22, 1899, the editor of a small newspaper wrote in a single hour an article that leaped like wildfire across the world. Over forty million copies have been printed in hundreds of languages.

What prompted the article? The initiative of Rowan, who delivered an important message from President McKinley to General Garcia in the jungles of Cuba during the Spanish-American war.

The article is a plea for others to follow his example. "Rowan took the letter and did not ask, 'Where is he?' He simply did the job he was asked to do! . . . [If you make this request of a staff member], 'Please look in the encyclopedia and make a brief memorandum for me concerning the life of Correggio,' . . . [w]ill your man quietly say, . . . 'Yes, sir,' and go do the task?

"On your life he will not. He will look at you out of a fishy eye and ask . . . [a series of foolish] questions . . . . This incapacity for independent action, . . . this unwillingness to cheerfully catch hold of a project . . . are the reasons why true Christianity does not gain its rightful victory over the world."

that things which are seen were not made of things which do appear" (Hebrews 11:3). The words of God are recorded in the creation account: "And God said, Let there be light: and there was light" (Genesis 1:3). "And God said, Let there be a firmament in the midst of the waters" (Genesis 1:6). Eight times God spoke and creation resulted. (See Genesis 1.)

Words are also basic to the initiative of redemption. Jesus is the Living Word of God. "In the beginning was the Word, and the Word was with God, and the Word was God" (John 1:1).

God initiated our salvation through words, and we receive salvation by words. "If thou shalt confess with thy mouth the Lord Jesus, and shalt believe in thine heart that God hath raised him from the dead, thou shalt be saved. For with the heart man believeth unto righteousness; and with the mouth confession is made unto salvation" (Romans 10:9).

When Does Initiative Become Iniquity?

We can take initiative to do many good things; however, they may actually be works of iniquity. If we are to avoid iniquity, we must follow Christ's example and allow the Holy Spirit to produce in us the right initiatives and guide us in properly carrying them out.

It is the Holy Spirit Who gives us grace, which is the desire and power to do God's will. It is also the Holy Spirit Who guides us with Scriptural truths (*rhemas*). We can take initiative with any of these Scriptural *rhemas* and know that we are in the will of God. This is the promise of John 15:7–8, "If ye

abide in me, and my words abide in you, ye shall ask what ye will, and it shall be done unto you. Herein is my Father glorified, that ye bear much fruit; so shall ye be my disciples."

How Did David Illustrate Initiative?

David wrote in Psalm 37:4, "Delight thyself also in the LORD; and he shall give thee the desires of thine heart." In other words, He will place His desires within us. It is then important for us to check these desires with Scripture and confirm them with Biblical *rhemas*.

Scripture gives David the awesome title of being "a man after God's own heart." (See Acts 13:22.) Even as a young boy, David demonstrated amazing initiative. As a shepherd, he could have spent all his time sitting around watching the sheep. Instead, he took initiative to meditate and memorize the Law of God, to skillfully play the harp, and to accurately sling stones at the predators of his sheep. These initiatives made him a skilled shepherd and prepared him to lead the nation of Israel.

As king, he decided to build a temple for God. Notice how his initiative began with words. "The king said unto Nathan the prophet, See now, I dwell in an house of cedar, but the ark of God dwelleth within curtains" (II Samuel 7:2). Even though God pointed out that it was impossible for a house to contain Him and that David was unqualified to build it, He honored David's initiative by allowing David's son to build the temple, and God made it a centerpiece of His dealings with Israel. (See II Samuel 7:6–17.)

How to Test Your Initiative

When our chief concern is to glorify God in all that we do and to "do good unto all men, especially those of the household of faith," (see Galatians 6:10) we will be in a good position to establish proper initiatives.

If we have failed to take initiative, it would be important to examine our relationship with the Lord and His Spirit. If we have grieved Him by unconfessed sin, we will not hear the prompting of His initiatives. If we have heard them and failed to obey them, we have grieved Him by disobedience. "If we confess our sins, he is faithful and just to forgive us our sins, and to cleanse us from all unrighteousness" (I John 1:9).

Biblical Examples of Initiative

1. Moses took initiative in delivering his people from bondage. His initial actions were not right, but God honored his goal and prepared him to fulfill that vision (see Exodus 2).

2. David demonstrated initiative while caring for his family's sheep. During this time, he developed skills that he later used to lead the nation (see I Samuel 17; Psalm 78:71–72).

3. Naaman took initiative by coming to Elijah for healing. When he followed God's instructions, he was healed (see II Kings 5).

4. Nehemiah took initiative to rebuild the walls around Jerusalem (see Nehemiah 1–2).

5. The rich young ruler took initiative in coming to Jesus (see Luke 18).

Personal Evaluation

How much initiative do you have?

- Do you show initiative by rising early in the morning and seeking the Lord?

- Do you take initiative to seek direction for your life in God's Word?

- Do you show initiative in memorizing and meditating on Scripture?

- Do you show initiative in asking forgiveness and being reconciled with your enemies?

- Do you display initiative in building and using a prayer list?

- Do you take initiative in setting aside times for fasting?

- Do you take initiative to honor the Lord's Day?

- Do you participate in other initiatives to do good works?

- Do you take initiative in sharing the Gospel with others?

- Do you exemplify initiative by keeping your home and car in good repair?

- Do you take initiative to search out the fatherless and the widows in your church and neighborhood and discover what their needs are?

- Do you exercise initiative in learning how to write down the truths that God is teaching you?

The older **whistling swan** shows initiative by taking the lead in a flock's "V" formation. As other swans follow the leader's example and take turns breaking the wind, a flock is able to fly 30 percent farther than if each swan flew alone.

Initiative is a building block of virtue.

"Who can find a virtuous woman? . . . She looketh well to the ways of her household, and eateth not the bread of idleness." —Proverbs 31:10, 27

"It is an erroneous notion that you have to wait for the call of God: see that you are in such a condition that you can realize it."

—Oswald Chambers

Joyfulness

vs. Self-Pity

Joyfulness is the bright spirit and radiant countenance that come by being in full fellowship with the Lord.

*J*oy is proof to the world that God can fully satisfy the human heart.

"In thy presence is fulness of joy; and at thy right hand there are pleasures for evermore." —Psalm 16:11

"Joy is not luxury or a mere accessory in the Christian life. It is the sign that we are really living in God's wonderful love, and that love satisfies us."

—Andrew Murray

*J*oy is the component that, when added to a trial, provides the strength to endure it.

"For the joy of the LORD is your strength." —Nehemiah 8:10

"Joy is not the absence of trouble but the presence of Christ."

—William VanderHaven

Definition

A primary Hebrew word for *joy* is *simchah*. It comes from the root word *samach*, which means "to brighten up, to make glad, to be merry." Related Biblical words are *rejoice* (Philippians 4:4), *exceeding glad* (Matthew 5:12), *delight* (Psalm 37:4), and *blessed*, which means to be happy and spiritually prosperous (Psalm 1:1).

How Can Joy and Sorrow Exist Together?

Paul stated that he had great heaviness and continual sorrow in his heart for those who refused to believe in the Lord, but at the same time, he had continuous joy for those who responded to the Gospel. (See Romans 9:2 and Philippians 4:4.) He also testified of both joy and sorrow in the following passage: "As sorrowful, yet alway rejoicing" (II Corinthians 6:10). It is possible to have joy and sorrow at the same time, because joy is an expression of the spirit, and sorrow is an expression of the soul. Joy or sorrow can affect our hearts so that we will have either a joyful heart or a sorrowful heart.

The Rewards of Joy

There are physical, psychological, and spiritual rewards of joy, both in the life of the one who is joyful and in the lives of those who are around a joyful person, as joy tends to be contagious. Joy releases hormones that strengthen the immune system. Thus . . .

1. **Joy is our strength**—"For the joy of the LORD is your strength" (Nehemiah 8:10).

2. **Joy is our health**—"A merry heart doeth good like a medicine" (Proverbs 17:22).

3. **Joy is our brightness**—"A merry heart maketh a cheerful countenance" (Proverbs 15:13).

What Produces Joy?

1. Our eternal salvation

Our greatest source of joy is eternal salvation. Jesus emphasized this point to His disciples when He said, "Rejoice not, that the spirits are subject unto you; but rather rejoice, because your names are written in heaven" (Luke 10:20). Unfortunately, the joy from our salvation can be diminished or lost if we allow sin in our lives. Therefore David prayed, "Restore unto me the joy of thy salvation; and uphold me with thy free spirit" (Psalm 51:12).

2. A good conscience

Because joy comes from fellowship with the Lord, anything hindering that fellowship will diminish our joy. Unconfessed sin and iniquity will damage that fellowship, because evil deeds are of darkness and usually done in darkness. God is light, and in Him is no darkness at all. "But if we walk in the light, as he is in the light, we have fellowship one with another, and the blood of Jesus Christ his Son cleanseth us from all sin" (I John 1:7). Based on this truth, Paul wrote: "For our rejoicing is this, the testimony of our conscience" (II Corinthians 1:12).

3. The statutes of God's Word

A statute is a practical application of the Law of God. When David and his six hundred men pursued and overcame the Amalekites who had captured their families and possessions, they returned with all they had lost plus an additional bounty of riches. Some of David's men decided that the two hundred men who were too weak to continue the chase should receive only their own possessions and none of the spoil that was taken in the battle. David replied that those who "stayed by the stuff" would share equally with those who went out to battle. This became a statute forever in Israel. (See I Samuel 30:24–25).

A statute rings with truth and thus causes our hearts to rejoice: "The statutes of the LORD are right, rejoicing the heart" (Psalm 19:8).

4. The commands of the Lord

The whole Law is fulfilled in the commandment to love God and love one another. Jesus, in the Gospel of John, reminds us of the joy that comes by keeping this commandment: "As the Father hath loved me, so have I loved you: continue ye in my love. If ye keep my commandments, ye shall abide in my love; even as

I have kept my Father's commandments, and abide in his love. These things have I spoken unto you, that my joy might remain in you, and that your joy might be full. This is my commandment, That ye love one another, as I have loved you. Greater love hath no man than this, that a man lay down his life for his friends" (John 15:9–13). "The commandment of the Lord is pure, enlightening the eyes" (Psalm 19:8).

5. The *rhemas* of Scripture

All Scripture is inspired by God and profitable for personal application. Because of this, the Holy Spirit will guide each believer to passages that have specific direction for a particular situation. As these *rhemas* are engrafted into our souls and made a living part of our lives, they produce special joy. "Thy words were found, and I did eat them; and thy word was unto me the joy and rejoicing of mine heart" (Jeremiah 15:16).

John confirms the joy that comes from *rhemas*. "If ye abide in me, and my words [*rhemas*] abide in you, ye shall ask what ye will, and it shall be done unto you. Herein is my Father glorified, that ye bear much fruit . . . These things have I spoken unto you, that my joy might remain in you, and that your joy might be full" (John 15:7–11).

6. The giving of a wise answer

Words have power for good or for evil—"Death and life are in the power of the tongue" (Proverbs 18:21). When we speak words that hurt others or do not effectively communicate truth, we experience sorrow and regret. However, when we give a wise and helpful

A joyful spirit is a fountain of health in those who have it, and with those who share it.

"A merry heart doeth good like a medicine." —Proverbs 17:22

"Joy is one of those rare treasures that is multiplied by giving it away."
—Unknown

Three types of *Smiles*

1. Obedient smile

Fulfilling the command to rejoice in all things, regardless of how I feel.

2. Ministry smile

Desiring to encourage the ones who have to look at my face.

3. Joyful smile

Expressing with my soul the joy of my spirit because of the work of God in my life.

*G*od can turn our greatest sorrows into our deepest joys.

"Weeping may endure for a night, but joy cometh in the morning."

—Psalm 30:5

"Our purest and noblest joys are transformed sorrows."

—Alexander Maclaren

The **river otter** makes even mundane chores a delight. Everything from conquering the fear of water to opening difficult mussel shells is turned into playful pursuits.

answer, we have joy. "Every man shall kiss his lips that giveth a right answer" (Proverbs 24:26). "A man hath joy by the answer of his mouth: and a word spoken in due season, how good is it!" (Proverbs 15:23).

Wise answers do not come naturally. "The heart of the wise teacheth his mouth, and addeth learning to his lips" (Proverbs 16:23).

7. The tests of persecution

The very trials that most people fear and react to are designed by God to be sources of joy. Jesus said, "Blessed [a condition of joy] are ye, when men shall revile you, and persecute you, and shall say all manner of evil against you falsely, for my sake. Rejoice and be exceeding glad [joyful], for great is your reward in heaven" (Matthew 5:11–12).

James gives further witness to this truth: "Count it all joy when ye fall into divers temptations; Knowing this, that the trying of your faith worketh patience" (James 1:2–3). Peter also explains how suffering produces joy: When you suffer, "rejoice, inasmuch as ye are partakers of Christ's sufferings; that, when his glory shall be revealed, ye may be glad also with exceeding joy" (I Peter 4:13).

8. The spiritual growth of our disciples

Our goal in life should be to bring as many people as we can to the Lord Jesus Christ and to help them grow to spiritual maturity (see Colossians 1:28–29 and Matthew 28:19–20). This requires great effort. However, the reward is great joy: "They that sow in tears shall reap in joy" (Psalm 126:5). Paul stated to those whom he won to Christ, "My little children, of whom I travail in birth again until Christ be

formed in you" (Galatians 4:19). "For what is our hope, or joy, or crown of rejoicing? Are not even ye in the presence of our Lord Jesus Christ at his coming?" (I Thessalonians 2:19). John stated, "I have no greater joy than to hear that my children walk in truth" (III John 4).

9. The power of the Holy Spirit

When we respond to "infirmities, reproaches, necessities, persecutions, and distresses" by thanking God, rejoicing, and when necessary, crying out, God will reward us with the power of the Holy Spirit (see II Corinthians 12:8–9). "If ye be reproached for the name of Christ, happy are ye; for the spirit of glory and of God resteth upon you . . ." (I Peter 4:14). The power of the Holy Spirit begins with love and joy (see Galatians 5:22).

10. The confidence of a job well-done

With the power of the Holy Spirit, God will be able to accomplish "great and mighty things" that will bring joy to us (Jeremiah 33:3). "But let every man prove his own work, and then shall he have rejoicing in himself alone, and not in another" (Galatians 6:4).

The ultimate joy for every believer is to meet the Lord at the end of his life and to hear Him say, "Well done, thou good and faithful servant thou hast been faithful over a few things, I will make thee ruler over many things: enter thou into the joy of thy lord" (Matthew 25:21).

What Are the Steps to Experience Joy?

Scripture contains a significant list of nine commands that, if followed, will cause our hearts to rejoice. This list may be found in I Chronicles 16:8–11 as well as in Psalm 105:1–4.

1. "Give thanks unto the LORD."

Our first response to every situation should be to thank God, because doing so is God's will for every believer. (See I Thessalonians 5:18.) We can thank God because:

1. All things come from the hand of God. (See Job 1:21 and Matthew 10:29.)

2. Everything that happens to us is ultimately for our good. (See Romans 8:28.)

3. Every circumstance can build character in us. (See Romans 8:29.)

4. Difficulties and afflictions can teach us God's ways. (See Psalm 119:71.)

By understanding these truths and developing a thankful spirit, we have the foundation for true joy.

2. "Call upon his name."

Sorrow and discouragement are often the result of trying to live the Christian life in our own energy. Joy is knowing that only God can work in us and give us the desire and power to do His will. (See Philippians 2:13.) Our natural tendency is to depend on our own strength and forget that we need the Lord. Therefore God continually puts us in situations that are beyond our human ability to deal with so that we will cry out to Him and experience His supernatural power in and through us.

Paul discovered that when he acknowledged his weakness, he became strong. "For when I am weak, them am I strong" (II Corinthians 12:10). The best way to express our weakness and dependence on God is to cry out to Him. This is what God invites us to do: "Call upon me in the day of trouble: I will deliver thee and thou shalt glorify me" (Psalm 50:15). This is further affirmed in Jeremiah 33:3: "Call unto me, and I will answer thee, and shew thee great and mighty things, which thou knowest not."

3. "Make known his deeds among the people."

The moment we cry out to God in an attitude of "unconditional surrender" to His will and total dependence on His power and provision, He will respond to us. It is then our responsibility to make known the great and mighty things He has done in response to our cries. Our rejoicing in His power and provision glorifies Him and strengthens the faith of others.

4. "Sing unto him, sing psalms unto him."

A psalm is a personal, musical expression of important events that happen to us. When God responds to our cries through mighty deeds, we can demonstrate our joy and gratefulness by composing a musical tribute to Him. This was David's practice, and we are instructed to follow it: "Be filled with the Spirit; Speaking to yourselves in psalms, and hymns and spiritual songs, singing and making melody in your heart to the Lord" (Ephesians 5:18–19). A joyful person is one who sings.

5. "Talk ye of all his wondrous works."

Our conversation will usually center around the people and events about which we are most excited. When we see the Lord

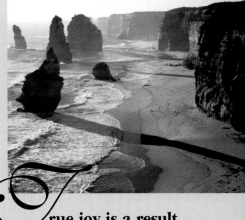

True joy is a result not of what happens in our lives but of what happens because of the One Who lives in our hearts.

Joy springs from tapping into eternal riches and fellowship with God.

"Where the soul is full of peace and joy, outward surroundings and circumstances are of comparatively little account."
—Hannah Whitehall Smith

"Who among us can be counted on for happiness? It is those who never take self into consideration."

—Amy Carmichael

The Treasured Gift of Joy

- Joy has no value until it is given away.

- No king is so rich or powerful that he does not need it.

- No person is so poor he cannot give it.

- Sharing joy takes only a moment, but those who receive it treasure it for a lifetime.

- The one who gives away joy becomes richer.

- The one who receives joy returns it and can still give it to others.

- Joy is far rarer than it needs to be, but the need for it only makes it more valuable.

- Joy is shown in a genuine smile from a joyful heart.

doing mighty things in and through us, it is a joy to tell about them to all those whom we meet.

6. "Glory ye in his holy name."

God has many names. Each one represents an aspect of life. When we call upon Him, we should use the name that identifies a specific area of need. Jesus promised, "If ye shall ask anything in my name, I will do it" (John 14:14). God's names also define His character. He is the Great Physician, Tireless Provider, and the Strong Protector. He is holy, just, and merciful.

7. "Let the heart of them rejoice that seek the Lord."

The trials and tribulations in life are designed by God to turn our affections away from temporal things. These trials and tribulations should motivate us to seek the Lord, in whose "presence is fullness of joy" (Psalm 16:11). The first requirement to seek the Lord is that we do it with a whole heart. "Ye shall seek me, and find me, when ye shall search for me with all your heart" (Jeremiah 29:13). When God has our whole hearts, He fills them with joy, because "no good thing will he withhold from them that walk uprightly" (Psalm 84:11).

8. "Seek the Lord and his strength."

The most important times to seek the Lord are during trials and difficulties. We can ask Him for wisdom to discern the benefits for allowing these things to happen, so we can then thank Him for them. The resulting joy strengthens us, because "the joy of the Lord is . . .[our] strength" (Nehemiah 8:10).

9. "Seek his face continually."

Seeking the face of the Lord can be done only when there are no sins or transgressions that would cause Him to hide His face from us (Isaiah 59:2) or cause us to not want to look up at His face. As His face shines upon us, our faces also shine and brighten the lives of others. This is the very essence of joy, which means "to brighten up." David prayed, "God be merciful unto us, and bless us; and cause [Your] face to shine upon us; That thy way may be known upon earth, thy saving health among all nations" (Psalm 67:1–2).

Personal Evaluation

How joyful are you?

- Do people see a bright countenance when they look at you?

- Do you cry out to God whenever you are faced with a difficult situation?

- Do you cry out to God and experience His working in response to your crying out?

- Do you joyfully share these experiences with everyone you can?

- Do you know which names of God to use when crying out?

- Do you enjoy times of rich, wholehearted fellowship with the Lord?

- Do you memorize *rhemas* from Scripture?

- Do you thank God for every trial you experience?

- Are you discipling others in their spiritual growth?

- Do you put your whole heart and mind into the jobs you are given?

Justice

vs. Fairness

Justice is carrying out wise judgments based on the laws and character of God.

Definition

A primary Hebrew word for *justify* is *tsadaq*. It means to be right in a moral and legal sense. It is significant that Scripture uses this same Hebrew word for *righteousness*. Righteousness is the perfection of the character of the Lord Jesus Christ. His righteousness becomes ours when we receive Him as our own Redeemer. Jesus fulfilled the just demands of the Law by substituting His sinless life for our sins through His death on the cross.

Justice is frequently used in conjunction with judgment. One Hebrew word for *judgment* is *mishpat*. It means "a verdict, a formal decree, a divine law." "Keep ye judgment, and do justice" (Isaiah 56:1). (See also Psalm 119:121 and Proverbs 21:3.)

The Rewards of Justice

- "The path of the **just** is as the shining light, that shineth more and more unto the perfect day" (Proverbs 4:18).

- "Teach a **just** man, and he will increase in learning" (Proverbs 9:9).

- "The **just** shall come out of trouble" (Proverbs 12:13).

- "There shall no evil happen to the **just**" (Proverbs 12:21).

- "The wealth of the sinner is laid up for the **just**" (Proverbs 13:22).

- "For a **just** man falleth seven times, and riseth up again" (Proverbs 24:16).

- "The memory of the **just** is blessed" (Proverbs 10:7).

The Requirements of Doing Justice

Justice is an active expression of the will and nature of God. Justice requires a person to verbally confirm God's truth and carry it out. Therefore, the word *do* often precedes the word *justice*. Psalm 82:3 states, "**Do justice** to the afflicted and needy." "David . . . executed judgment and justice" (I Chronicles 18:14).

The same point is emphasized in Romans 2:13, "For not the hearers of the law are **just** before God, but the **doers** of the law shall be justified." God provides a detailed description of a just man:

"If a man be just, and do that which is lawful and right and . . . ."

- Has not looked to the false gods of his day

- Has not defiled his neighbor's wife

- Has not violated commands of personal uncleanness

- Has not oppressed anyone

- Has not taken advantage of a creditor

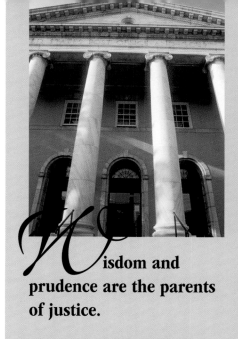

*W*isdom and prudence are the parents of justice.

"I wisdom dwell with prudence . . . By me kings reign, and princes decree justice." —Proverbs 8:12–15

"Justice is the activity of God's holiness." —Proverb

"Justice means rightness with God; nothing is just until it is adjusted to God." —Oswald Chambers

"Yea, let God be true, but every man a liar; as it is written, That thou mightest be justified in thy sayings, and mightest overcome when thou art judged." —Romans 3:4

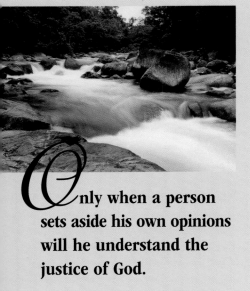

*O*nly when a person sets aside his own opinions will he understand the justice of God.

"The meek will he guide in judgment: and the meek will he teach his way."
—Psalm 25:9

"He hath shewed thee, O man, what is good; and what doth the LORD require of thee, but to do justly, and to love mercy, and to walk humbly with thy God?"
—Micah 6:8

Mature bull elephants keep the peace on the plains of Africa by preventing unruly "teenagers" from disrupting the social order.

- Has given food to the hungry
- Has provided clothes for the poor
- Has not gotten rich by high interest
- Has not engaged in iniquity
- Has carried out wise judgment between parties
- Has walked in God's statutes and judgments

". . . he is just, he shall surely live" (Ezekiel 18:5–9).

Based on this list, justice requires the following:

1. "The mouth of the just bringeth forth wisdom" (Proverbs 10:31).
2. "The tongue of the just is as choice silver" (Proverbs 10:20).
3. "The just man walketh in his integrity" (Proverbs 20:7).

An Example of a Just Man Doing Justice

"For the kingdom of heaven is like unto a man that is an householder, which went out early in the morning to hire labourers into his vineyard. And when he had agreed with the labourers for a penny a day, he sent them into his vineyard.

"And he went out about the third hour, and saw others standing idle in the marketplace, And said unto them; Go ye also into the vineyard, and whatsoever is **right** [just] I will give you. And they went their way. Again he went out about the sixth and ninth hour, and did likewise. And about the eleventh hour he went out, and found others standing idle, and saith unto them, Why stand ye here all the day idle? They say unto him, Because no man hath hired us. He saith unto them, Go ye also into the vineyard; and whatsoever is **right** [just], that shall ye receive.

"So when even was come, the lord of the vineyard saith unto his steward, Call the labourers, and give them their hire, beginning from the last unto the first. And when they came that were hired about the eleventh hour, they received every man a penny. But when the first came, they supposed that they should have received more; and they likewise received every man a penny. And when they had received it, they murmured against the goodman of the house, Saying, These last have wrought but one hour, and thou hast made them equal unto us, which have borne the burden and heat of the day.

"But he answered one of them, and said, Friend, I do thee no wrong: didst not thou agree with me for a penny? Take that thine is, and go thy way: I will give unto this last, even as unto thee. Is it not lawful for me to do what I will with mine own? Is thine eye evil, because I am good?" (Matthew 20:1–15).

The Issue of Justice

The justice in this case is the question that the householder asked the last labourers. "Why stand ye here all the day idle?" Even though the labourers worked only an hour, they had made themselves available all day long. Thus, by engaging them for the one hour the householder assumed responsibility for their readiness all day. Those who are greedy tend to be unjust because they do not see the bigger picture or consider all the factors of a situation.

How Justice Competes With Fairness

Most people demand fairness. However, absolute fairness requires that all get the same things at the same time. This is impossible; thus, we must look to God, Who is totally just.

When we focus on fairness, we fail to see the just compensation of God. For example, if God gives more money to one, He will give more faith to another, who can appropriate needed funds. "Hath not God chosen the poor of this world rich in faith?" (James 2:5.).

- Justice is based on the universal, unchanging principles of God's Word; fairness, on the variable will of the majority.

- Justice establishes guilt when God's standards are violated. Fairness tries to remove guilt by lowering God's standards.

- Justice causes us to confess our failures and plead for mercy; fairness, to justify our failures so we do not think we need mercy.

- Justice is based on personal responsibility and yields revival; fairness, on personal rights and produces rebellion.

- Justice expresses God's wisdom. Fairness expresses man's reason.

- Justice is impartial and objective; fairness is partial and subjective.

- Justice requires swift prosecution of criminals. Fairness results in slow punishment of criminals.

- Justice limits the punishment of criminals. Fairness produces inconsistent punishment of criminals.

How Good Judgment and Justice Work Together

Proverbs was written to give "the instruction of wisdom, justice, and judgment, and equity" (Proverbs 1:3). The ability to judge wisely is given to the meek. "The meek will he guide in judgment: and the meek will he teach his way" (Psalm 25:9).

Judgment is acquired through a sequence identified in Psalm 37:4–6: "Delight thyself also in the LORD; and he shall give thee the desires of thine heart. Commit thy way unto the LORD; trust also in him; and he shall bring it to pass. And he shall bring forth thy righteousness as the light, and thy judgment as the noonday."

—Personal Evaluation—

How just are you?

- Have you read God's Law, and do you memorize and meditate on it day and night?

- When you are dealing with a matter that requires justice, do you find comparable Biblical examples on which to base your decisions?

- Have you asked God for an understanding heart so you can make wise and just judgments?

- Do you have a meek spirit so God can guide you in justice and judgment?

- Do you understand the difference between justice and fairness?

- Do you cry out to God when required to make a decision based on justice?

Justice is the response of one who memorizes and meditates on God's Law day and night.

A ruler was to make his own copy of the law and read it daily so he would make wise decisions and establish his kingdom with justice. (See Deuteronomy 17:18–19.)

If you want to promote revival, tell people about their responsibilities. If you want to promote rebellion, tell people about their rights.

"I will praise thee with uprightness of heart, when I shall have learned thy righteous judgments." —Psalm 119:7

Until a person is brought to justice, he will neither desire nor appreciate mercy.

"Such is the way of an adulterous woman; she eateth, and wipeth her mouth, and saith, I have done no wickedness." —Proverbs 30:20

Loyalty
vs. Infidelity

Loyalty is the bonding of individuals in a long-term commitment of sacrificial support and defense.

*L*oyalty is exchanging "open accounts" on our time, energy, and possessions.

"For ye know the grace of our Lord Jesus Christ, that, though he was rich, yet for your sakes he became poor, that ye through his poverty might be rich." —II Corinthians 8:9

*O*ne of the benefits of being falsely accused is discovering the level of loyalty of those around you.

The **Canada goose** protects its nest from intruders and will even lay down its own life in defense of its lifelong mate.

Definition

The word *loyalty* is not found in Scripture. The word *faithfulness* would at first appear to be a synonym. However, faithfulness and dependability relate to the work or service that a person performs, whereas loyalty involves a much deeper, long-term relationship. The Biblical concepts that best describe loyalty are blood covenants, bond servant relationships, and marriage vows.

Why Is Loyalty Important?

Every important relationship in life must be built on loyalty. Marriages must be based on this quality or they will not survive. Leaders look for this quality as a primary qualification for those who serve. Most of all, God requires loyalty of His disciples, and especially in the lives of those whom He uses mightily.

Loyalty in Covenants

The Hebrew word for *covenant* is *beriyth*. It means "a cutting" and involves a compact made by passing between pieces of flesh. God illustrates this word in the covenant that He made with Abraham. This and other covenants are rich with symbolism that describes the depth and meaning of loyalty.

1. A covenant is made with those of like spirit. God said to Abraham, "I am the Almighty God; walk before me, and be thou perfect" (Genesis 17:1). Note: Scripture calls Abraham the friend of God and the father of faith. (See James 2:23 and Galatians 3:9.)

2. A covenant requires an initiator who assumes the greater responsibility in maintaining the covenant. "I will make my covenant between me and thee" (Genesis 17:2). Note: In marriage the man initiates the covenant and therefore has the greater responsibility to maintain it.

3. A covenant often involves a name change. "Neither shall thy name any more be called Abram" (Genesis 17:5). Note: A name change also occurs in a marriage as the wife takes on the husband's name and in salvation as we take on Christ's name.

4. The purpose of a covenant is to multiply benefits and fruitfulness. "I will make thee exceeding fruitful" (Genesis 17:6). Note: These purposes are fulfilled with children in a marriage and spiritual children in salvation.

5. A covenant has relationships that last beyond the lifetimes of the covenant makers. "Thou shalt keep my covenant therefore, thou, and thy seed after thee in their generations" (Genesis 17:9).

Although marriage does not continue after death, the relationships between the children and relatives do. Also, covenants with land continue with the land even under new ownership. The covenant of salvation continues beyond one's lifetime. David honored his covenant with Jonathan after Jonathan died.

6. A blood covenant requires the shedding of blood. Every man child "must needs be circumcised: and my covenant shall be in your flesh" (Genesis 17:13). When God made a covenant with Abraham, He instructed Abraham to take five different animals and "divide them in the midst." (See Genesis 15.)

A Covenant of Friends

A powerful example of loyalty in Scripture is the friendship between Jonathan and David and the covenant they made with each other. The symbolism of this covenant is rich with meaning.

1. They had a oneness of spirit— "The soul of Jonathan was knit with the soul of David, and Jonathan loved him as his own soul" (I Samuel 18:1).

2. They exchanged their outer garments—"Jonathan stripped himself of the robe that was upon him, and gave it to David" (I Samuel 18:4). Note: In salvation, Christ gives us robes of righteousness in exchange for our filthy rags.

3. They gave their weapons—When danger comes, the covenant makers will protect each other even to the point of death. Jonathan gave David his sword and his bow. (See I Samuel 18:4.)

4. They exchanged belts—The belt (translated *girdle* in I Samuel 18:4) symbolizes the strength of a person. Covenant makers pledge their strength to one another. In salvation, God's strength is made available to us in exchange for our weakness.

A Covenant of Servants

Scripture illustrates the long-term relationship of loyalty in the provisions of a bond servant's decision to continue serving his master for the rest of his life out of love for his master. (See Exodus 21:1–6 and Deuteronomy 15:16–17.)

1. The covenant of a bond servant was voluntary and based on love. If a servant chooses this covenant, then "the servant shall plainly say, I love my master, my wife, and my children; I will not go out free" (Exodus 21:5).

2. A bond-servant covenant was confirmed in a legal document. "Then his master shall bring him unto the judges" (Exodus 21:6).

3. A bond servant covenant was made public through a symbol. "He shall also bring him to the door, or unto the door post; and his master shall bore his ear through with an awl; and he shall serve him for ever" (Exodus 21:6).

A Covenant of Family

Ruth's loyalty to Naomi is one of history's most inspiring stories. After Ruth's husband died, Naomi told Ruth to return to her own people, because there was nothing more Naomi could do for Ruth. Ruth's famous response was this, "Whither thou goest, I will go; and where thou lodgest, I will lodge:

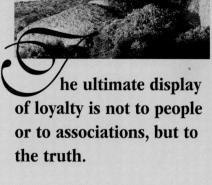

*T*he ultimate display of loyalty is not to people or to associations, but to the truth.

"From that time many of his disciples went back, and walked no more with him. Then said Jesus unto the twelve, Will ye also go away? Then Simon Peter answered him, Lord, to whom shall we go? thou hast the words of eternal life." —John 6:66–68

*B*uilding loyalty in others is done by demonstrating loyalty to them.

"We love him, because he first loved us." —I John 4:19

"I never made a sacrifice. Of this we ought not to talk when we remember the great sacrifice which He made Who left His Father's throne on high to give Himself for us." —David Livingstone

*L*oyalty is demonstrating our commitment to God by staying with those whom He has called us to serve.

"Loyalty is the one thing a leader cannot do without."

—A. P. Gouthey

Covenants vs. Contracts

- A covenant is based on trust; a contract is based on distrust.

- A covenant is built on unlimited liability; a contract is based on limited liability.

- A covenant is a sealed agreement; a contract is open to more debate.

- A covenant cannot be broken; a contract can be set aside.

thy people shall be my people, and thy God my God: Where thou diest, will I die, and there will I be buried: the LORD do so to me, and more also, if aught but death part thee and me" (Ruth 1:16–17).

A Covenant of Marriage

Marriage is a blood covenant, not just a legal contract. All the rich symbolisms of a Biblical blood covenant are contained in marriage. Beginning with the groom as the covenant initiator (and therefore the one with the greater responsibility to maintain the marriage), the seriousness of marriage vows is emphasized in the following warning. "When thou vowest a vow unto God, defer not to pay it; for he hath no pleasure in fools: pay that which thou hast vowed. Better is it that thou shouldest not vow, than that thou shouldest vow and not pay" (Ecclesiastes 5:4–5).

A Covenant of Believers

When Jesus established communion among His disciples, He actually presented it as a blood covenant. This is clear from the very words He used to describe it: "Take, eat; this is my body. And he took the cup, and gave thanks, and gave it to them, saying, Drink ye all of it; For this is my blood of the new testament, which is shed for many for the remission of sins" (Matthew 26:26–28).

"The cup of blessing which we bless, is it not the communion of the blood of Christ? The bread which we break, is it not the communion of the body of Christ?" (I Corinthians 10:16). The word *communion* signifies the Greek word *koinonia*, which is a deep and bonding fellowship with one another. This is consistent with the many commands of Scripture to love one another, because we are all members of the same body.

When we show disloyalty toward other believers, we violate the blood covenant that is made at the communion table and receive the condemnation that accompanies such a violation. "For he that eateth and drinketh unworthily, eateth and drinketh damnation to himself, not discerning the Lord's body. For this cause many are weak and sickly among you, and many sleep [die prematurely]" (I Corinthians 11:29–30).

Personal Evaluation

How loyal are you?

- Do you doubt God's sovereignty during adversity, or do you draw nearer to Him?

- Do you speak well of your authorities even during difficult times, or do you murmur?

- Do you protect your family even when circumstances make it difficult?

- Do you treat other believers as you would want to be treated?

- Do you commit to the success of those God has called you to serve?

- Are you willing to lay down your life for your family and friends?

- Are you committed to keeping your marriage vows, no matter what the cost?

Meekness
vs. Anger

Meekness is yielding our rights to God so He can demonstrate His peace and power through us.

Definition

The Hebrew word for *meekness* is *anavah*. It comes from a word that means "to abase oneself, to chasten and humble oneself, to look down."

The Greek word for *meek* is *praus*. It simply means "humble." The word *meekness* is often used in combination with other words such as *lowliness* (see Ephesians 4:2), *righteousness* (see Psalm 45:4), *gentleness* (see II Corinthians 10:1), and *fear* (see I Peter 3:15).

Significance of Meekness

Meekness is vital because it is the one quality that Jesus used to describe Himself: "Learn of me; for I am meek and lowly in heart" (Matthew 11:29). Thus, the more we understand and develop meekness, the more we take on the nature of the Lord Jesus Christ.

It is therefore understandable that Jesus would begin His discourse on discipleship by praising the qualities of meekness: "Blessed are the poor in spirit. . . . Blessed are they that mourn. . . . Blessed are the meek . . ." (Matthew 5:3–5).

Rewards of Meekness

1. Knowing Jesus Christ

The goal of the Apostle Paul was "to know Jesus Christ and the power of His resurrection." (See Philippians 3:10.) The importance of this goal is indicated by what he gave to achieve it. "Yea doubtless, and I count all things but loss for the excellency of the knowledge of Christ Jesus my Lord: for whom I have suffered the loss of all things, and do count them but dung, that I may win Christ" (Philippians 3:8).

2. Comprehending the Gospel

The good news of salvation is available to everyone. However, it is only the meek who will understand it and respond to it. Jesus explained this when He opened the scroll of Isaiah and read, "The spirit of the Lord GOD is upon me; because the LORD hath anointed me to preach good tidings unto the **meek**" (Isaiah 61:1). David wrote, "The LORD taketh pleasure in his people: he will beautify the **meek** with salvation" (Psalm 149:4) He will "save all the **meek** of the earth" (Psalm 76:9).

3. Transforming our souls

It is by the quality of meekness that one is able to make God's Word a vital part of his mind, will, and emotions and thereby conquer the destructive habits of life. "Wherefore lay apart all filthiness and superfluity of naughtiness, and receive with **meekness** the engrafted word, which is able to save your souls" (James 1:21). Since Jesus is the Living Word of God, the more we know about

Meekness is not weakness. It is strength under God's control.

Jesus said, "I seek not mine own will, but the will of the Father which hath sent me." —John 5:30

Meekness must be taught, whereas anger is contagious.

"Make no friendship with an angry man; and with a furious man thou shalt not go: Lest thou learn his ways, and get a snare to thy soul." —Proverbs 22:24

The strength of a **horse** under the control of a bridle and bit illustrates a true picture of meekness.

*M*eekness is exchanging the burdens of my life, which are hard and heavy, for the yoke of Christ, which is easy and light.

"Come unto me, all ye that labour and are heavy laden, and I will give you rest. Take my yoke upon you, and learn of me; for I am meek and lowly in heart: and ye shall find rest unto your souls. For my yoke is easy, and my burden is light."

—Matthew 11:28–30

"The greatness of man's power is the measure of his surrender." —William Booth

"Is there a heart o'erbound by sorrow? Is there a life weighed down by care? Come to the cross, each burden bearing. All your anxiety, leave it there." —E. H. Joy

Him, the more we will understand God's Word. (See John 1:1.)

4. Receiving God's guidance

One of the most important challenges in life is making wise decisions. We often make decisions that we are sure are right, but they turn out to be wrong. How, then, do we gain the judgment to make wise decisions? "The **meek** will he guide in judgment: and the **meek** will he teach his way" (Psalm 25:9).

5. Developing true character

Scripture explains that the "hidden man of the heart" is more important to adorn than the outward appearance of a person. This adornment is to be meekness. "Whose adorning let it not be that outward adorning of plaiting the hair, and of wearing of gold, or of putting on of apparel; But let it be the hidden man of the heart, in that which is not corruptible, even the ornament of a **meek** and quiet spirit, which is in the sight of God of great price" (I Peter 3:3–4).

6. Enjoying life to the fullest

Many people own possessions but do not enjoy them. They eat food, but it does not satisfy their appetites. However, "The **meek** shall eat and be satisfied: they shall praise the LORD that seek him: your heart shall live for ever" (Psalm 22:26).

7. Getting a lasting inheritance

Jesus promises: "Blessed are the **meek**: for they shall inherit the earth" (Matthew 5:5). An expanded explanation of this promise is in Psalm 37:9–11: "For evildoers shall be cut off: but those that wait upon the LORD, they shall inherit the earth. For yet a little while, and the wicked shall not be: yea, thou shalt diligently consider his place, and it shall not be. But the **meek** shall inherit the earth; and shall delight themselves in the abundance of peace."

Basic Functions of Meekness

Since meekness describes the nature of Jesus Christ, it is expected that the basic functions in the life of a believer require meekness.

1. Producing spiritual fruit

The fruit of the Spirit is possible only when we yield our rights to live in the works of the flesh. "But the fruit of the Spirit is . . . **Meekness**" (Galatians 5:22–23).

2. Restoring a fellow believer

Restoring an erring brother will be effective only if one yields his right to feel superior or to think that he cannot fall like his brother did. "Brethren, if a man be overtaken in a fault, ye which are spiritual, restore such an one in the spirit of **meekness**; considering thyself, lest thou also be tempted" (Galatians 6:1). "In **meekness** instructing those that oppose themselves; if God peradventure will give them repentance to the acknowledging of the truth" (II Timothy 2:25).

3. Walking worthy of Christ

The ability to walk worthy of our profession requires that we yield our rights to hold grudges against fellow believers. "I therefore, the prisoner of the Lord, beseech you that ye walk worthy of the vocation wherewith ye are called, With all lowliness and **meekness**, with longsuffering, forbearing one another in love" (Ephesians 4:1–2). "Put on therefore, as the elect of God, holy and beloved, bowels of mercies, kindness, humbleness of mind, **meekness,** longsuffering; Forbearing one another, and forgiving one another, if any man have a quarrel against any: even as Christ forgave you, so also do ye" (Colossians 3:12–13).

4. Respecting authorities

The proper respect for God-given authorities means that we yield our rights to give bad reports about them. "Put them in mind to be subject to principalities and powers, to obey magistrates, to be ready to every good work, To speak evil of no man, to be no brawlers, but gentle, shewing all **meekness** unto all men" (Titus 3:1–2).

5. Doing good works

In doing good works, one must yield his right to get the credit for them and defer the honor to others. "Who is a wise man and endued with knowledge among you? let him shew out of a good conversation his works with **meekness** of wisdom" (James 3:13).

6. Explaining our hope

When people see our lives, they should marvel at the hope that we have about the future, but they will not notice this unless we yield our right to have a life without trials and sorrows. "But and if ye suffer for righteousness' sake, happy are ye: and be not afraid of their terror, neither be troubled; But sanctify the Lord God in your hearts: and be ready always to give an answer to every man that asketh you a reason of the hope that is in you with **meekness** and fear" (I Peter 3:14–15).

How Do We Learn Meekness?

We learn meekness by coming to Christ with the recognition of our own weaknesses and being united with Him by belief in His finished work on the cross. Then we must grow in the experiential knowledge of Christ, Who humbled Himself for us, that we might be conformed to His image.

Personal Evaluation

How meek are you?

- Have you dedicated yourself to God and yielded all your rights to Him?
- Do you have full confidence that God controls all that happens to you?
- Is it your goal to become more like the Lord Jesus Christ?
- Have you received and responded to the good tidings of the Gospel?
- Do others praise you for a meek and quiet spirit, or do they react to an angry spirit?
- Do people resist your advice or counsel when you try to help them?
- Do you speak evil of those in positions of leadership?
- Do people ask you why you are so peaceful when serious adversities come into your life?
- Have you exchanged your burdens for the yoke of Christ?
- When you do good works and are praised for them, do you deflect the honor to others who helped you?

*A*nger is the signal that we need to check the quality of our meekness.

Emotions are like fire—a good servant but a bad master! The controlling overseer is meekness.

One of the most difficult rights to yield is the right to make final decisions.

"Anger is an acid that can do more harm to the vessel in which it is stored than to anything on which it is poured." —Unknown

*W*hen we are meek, we will not be concerned about having the first word or the last word.

Obedience
vs. Willfulness

Obedience is freedom to be creative under the protection of divinely appointed authorities.

Obedience is a relationship between two servants who must both answer to God.

"Yea, all of you be subject one to another, and be clothed with humility: for God resisteth the proud, and giveth grace to the humble."

—I Peter 5:5

The alternative to obedience is not freedom, but tyranny.

"An evil man seeketh only rebellion: therefore a cruel messenger shall be sent against him." —Proverbs 17:11

"How will you find good? It is not a thing of choice; it is a river that flows from the foot of the Invisible Throne and flows by the path of obedience."

—George Elliot

Definition

The primary Hebrew word for *obey* is *shama*. It is a root word meaning "to hear intelligently; to consider and consent with contentment; to diligently discern and perceive with the ear; to give ear."

The Greek word *hupakouo* expands the Hebrew meaning of *obey*. *Hupo* means "under; a place beneath; an inferior position." *Akouo* means "to hear and understand." *Hupakouo* means "to listen attentively; to heed or conform to a command or authority."

A second Greek word for *obey* is *peitharcheo*, meaning "to be persuaded by a ruler; to submit to authority." The disciples declared to the religious ruler who commanded them not to preach in the name of Jesus: "We ought to obey God rather than men" (Acts 5:29).

A word related to *obedience* is *submission*. The Greek word translated *submit* is *hupotasso*. It means "to put oneself under authority." It is a voluntary action of one person to become subordinate to another.

Life and Death Choices

Obedience is not an optional quality. A lack of it results in personal destruction. "Behold, I set before you this day a blessing and a curse; A blessing, if ye obey the commandments of the LORD your God, which I command you this day: And a curse, if ye will not obey the commandments of the LORD your God, but turn aside out of the way which I command you this day, to go after other gods, which ye have not known" (Deuteronomy 11:26–28).

"The eye that mocketh at his father, and despiseth to obey his mother, the ravens of the valley shall pick it out, and the young eagles shall eat it" (Proverbs 30:17). "He, that being often reproved hardeneth his neck, shall suddenly be destroyed, and that without remedy" (Proverbs 29:1).

Ministers of God

All legitimate authority comes from God. He is the One Who sets up rulers and takes them down. (See Psalm 75:7.) Therefore, when we disobey a God-given authority, we experience God's judgment.

"Let every soul be subject unto the higher powers. For there is no power but of God: the powers that be are ordained of God. Whosoever therefore resisteth the power, resisteth the ordinance of God: and they that resist shall receive to themselves damnation" (Romans 13:1–2).

Three times in this passage, God-given authorities are defined as "ministers of God" (Romans 13:4–6). Therefore, they carry out the will of God through authority entrusted to them.

Two Ways to Obey

Three military men were standing on the deck of an aircraft carrier. Suddenly their commanding officer spotted an approaching missile. He shouted to them to "drop." Two of the men dropped to the deck. The third one looked around to see what the problem was. Just as he turned, the missile struck him, and he was killed. This account illustrates the two philosophies of obedience.

The Greek approach is to understand first and then obey. The soldier who turned around wanted to know *why* he should "drop"—and then he would decide whether or not to obey. The second approach is the Hebrew model—obey first, and then understand why. This is the method that God used in His training of Abraham when He asked him to leave his homeland and to offer up his son. It is on this basis also that the Scriptures are written so that every believer would obey God and then understand why.

The Hebrew approach to obedience presupposes a close relationship between the one giving the command and the one who is to carry it out. Jesus emphasized this when He said, "My sheep hear my voice, and I know them, and they follow me" (John 10:27). Sheep will not follow a stranger, because they do not know the stranger's voice.

The Motive of Obedience

Two words in Deuteronomy 11:1 are foundational to obedience: *love* and *keep*. "Therefore thou shalt **love** the LORD thy God, and **keep** his charge, and his statutes, and his judgments, and his commandments, alway."

True obedience must be based on love. Therefore, Jesus said, "If ye love me, keep my commandments" (John 14:15). When we truly love the Lord, "his commandments are not grievous" (I John 5:3).

To "keep" God's commandments is to place them before our eyes with the intent of obeying them. In Deuteronomy 11:1 he Hebrew word translated *keep* is *shamar*, which means "to guard about; to preserve; to observe." God's people were told to write out God's commandments and keep them before their eyes so they would not forget them—even writing them on their doorposts so they would see them as they went out and came in.

The word *keepeth* is used in John 14:21: "He that hath my commandments, and keepeth them, he it is that loveth me: and he that loveth me shall be loved of my Father, and I will love him, and will manifest myself to him." The Greek word for *keepeth* is *tereo*, meaning "to guard (from loss or injury) by keeping the eye upon."

The best way to keep God's commandments before our eyes is to follow the instruction of Deuteronomy 11:18: "Therefore shall ye lay up these my words in your heart and in your soul, and bind them for a sign upon your hand, that they may be as frontlets between your eyes."

A third word that is basic to obedience is found in Deuteronomy 11:13: "And it shall come to pass, if ye shall **hearken** diligently unto my commandments which I command you this day, to love the LORD your God, and to serve him with all your heart and with all your soul." The word *hearken* is *shama*, the same word translated *obey* in Deuteronomy 11:27.

Wood ducks provide a profound illustration of obedience. Although the eggs are laid over an eleven-day period, they all hatch within a few minutes of each other in response to their mother's call.

Shortly thereafter, the mother stands at the base of the tree and calls out for the ducklings to jump. Those that obey find safety in nearby ponds. Those that disobey perish in the abandoned nest.

"Obedience is the one qualification for further vision."
—G. Campbell Morgan

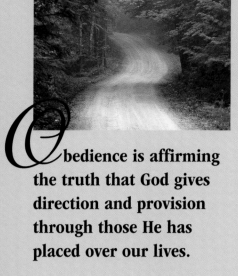

*O*bedience is affirming the truth that God gives direction and provision through those He has placed over our lives.

"Submit yourselves to every ordinance of man for the Lord's sake: whether it be to the king, as supreme; Or unto governors, as unto them that are sent by him for the punishment of evildoers, and for the praise of them that do well."

—I Peter 2:13–14

"Obedience to God's will is the secret of spiritual knowledge and insight. It is not willingness to know, but willingness to do God's will that brings certainty."

—Eric Liddell

How Obedience Relates to Wisdom

When God told Solomon to ask for whatever he wanted, Solomon asked for an understanding heart. "Give therefore thy servant an understanding heart to judge thy people, that I may discern between good and bad: for who is able to judge this thy so great a people?" (I Kings 3:9).

The Hebrew word for *understanding* in this verse is *shama*, the very same word used for *obey* and for *hearken*. God was pleased with Solomon's request and said, "Because thou hast asked this thing, and hast not asked for thyself long life; neither hast asked riches for thyself, nor hast asked the life of thine enemies; but hast asked for thyself understanding [*biyn*] to discern judgment; Behold, I have done according to thy words: lo, I have given thee a wise and an understanding [*biyn*] heart; so that there was none like thee before thee, neither after thee shall any arise like unto thee" (I Kings 3:11–12).

The understanding heart that God gave Solomon was not just a hearing (*shama*) heart, it was a *biyn* heart. A *biyn* heart involves a wide range of skills and abilities including "to separate and distinguish important matters; to be cunning; to be informed; to know with intelligence; to be prudent, and to be skillful in thinking and teaching."

How Obedience Avoids Tyranny and Bondage

Sometimes those in positions of authority misuse their power and should be reproved by those who are over them. Other times, those under authority want to be free from all restrictions and rebel— only to find themselves in new relationships that are even more restrictive.

Defining Jurisdictions for Obedience

When there are conflicting commands between different authorities or when one authority tells us to do what we know is morally wrong, we must discern whether the one who is giving the command is operating within the proper jurisdiction. There are four possible areas of jurisdiction.

1. Parental jurisdiction

Parents are given jurisdiction by God to train up their children to reverence Him and do what is right. Sons and daughters are instructed to obey their parents in all areas. (See Ephesians 6:1–2.) However, if parents command their children to do things contrary to the Laws of God or the laws of man, they are operating outside their jurisdiction.

2. Governmental jurisdiction

God ordained government to carry out His will in matters of justice. Rulers are to praise those who do well and punish those who do evil. (See Romans 13:3–4.) Because civil authorities derive their power from God, they will be judged if they violate the Laws of God. Therefore, citizens are to make wise appeals to contest unwise or unjust laws.

3. Ecclesiastical jurisdiction

The heads of households are to voluntarily submit to the leadership of wise and Godly elders in the church. The elders are not to go beyond their jurisdiction by instructing wives or children to disregard the guidance and wishes of the father, as long as his instruction is consistent with Scripture. (See Galatians 4:1–2.)

4. Vocational jurisdiction

Employees are to obey employers with wholehearted service. If an employer requires action that violates the Biblical convictions of an employee, the employee should make a wise appeal and then, if the appeal is rejected, he should consider resigning. (See Acts 5:29 and Colossians 3:22–23.)

Personal Evaluation

How obedient are you?

1. Do you obey regardless of what you are told to do?

    Obedience is based on what God says is true and right—no blind obedience; no surrender of personal responsibilities.

2. Do you ask for reasons when your request is turned down?

    Obedience is accepting "no" as the final answer—not asking challenging questions, making immediate appeals, or delaying discussions, but gaining only vital new information.

3. Do you stop what you are doing when given instructions?

    Obedience is acting immediately on command—no delays, no objections, no excuses such as "Let me finish this first."

4. Do you smile when you are told to do something?

    Obedience is cheerfully responding to requests—no frowns, no murmurs, no groans, no rolling of the eyes.

5. Do you ever give reasons why you cannot do a job?

    Obedience is finding ways to overcome obstacles—no negative thinking, no failure to be creative, no "I can't."

6. Have you ever had to be reminded to do little tasks?

    Obedience is fulfilling little commands as well as big ones—no excuses, no frustration, no reaction, no justification.

7. Do you ever have to redo a job you initially did the wrong way?

    Obedience is following all the instructions the first time—no assuming, no guessing, no forgetting, no self-will.

8. Do ever think that a job is "stupid"?

    Obedience is doing jobs and understanding the reasons later—no mocking, no whining, no cynical questioning.

9. Do you ever ask one parent after the other said "No"?

    Obedience is not pitting one authority against another—no scheming, no withholding of important facts, no repeat requests.

10. While working on chores, do you ever plan recreation?

    Obedience is putting all your energies into a task—no halfhearted effort, no holding back energy, no daydreaming.

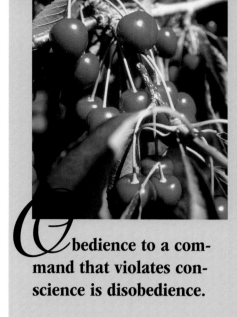

Obedience to a command that violates conscience is disobedience.

"Then Peter and the other apostles answered and said, We ought to obey God rather than men."
—Acts 5:29

When Jesus taught His disciples to pray, He gave them principles for a wise appeal.

1. **Protect authority's reputation—**
    "Hallowed be thy name."
    (i.e., "I want to give a good report about you and your work.")

2. **Advance authority's program—**
    "Thy kingdom come."
    (i.e., "I want to help you reach the goals that you have.")

3. **Honor authority's position—**
    "Thy will be done."
    (i.e., "I want others to respect your authority as much as I do.")

"Obedience is the fruit of faith; patience, the bloom on the fruit."
—Christina Rossetti

Orderliness

vs. Confusion

Orderliness is keeping everything that is under our jurisdiction neat, clean, functional, and in its proper place.

rderliness is knowing what to remove from my life and surroundings and having the courage to do it.

The Second Law of Thermodynamics:

Without intervention, things tend to go from order to disorder.

"God is not the author of confusion, but of peace. . . . Let all things be done decently and in order."

—I Corinthians 14:33, 40

leanliness is not ***next*** *to Godliness; it is* ***part*** *of Godliness.*

"That ye may put difference between holy and unholy, and between unclean and clean." —Leviticus 10:10

Definition

Several Hebrew words are translated *order*. One such word is *arak*. It means "to arrange; to put in order." Another is *taqan*. This word describes Solomon's putting the Proverbs in order. It means "to equalize; to straighten; to compose." (See Ecclesiastes 12:9)

The Greek word *epidiorthoo* means "to strengthen further, to arrange additionally" and is translated "order." While this word is used only once, other Greek words translated *order* have similar meanings. For example, the word used most frequently is *taxis*. It means "an arranging or an arrangement."

Interestingly, *taxis* is a derivative of *tasso*, a word similar in meaning to the Hebrew word *arak*. Both of these words can be used to refer to a military company that keeps rank, such as the valiant men of war who came to make David king. "All these men of war, that could keep rank [*ma'arakah*— derivative of *arak*], came with a perfect heart to Hebron, to make David king" (I Chronicles 12:38).

How to Be Orderly

1. Follow a wise schedule.

God's first act in creation was a demonstration of orderliness. He created light and then separated the light from the darkness. "And God called the light Day, and the darkness he called Night" (Genesis 1:5).

God designed the day for labor and the night for rest. Jesus stated, "I must work the works of him that sent me, while it is day: the night cometh, when no man can work" (John 9:4). He also intended the day to begin in the evening. "And the evening and the morning were the first day" (Genesis 1:5). The hours before midnight have been found to be more beneficial for sleep than the hours after midnight. This discovery affirms the time-honored proverb: "Early to bed and early to rise makes a man healthy, wealthy, and wise."

The truth of this saying is guaranteed if we meditate on Scripture while going to sleep and waking up in the morning. "Blessed is the man . . . [whose] delight is in the law of the LORD; and in his law doth he meditate day and night. . . . whatsoever he doeth shall prosper" (Psalm 1:1–3). By beginning our day in the evening, we can experience creative thinking during the night in the same way that David did. "I will bless the LORD, who hath given me counsel: my reins also instruct me in the night seasons" (Psalm 16:7).

As orderly people, we should make the best use of every minute, because time is one of our most valuable, yet most limited, assets.

2. Listen to orderly music.

Orderly music is consistent with the nature and ways of God. God has described Himself as the beginning and the ending: "I am Alpha and Omega, the beginning and the ending" (Revelation 1:8). Orderly music has a beginning and an ending and structured progressions in between that lead to resolution.

God is a triune God; each Person in the Trinity is in harmony with the others. God the Father is preeminent, just as the melody in music should be dominant. (See Ephesians 5:19.) Jesus subjected Himself to the will of the Father and magnified the Father through His obedience. "For I came down from heaven, not to do mine own will, but the will of him that sent me" (John 6:38). This is the function of harmony in orderly music. It is under the control of the melody and enhances and reinforces it.

The rhythm in music is analogous to the Holy Spirit. He did not come to magnify Himself but rather the Father and the Son. His position of being listed third confirms His subservient and supportive role. (See Matthew 28:19.) He did not come to draw attention to Himself but to glorify the Father and the Son. When rhythm becomes dominant and independent of the melody and the harmony, it causes the music to be disorderly.

God is the Creator and has infinite variety in what He creates. Likewise, orderly music has recurring themes, but the same melody, harmony, or rhythm does not repeat itself more than once. Disorderly music often majors in repetition. After three or four repetitions of either a melodic, harmonic, or rhythmic progression, the listener either reacts to it or becomes passive by it and addicted to it. Those addicted to disorderly music are motivated to violate the order of Godly thinking, behavior, and relationships.

3. Practice orderly behavior.

Orderly behavior is in harmony with the will of God and produces the fruit of the Spirit. "The fruit of the Spirit is love, joy, peace, longsuffering, gentleness, goodness, faith, Meekness, temperance: against such there is no law" (Galatians 5:22–23). Disorderly conduct is described in Galatians 5:19–21: "Now the works of the flesh are manifest, which are these; Adultery, fornication, uncleanness, lasciviousness, Idolatry, witchcraft, hatred, variance, emulations, wrath, strife, seditions, heresies, Envyings, murders, drunkenness, revellings, and such like: of the which I tell you before, as I have also told you in time past, that they which do such things shall not inherit the kingdom of God."

Perverted behavior is taking that which God created for one purpose and using it for an adverse and damaging purpose. God refers to immorality and perversion as "confusion." (See Leviticus 18:23; 20:12.)

4. Maintain clean surroundings.

Clutter breeds filth and confusion. The saying, "cleanliness is next to Godliness" is not quite accurate, because cleanliness is indeed part of Godliness (See Exodus 19:10, Leviticus 10:10, and II Corinthians 6:17.)

God illustrated the need for cleanliness in the world by His creating scavenger animals, bringing regular rains, and causing dead matter to decompose and return to dust.

Orderliness requires that we

*O*rderliness is having a place for everything and everything in its place.

Clutter is the enemy of order. Clutter is what we could never remember having if our house burned down.

"And he said unto them, Take heed, and beware of covetousness: for a man's life consisteth not in the abundance of the things which he possesseth." —Luke 12:15

The power of order is demonstrated by an army of locusts. Though locusts are small, when they march in perfect cadence, the ground actually swells and heaves before them.

*W*here there is disorder, there is uncleanness. Where there is uncleanness and filth, there is usually moral corruption.

As you clean out cluttered drawers, remember that an empty drawer is a clean drawer.

Keeping possessions organized and in good working order is a way of expressing gratefulness to God for providing them.

The **chipmunk** illustrates orderliness by designing its home with a room specific to each need. Chipmunks build storage rooms, kitchens, bedrooms, and even toilets in their underground burrows.

keep only those things that are needed, have a place for everything we keep, and keep things in good repair.

5. Have order in God's house.

Church order begins with qualified leadership. "For if a man know not how to rule his own house, how shall he take care of the church of God?" (I Timothy 3:5). Order also involves coming to the house of God with reverence for the King of all the earth.

Orderliness includes the sequence in which we give gifts to God. We are to give Him the firstfruits of all our increase, including the first part of our day, our week, and our income. "Honour the LORD with thy substance, and with the firstfruits of all thine increase: So shall thy barns be filled with plenty, and thy presses shall burst out with new wine" (Proverbs 3:9–10).

The four major functions of the first-century church are listed in Acts 2:42. The order of this list is significant: "And they continued stedfastly in the apostles' doctrine and fellowship, and in breaking of bread, and in prayers" (Acts 2:42).

Often the last item in a Biblical list is the most important. In I Corinthians 13:13 love is listed last, but it is the most important. (See also II Peter 1:1–10 and Proverbs 6:16–19.)

Applying this principle to Acts 2:42 reveals that doctrine, fellowship, and Communion are all important, but their primary function is to prepare the worshipper for powerful prayer. The goal of Jesus for His Church is that it be a "house of prayer for all people." (See Isaiah 56:7.)

Order within the church service is also necessary to avoid reaction by visitors and to convict them of their sin and bring them to repentance. "If therefore the whole church be come together into one place, and all speak with tongues, and there come in those that are unlearned, or unbelievers, will they not say that ye are mad? . . . For God is not the author of confusion, but of peace, as in all churches of the saints" (I Corinthians 14:23–33).

Personal Evaluation

How orderly are you?

- Do you begin your day by wise planning and quality time with the Lord?

- Do you go to bed early and go to sleep meditating on Scripture?

- Do you seek to discern God's will for every decision?

- Do you listen to music that is in harmony with the character of God and honoring to your parents and other Christians?

- Do your dress and appearance reflect order and show respect for how God made you.

- Do you maintain an orderly system for necessary records?

- Do you steward your home, yard, and car carefully?

- Do you have a place for everything and keep everything in its place or do you own more than you can keep organized?

- Do you keep your home ready to receive guests on short notice?

- Do you come to God's house prepared to listen and give a testimony?

- Do I encourage younger brothers and sisters to be orderly and attentive?

Patience

vs. Restlessness

Patience is welcoming trials and tribulations as friends and allowing them to perfect our character.

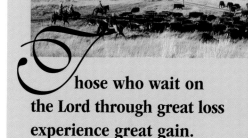

Definition

The word *patience* presupposes an adverse situation that must be endured. Thus, patience is accepting a difficult situation from God without giving Him a deadline to remove it.

The Hebrew word *chiyl* is used is used in the verse "Rest in the LORD, and wait patiently for him" (Psalm 37:7). This word means "to writhe in pain as in bringing forth a child, to bear, to bring forth, to be sorrowful, and to travail."

In Psalm 40:1, David used a different Hebrew word with the same underlying connotation. "I waited patiently for the LORD; and he inclined unto me, and heard my cry." The word he used here is *qavah*. It means "to bind together by twisting, to collect, to gather together, to tarry, to expect."

Two primary Greek words are translated *patience*. *Hupomone* is a word that comes from *hupo*, which means "under," and *meno*, which means "to stay or remain." It means "to endure with cheerfulness, and to be constant." Its root meaning is "to undergo and to bear trials, to have fortitude, to persevere."

The second word is *makrothumeo*. It means "to be forbearing, long-spirited, and longsuffering." It is by faith and *makrothumeo* that we inherit the promises of God. (See Hebrews 6:12.)

How Patience Is Developed

Patience is a reward for properly responding to trials and tribulations. Therefore, Paul wrote: "We glory in tribulations also: knowing that tribulation worketh **patience**; And **patience**, experience; and experience, hope." (Romans 5:3–4).

In order to "glory" in tribulations, we must thank God for them and rejoice in the benefits that He designed them to produce. The end result of glorying in tribulations is that we experience the power of God's love through the power (*dunamis*) of His Holy Spirit. "Hope maketh not ashamed; because the love of God is shed abroad in our hearts by the Holy Ghost which is given unto us" (Romans 5:5).

Paul reaffirms this in his letter to the Corinthian believers: "And he said unto me, My grace is sufficient for thee: for my strength is made perfect in weakness. Most gladly therefore will I rather glory in my infirmities, that the power of Christ may rest upon me. Therefore I take pleasure in infirmities, in reproaches, in necessities, in persecutions, in distresses for Christ's sake: for when I am weak, then am I strong" (II Corinthians 12:9–10).

The development of patience through tribulations is also

Those who wait on the Lord through great loss experience great gain.

Job lost . . .

- 7,000 sheep
- 3,000 camels
- 500 yoke of oxen
- 500 donkeys

Job received . . .

- 14,000 sheep
- 6,000 camels
- 1,000 yoke of oxen
- 1,000 donkeys

"Except a corn of wheat fall into the ground and die, it abideth alone: but if it die, it bringeth forth much fruit." —John 12:24

"No one will ever know the full depth of his capacity for patience and humility as long as nothing bothers him. It is only when times are troubled and difficult that he can see how much of either is in him."

—St. Francis of Assisi

*T*ime ceases to be a factor when patience is motivated by love.

Jacob's seven years of waiting seemed like "a few days" because of the great love that he had for Rachel. (See Genesis 29:20.)

*P*atience is enjoying the fellowship of Christ's sufferings in order to give life to others.

"**Quiet waiting before God would save from many a mistake and from many a sorrow.**"
—J. Hudson Taylor

confirmed by James: "My brethren, count it all joy when ye fall into divers temptations; Knowing this, that the trying of your faith worketh **patience**. But let **patience** have her perfect work, that ye may be perfect and entire, wanting nothing" (James 1:2–4).

The Greek word for *perfect* is *teleios*. It means "complete (in various applications of labor, growth, mental and moral character, etc.)."

Tribulation Is Necessary for Patience

Scripture identifies Job as an ultimate example of patience. "Behold, we count them happy which endure. Ye have heard of the **patience** of Job, and have seen the end of the Lord; that the Lord is very pitiful, and of tender mercy" (James 5:11).

The trials Job endured were classic examples of disasters. "There came a messenger unto Job, and said, The oxen were plowing, and the asses feeding beside them: And the Sabeans fell upon them, and took them away; yea, they have slain the servants with the edge of the sword; and I only am escaped alone to tell thee.

"While he was yet speaking, there came also another, and said, The fire of God is fallen from heaven, and hath burned up the sheep, and the servants, and consumed them; and I only am escaped alone to tell thee.

"While he was yet speaking, there came also another, and said, The Chaldeans made out three bands, and fell upon the camels, and have carried them away, yea, and slain the servants with the edge of the sword; and I only am escaped alone to tell thee.

"While he was yet speaking, there came also another, and said, Thy sons and thy daughters were eating and drinking wine in their eldest brother's house: And, behold, there came a great wind from the wilderness, and smote the four corners of the house, and it fell upon the young men, and they are dead; and I only am escaped alone to tell thee" (Job 1:14–19).

The suffering that Job endured is astonishing. Yet his response reveals the purifying and perfecting that patience in trials produces in a believer's life.

After learning that all his herds and flocks had been stolen or killed, all but three of his herdsmen had been killed, and his seven sons and three daughters had been killed, Job "arose, and rent his mantle, and shaved his head, and fell down upon the ground, and worshipped. And said, Naked came I out of my mother's womb, and naked shall I return thither: the LORD gave, and the LORD hath taken away; blessed be the name of the LORD" (Job 1:20–21).

In this response, we see the following perfection of character.

1. **Tribulation produced humility.** Job "arose, and rent his mantle, and shaved his head, and fell down upon the ground."

2. **Tribulation increased reverence.** Job "fell down upon the ground, and worshiped."

3. **Tribulation prompted meekness.** "Naked came I out of my mother's womb."

4. **Tribulation clarified priorities.** "Naked shall I return thither."

5. **Tribulation caused gratefulness.** "The Lord gave."

6. Tribulation strengthened discernment. "The Lord hath taken away" (not Satan although he carried it out).

7. Tribulation resulted in honor. "Blessed be the name of the Lord."

The Significance of Anguish in Patience

The quality of patience presupposes suffering and anguish. It is in the definition of the words.

The trials and tribulations requiring patience have a purifying effect on those who endure them. Peter emphasizes this. "But the God of all grace, who hath called us unto his eternal glory by Christ Jesus, after that ye have suffered a while, make you perfect, stablish, strengthen, settle you." (I Peter 5:10).

The suffering we are to endure with patience also powerfully benefits the lives of those who watch our faith grow through trials.

Paul explains that the more we experience suffering and death, the more power we will have to impart life to others. "But we have this treasure in earthen vessels, that the excellency of the power may be of God, and not of us. We are troubled on every side, yet not distressed; we are perplexed, but not in despair; Persecuted, but not forsaken; cast down, but not destroyed; Always bearing about in the body the dying of the Lord Jesus, that the life also of Jesus might be made manifest in our body.

"For we which live are alway delivered unto death for Jesus' sake, that the life also of Jesus might be made manifest in our mortal flesh. So then death worketh in us, but life in you" (II Corinthians 4:7–12).

Paul uses this same Hebrew word for patience to describe bringing others to salvation and to maturity in the Christian life. "My little children, of whom I travail in birth again until Christ be formed in you" (Galatians 4:19).

Why Patience Is Necessary

1. **To see the end of the wicked—** "Rest in the LORD, and wait **patiently** for him: fret not thyself because of him who prospereth in his way, because of the man who bringeth wicked devices to pass." (Psalm 37:7).

2. **To produce a good harvest—** "But that on the good ground are they, which in an honest and good heart, having heard the word, keep it, and bring forth fruit with **patience**" (Luke 8:15).

3. **To possess our souls—** "In your **patience** possess ye your souls" (Luke 21:19).

4. **To seek after glory and honor—** "To them who by **patient** continuance in well-doing seek for glory and honour and immortality, eternal life" (Romans 2:7).

5. **To be approved for ministry—** "But in all things approving ourselves as the ministers of God, in much **patience**, in afflictions, in necessities, in distresses" (II Corinthians 6:4).

6. **To prepare for Christ—** "And the Lord direct your hearts into the love of God, and into the **patient** waiting for Christ" (II Thessalonians 3:5). Be

Patience is staying in God's crucible until His purification is finished.

"So then death worketh in us, but life in you." —II Corinthians 4:12

"Never think that God's delays are God's denials. Hold on; hold fast; hold out. Patience is genius."

—Comte Leclerc de Buffon

When the chrysalis of a **butterfly** finally splits open, the butterfly must quickly free itself. The pressure of this struggle inflates the butterfly's wrinkled wings with vital fluids. Without the struggle, a butterfly's wings harden into misshapen stubs.

$\mathcal{P}$atience is letting God choose the time for reaping the fruit of my labors.

Personal Evaluation

How patient are you?

- Do you realize that the final results of life's situations are in God's hands?

- Do you use waiting on others as an opportunity to learn to wait on God?

- Do you take time to listen to God's voice when you pray?

- Do you wait for God to answer your prayers in His timing?

- Do you fulfill your responsibilities while waiting on the Lord or others?

- Do you look to the face of God while waiting for provisions from His hand?

- Do you joyfully endure pain and suffering?

- Do you patiently instruct those for whom you are responsible?

- Do you rejoice in trials instead of becoming bitter?

ye also **patient**; stablish your hearts: for the coming of the Lord draweth nigh" (James 5:7).

7. **To be a qualified leader—**
"The servant of the Lord must not strive; but be gentle unto all men, apt to teach, **patient**" (II Timothy 2:24).

8. **To run a good race—**
"Wherefore seeing we also are compassed about with so great a cloud of witnesses, let us lay aside every weight, and the sin which doth so easily beset us, and let us run with **patience** the race that is set before us" (Hebrews 12:1).

The Rewards of Patience

1. **Seeing God answer our cries—**
"I waited **patiently** for the LORD; and he inclined unto me, and heard my cry" (Psalm 40:1).

2. **Having hope in the Lord—**
"For whatsoever things were written aforetime were written for our learning, that we through **patience** and comfort of the scriptures might have hope" (Romans 15:4).

3. **Being renewed with strength—**
"Strengthened with all might, according to his glorious power, unto all **patience** and longsuffering with joyfulness" (Colossians 1:11). "But they that wait upon the LORD shall renew their strength; they shall mount up with wings as eagles; they shall run, and not be weary; and they shall walk, and not faint" (Isaiah 40:31).

4. **Inheriting God's promise—**
"That ye be not slothful, but followers of them who through faith and **patience** inherit the promises . . . And so, after he had **patiently** endured, he obtained the promise" (Hebrews 6:12–15). "For ye have need of **patience**, that, after ye have done the will of God, ye might receive the promise" (Hebrews 10:36).

5. **Becoming a mature believer—**
"But let **patience** have her perfect work, that ye may be perfect and entire, wanting nothing" (James 1:4).

6. **Gaining God's approval—**
"For what glory is it, if, when ye be buffeted for your faults, ye shall take it **patiently**? but if, when ye do well, and suffer for it, ye take it **patiently**, this is acceptable with God" (I Peter 2:20).

In the instruction that James gives to be patient, he emphasizes both the importance of it and the rewards from it. "Be **patient** therefore, brethren, unto the coming of the Lord. Behold, the husbandman waiteth for the precious fruit of the earth, and hath long **patience** for it, until he receive the early and latter rain.

"Be ye also **patient**; stablish your hearts: for the coming of the Lord draweth nigh. . . . Take, my brethren, the prophets, who have spoken in the name of the Lord, for an example of suffering affliction, and of **patience**. Behold, we count them happy which endure. Ye have heard of the **patience** of Job, and have seen the end of the Lord; that the Lord is very pitiful, and of tender mercy" (James 5:7–11).

After Job successfully passed the test of persecution, God rewarded him with double of everything that he lost.

Persuasiveness
vs. Contentiousness

Persuasiveness is convincing others to follow God's ways because of how His ways are working in our lives.

Definition

Several Greek words reveal the fuller meaning of persuasiveness. *Peitho* (persuade) means "to induce by words to believe; to convince by sound reasoning." It carries with it the concept of guiding a person's thoughts by a sequence of convincing statements. *Elegcho* (convince) means "to confute, to admonish, to convict, to find fault with; to correct, to rebuke, and to reprove." *Dialogizomai* (reason) means "to bring together different reasons, to reckon."

Why Persuasiveness Is Important

God's primary purpose for every believer is to be a witness of His truth. Persuasiveness is communicating truth to a person's spirit through sound reasoning and convincing him to follow the ways of God. The more persuasive we are in talking to another person about the ways of God, the more effective we will be as witnesses and the greater number of people we will be able to turn from the way of death to the path of life.

The eternal torments of hell should be a powerful motivation for us to develop the skills of persuasiveness so that we can turn unbelievers from such a place.

This was the motivation of Paul: "Knowing therefore the terror of the Lord, we persuade men" (II Corinthians 5:11).

When we talk to people, they tend to have two questions in their minds: (1) Why is this important for me to hear? (2) How can I apply it to my life? Our first words should answer these two questions.

How Paul Used Persuasiveness

Paul was a master at persuading many to turn to Christ.

- He "**persuaded them** [hearers] to continue in the grace of God" (Acts 13:43).

- He "reasoned in the synagogue every sabbath, and **persuaded** the Jews and the Greeks" (Acts 18:4).

- He "went into the synagogue, and spake boldly for the space of three months, disputing and **persuading** the things concerning the kingdom of God" (Acts 19:8).

- He "expounded and testified the kingdom of God, **persuading** them concerning Jesus, both out of the law of Moses, and out of the prophets, from morning till evening" (Acts 28:23).

The most significant testimony of Paul's effectiveness in persuasion came from his oppo-

Persuasion is helping people find out what they need and then showing them the best way to get it.

"Knowing therefore the terror of the Lord, we persuade men."
—II Corinthians 5:11

"We are all missionaries . . . Wherever we go, we either bring people nearer to Christ, or we repel them from Christ." —Eric Liddell

Convincing people requires a confidence in our voices that matches the truth and love in our hearts.

"That we henceforth be no more children, tossed to and fro, and carried about with every wind of doctrine . . . But speaking the truth in love, may grow up into him."
—Ephesians 4:14–15

The most effective persuasion is convincing a person that an idea originated with him.

Two Basic
Motivations
for Persuasiveness

1. What will I gain if I do it?

2. What will I lose if I don't?

God has set these two motivations in the heart of man. Therefore, we must answer them when motivating others to do what is right. The ultimate gain is Heaven; the ultimate loss is hell.

The impending judgment of the wicked is the urgency of persuasion.

"When I say unto the wicked, Thou shalt surely die; and thou givest him not warning . . . the same wicked man shall die in his iniquity; but his blood will I require at thine hand."

—Ezekiel 3:18

nents. The silversmiths of Ephesus exclaimed, "Moreover ye see and hear, that not alone at Ephesus, but almost throughout all Asia, this Paul hath persuaded and turned away much people, saying that they be no gods, which are made with hands" (Acts 19:26).

The Secrets of Persuasiveness

1. The authority of a clear conscience

Paul continually exercised himself to have a conscience void of offense toward God and men. In II Corinthians 5:11, he associated a clear conscience with persuasiveness. He also identified a good conscience as a weapon in the battle for truth: "That thou by them mightest war a good warfare; Holding faith, and a good conscience; which some having put away concerning faith have made shipwreck" (I Timothy 1:18–19). If we do not have a clear conscience, we will not be able to speak convincingly about the work and ways of a Holy God.

2. The authority of Scripture

Persuasiveness is based on the authority that is behind it, and there can be no greater authority than "Thus saith the Lord." The use of Scripture was the key to the persuasiveness of Paul, Apollos, and others. Apollos "mightily convinced the Jews, and that publicly, shewing by the scriptures that Jesus was Christ" (Acts 18:28). In order to have this authority, we must learn how to skillfully use the Word of God, "rightly dividing the word of truth" (II Timothy 2:15).

3. The authority of personal testimony

Paul often used his own testimony to convince his hearers of the power and truth of God. He even used his testimony in talking to King Agrippa and almost persuaded him to become a believer. (See Acts 26:13–28.) The saints spoken of in Revelation 12:11 overcame Satan by the word of their testimony. The power of testimonies to persuade unbelievers or those unlearned in the things of God is described in I Corinthians 14:25: "And thus are the secrets of his heart made manifest; and so falling down on his face he will worship God, and report that God is in you of a truth."

4. The authority of appealing to the conscience

Paul learned on Mars Hill the limitations of trying to persuade hearers by appealing to their minds. They listened until he spoke of the resurrection which was beyond their capacity to understand. A more effective method of persuasion was explained by Paul in II Corinthians 4:2: We "have renounced the hidden things of dishonesty, not walking in craftiness, nor handling the word of God deceitfully; but by manifestation of the truth commending ourselves to every man's conscience in the sight of God." In order to appeal to the conscience of a person, it is important to get his permission to ask personal questions about past failures.

5. The effectiveness of using gracious words

God gives us grace, which produces the desire and power to

do His will. In the same way, we must use gracious words to persuade others to do what is right. "Let your speech be alway with grace, seasoned with salt, that ye may know how ye ought to answer every man" (Colossians 4:6).

Even when others argue with us, we are to not be contentious. "And the servant of the Lord must not strive; but be gentle unto all men, apt to teach, patient, In meekness instructing those that oppose themselves; if God peradventure will give them repentance to the acknowledging of the truth; And that they may recover themselves out of the snare of the devil, who are taken captive by him at his will" (II Timothy 2:24–26).

Biblical Examples of Persuasiveness

1. Ahithophel was such a wise counselor that he spoke "as the oracle of God." Yet, Hushai saved David's life by persuading Absalom to disregard Ahithophel's wise counsel. (II Samuel 16:23 and chapter 17)

2. Haman was a skilled and clever diplomat, yet Esther persuaded King Ahasuerus to listen to her appeal which exposed Haman's plot against her people. (Esther 7)

3. Jesus was sent to the Jewish nation, however a Syrophenician woman persuaded Him to include her healing in His agenda. (Mark 7:24–30)

4. Israel was commanded not to make a league with any other nation, but the Gibeonites persuaded them to violate this instruction. (Joshua 9)

Personal Evaluation

How persuasive are you?

- Do you persuade Christian friends to join you in doing good works for others who are in need?

- Do you have a written testimony concerning various areas of the Christian life so that others would be persuaded to follow your example?

- Do you persuade others to believe on Jesus Christ?

- Do you persuade rebellious sons or daughters to clear their consciences and get back under the authority of God and their parents?

- Do you convince friends who are considering a divorce not to go through with it?

- Do you persuade brothers or sisters to reject wrong decisions?

- Do you persuade others to dedicate their lives to God?

- Do you persuade those who use Scripture to justify wrong activities that they are misusing God's Word?

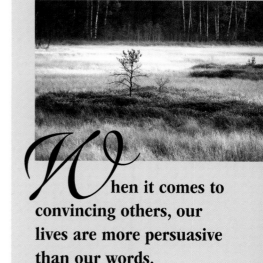

When it comes to convincing others, our lives are more persuasive than our words.

"Whereas they speak against you as evildoers, they may by your good works, which they shall behold, glorify God in the day of visitation."
—I Peter 2:12

Reduce contention by finding common ground with someone who disagrees with you.

"What man is he that desireth life, and loveth many days, that he may see good? Keep thy tongue from evil, and thy lips from speaking guile. Depart from evil, and do good; seek peace, and pursue it."—Psalm 34: 12–14

The **peacock** uses the fullest measure of his iridescent fan of feathers and enthusiastic display to attract the attention of a prospective mate.

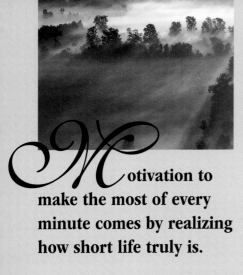

*M*otivation to make the most of every minute comes by realizing how short life truly is.

"For what is your life? It is even a vapour, that appeareth for a little time, and then vanisheth away."
—James 4:14

Punctuality is respecting the time of others. My five-minute delay means that each one waiting for me loses five minutes of irreplaceable time.

"I ought not to insult any one by supposing that his time is worth nothing, and that he himself is a nobody, who may as well wait for me as not."
—C. H. Spurgeon

*P*eople tend to count the faults of those who keep them waiting. The longer they wait, the more faults they find.

"Procrastination is the thief of time." —Unknown

Punctuality

vs. Tardiness

Punctuality is demonstrating the worth of people and time by arriving for appointments before they begin.

The Importance of Punctuality

Punctuality is based on two important factors. The first is a reverence for time, and the second is a respect for other people. Punctuality is being present, prepared, and alert for appointed times and seasons. Being punctual is living in harmony with the nature of God (Who is always precisely on time). Failing to be punctual hinders God's purposes in our lives and offends those who are then forced to wait for us. People tend to count the faults of those who keep them waiting. The longer they wait, the more faults they find.

A Reverence for Time

We are to reverence time, because God created it. He created days, nights, weeks, months, and years. He also established seasons of the year and seasons of life. God designed the day for work and the night for rest. He wants us to make full use of every day and finish one week's work in six days. We are then to honor Him with "the first fruits of all our increase," including the first portion of a paycheck, the first part of the day, and the first day of the week.

If you have not been punctual toward God, consider the Word of the Lord, "Therefore to him that knoweth to do good, and doeth it not, to him it is sin" (James 4:17). Confess your sins to God, and write out the steps you plan to take to establish punctuality before the Lord.

Personal Evaluation

How punctual are you toward God?

- Do you meet God punctually each morning for prayer and reading Scripture?

- Do you go to bed early so that you can get up early?

- Do you arrive for church early so that you are ready at the appointed time?

- Do you tithe punctually?

- Do you quickly do all you can to meet a need that God brings to your attention?

- Do you seize opportunities to share the Gospel as God directs you?

A Respect for People

The second factor required for punctuality is a respect for other people and the time God has entrusted to them. Time is one of our most precious assets.

We are given a limited amount of it and are accountable to God for how we use it.

When we keep other people waiting, we actually rob them of their time and hinder them from accomplishing God's will. We fail to obey the command to "walk circumspectly. . . . Redeeming the time, because the days are evil" (Ephesians 5:15–16).We also fail to comprehend the truth of the following quote:

**"Lost yesterday,
Somewhere between
   sunrise and sunset,
Two golden hours,
Each set with sixty
   diamond minutes.
No reward is offered
For they are gone
   forever."**

—Horace Mann

If you have robbed others of time by your lack of punctuality, make a list of those whom you have wronged and ask for their forgiveness. Fulfill the promises that you have made to others, and design ways for others to hold you accountable for punctuality. Make this a priority until punctuality is a consistent discipline in your life.

Personal Evaluation

How punctual are you toward others?

- Do you arrive punctually for mealtimes and other family gatherings?
- Do you arrive early at your place of employment?
- Do you keep appointments that you make with others?
- Do you promptly pay your bills ?

- Do you write thank-you letters and notes in a timely fashion?
- Do you punctually return books and other items that you borrow?
- Do you fulfill the promises you have made to others?

Related Character Qualities Necessary for Punctuality

- Organization—Organizing our lives and surroundings so that we can be on time.
- Creativity—Designing more efficient ways to accomplish tasks so as to be on time.
- Initiative—Taking the lead in doing what needs to be done in order to be punctual.
- Patience—Forgiving the lack of punctuality in others.

The punctual migration of swallows has been documented for thousands of years. Each fall, swallows fly south, and each spring they return—usually within twenty-four hours of their anticipated arrival.

Punctuality is saying "yes" to wise planning and "no" to delightful distractions.

"So teach us to number our days, that we may apply our hearts unto wisdom." —Psalm 90:12

"Time is the passing of life. Redeeming the time means rescuing it from going to waste." —Rick Grubbs

Time is a valuable asset which is multiplied when we give the first part back to God.

"Honour the LORD with thy substance, and with the firstfruits of all thine increase: So shall thy barns be filled with plenty." —Proverbs 3:9–10

Time is like a coupon; it does nothing for us until we exchange it for something of value. We get the most value for it when we invest it in eternal treasures.

Resourcefulness
vs. Wastefulness

Resourcefulness is increasing assets by seeing value in what others overlook or discard.

The waste of the slothful is the wealth of the resourceful.

The ultimate example of resourcefulness is the great value God sees in each person and the loving diligence He exerts to "seek and to save" that which is lost. (See Luke 19:10.)

God provides food for the fowls of the air, but they must exercise resourcefulness to get it!

When we give away assets in times of plenty, we will have what we need in times of want.

(See II Corinthians 8:14.)

Definition

A resource is an asset that is available for anticipated needs. The Biblical concept of resourcefulness is "to gather." "Wealth gotten by vanity shall be diminished: but he that gathereth by labour shall increase" (Proverbs 13:11). In this verse, the Hebrew word for *gather* is *qabats* and literally means "to grasp." Another Hebrew word for *gather* is *agar* and means "to harvest." "He that gathereth in summer is a wise son: but he that sleepeth in harvest is a son that causeth shame" (Proverbs 10:5).

The Importance of Resourcefulness

The result of resourcefulness is the increase of our net worth. The goal of increasing our assets must not be to heap up treasures for ourselves, but to increase the ability to give to others. "That ye, always having all sufficiency in all things, may abound to every good work" (II Corinthians 9:8).

Jesus told a parable about the kingdom of Heaven; however, it also has an application on the importance of resourcefulness.

"For the kingdom of heaven is as a man travelling into a far country, who called his own servants, and delivered unto them his goods. And unto one he gave five talents, to another two, and to another one; to every man according to his several ability; and straightway took his journey.

"Then he that had received the five talents went and traded with the same, and made them other five talents. And likewise he that had received two, he also gained other two. But he that had received one went and digged in the earth, and hid his lord's money.

"After a long time the lord of those servants cometh, and reckoneth with them. And so he that had received five talents came and brought other five talents, saying, Lord, thou deliveredst unto me five talents: behold, I have gained beside them five talents more. His lord said unto him, Well done, thou good and faithful servant: thou hast been faithful over a few things, I will make thee ruler over many things: enter thou into the joy of thy lord.

"He also that had received two talents came and said, Lord, thou deliveredst unto me two talents: behold, I have gained two other talents beside them.

"His lord said unto him, Well done, good and faithful servant; thou hast been faithful over a few things, I will make thee ruler over many things: enter thou into the joy of thy lord.

"Then he which had received the one talent came and said, Lord, I knew thee that thou art an hard man, reaping where thou hast not sown, and gathering where thou hast not strawed: And I was afraid, and went and hid thy talent in the earth: lo, there thou hast that is thine.

"His lord answered and said unto him, Thou wicked and slothful servant, thou knewest that I reap where I sowed not, and gather where I have not strawed:

"Thou oughtest therefore to have put my money to the exchangers, and then at my coming I should have received mine own with usury" (Matthew 25:15–27).

How Gleaning Laws Emphasize Resourcefulness

When God designed laws, statutes, and judgments for the nation of Israel, He made provisions for "social welfare." However, resourcefulness was necessary for the program to work.

"When ye reap the harvest of your land, thou shalt not wholly reap the corners of thy field, neither shalt thou gather the gleanings of thy harvest.

"And thou shalt not glean thy vineyard, neither shalt thou gather every grape of thy vineyard; thou shalt leave them for the poor and stranger" (Leviticus 19:9–10).

This "welfare program" kept Naomi and Ruth alive after their return from Moab and gave Boaz an opportunity to be generous.

How Life Was Preserved Through Resourcefulness

1. During the Flood

After God determined to judge the world with a flood, He instructed Noah to build an ark in order to preserve his family and all the creatures that could not swim. In addition to preparing the space needed to house the animals, Noah and his family had to demonstrate resourcefulness to gather the food that was needed to survive.

"Of every living thing of all flesh, two of every sort shalt thou bring into the ark, to keep them alive with thee; they shall be male and female. . . . And take thou unto thee of all food that is eaten, and thou shalt gather it to thee; and it shall be for food for thee, and for them" (Genesis 6:19, 21).

2. During a Famine

A second excellent example of resourcefulness was the preparation made for a famine during the days of Joseph.

Through a dream, God warned Pharaoh that there would be seven years of abundant harvest followed by seven years of famine. Joseph designed a resourceful plan to prepare for the famine.

"Let them gather all the food of those good years that come, and lay up corn under the hand of Pharaoh, and let them keep food in the cities.

"And that food shall be for store to the land against the seven years of famine, which shall be in the land of Egypt; that the land perish not through the famine" (Genesis 41:35–36).

Believers are instructed to establish personal programs of resourcefulness in order to distribute to the necessity of saints. (See Romans 12:13.)

"Now concerning the collection for the saints, as I have given order to the churches of Galatia, even so do ye. Upon the first day of the week let every one of you

Known as one of the most difficult of all fish to catch, the **muskie** demonstrates resourcefulness by doing anything in its power to escape. It twists, jumps, dives, and even lies motionless on the bottom in order to free itself from a fisherman's lure.

*R*esourcefulness is finding the assets that God has already provided.

"For every one that asketh receiveth; and he that seeketh findeth."

—*Luke 11:10*

*R*esourcefulness is taking what others view as "nothing" and making it into something.

Resourceful people think in terms of percentages. Buying a can of food for eight cents, rather than ten cents, is not just saving two cents; it is saving 20 percent.

"Take care of the minutes; the hours will take care of themselves." —Lord Chesterfield

*I*dle talk is the enemy of resourcefulness, because it consumes one of our most valuable assets.

"The talk of the lips tendeth only to penury." —Proverbs 14:23

lay by him in store, as God hath prospered him, that there be no gatherings when I come" (I Corinthians 16:1–2).

The Power Behind Resourcefulness

As resources are increased through wise and creative gathering, it is easy to convince ourselves that we are the ones responsible for the added wealth. Therefore, we must continually remind ourselves that it is God "that giveth thee power to get wealth" (Deuteronomy 8:18).

"Every good gift and every perfect gift is from above, and cometh down from the Father of lights, with whom is no variableness, neither shadow of turning" (James 1:17).

The Threefold Procedure to Gather Resources

God uses physical needs to motivate us to maintain a daily dependence upon Him. Therefore, He instructs us to pray, "Give us this day our daily bread" (Matthew 6:11).

God has established a threefold procedure to gain resources in answer to prayer:
1. **Ask and receive**—When we ask God for needed resources, He has promised to provide them for us. However, in order to get them, we must take the next two steps.
2. **Seek and find**—Even though God has already given what we have asked for, we must be diligent to search out that which He has given. This will require insight, initiative, and creativity.
3. **Knock and open**—When we believe we have found what God has given, we must make contact with the people who are

involved. By explaining to them our goals and how God has previously led us, we can then see whether God has prepared their hearts to complete the acquisition of the resource.

Many people ask God for things and are given them, but they never take the next two steps. Thus, they conclude that God did not hear or answer their prayer.

"Ask, and it shall be given you; seek, and ye shall find; knock, and it shall be opened unto you: For every one that asketh receiveth; and he that seeketh findeth; and to him that knocketh it shall be opened" (Matthew 7:7–8).

Personal Evaluation

How resourceful are you?

- Do you keep accurate records of the resources God has given you?
- Would God be pleased with the way you are using the assets He has given to you?
- Have you searched out valuable resources that others are discarding?
- As you increase personal assets, is your real motive to have more to give away or to heap up these assets for your own security?
- Have you asked God for things and expected Him to give them to you without first seeking and finding them?
- Have you multiplied the value of your assets, or has their value been eaten up with depreciation, rust, and moths?

Responsibility
vs. Unreliability

Responsibility is knowing and doing what God and others are expecting of me.

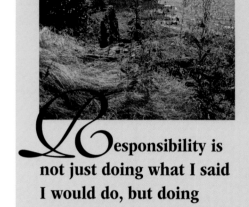

Definition

The Biblical word *duty* describes the concept of responsibility. It is translated from the Greek word *opheilo*. It means "to owe" or "the good will due to another."

The word *opheilo* is translated different ways in the New Testament. These include *ought, due, need, owe,* and *bound.* "We then that are strong ought [*opheilo*] to bear the infirmities of the weak" (Romans 15:1); "Let the husband render unto the wife due [*opheilo*] benevolence" (I Corinthians 7:3); "But if any man think that he behaveth himself uncomely toward his virgin, if she pass the flower of her age, and need [*opheilo*] so require, let him do what he will, he sinneth not: let them marry" (I Corinthians 7:36).

"Owe [*opheilo*] no man any thing, but to love one another: for he that loveth another hath fulfilled the law" (Romans 13:8); "We are bound [*opheilo*] to give thanks alway to God for you, brethren" (II Thessalonians 2:13).

Duties That Are Our Responsibility

- **Paying on a debt of love—** "Owe [*opheilo*] no man any thing, but to love one another: for he that loveth another hath fulfilled the law" (Romans 13:8).

- **Supporting faithful ministers—** "It hath pleased them verily; and their debtors they are. For if the Gentiles have been made partakers of their spiritual things, their **duty** [*opheilo*] is also to minister unto them in carnal things" (Romans 15:27).

- **Protecting weaker believers—** "We then that are strong **ought** [*opheilo*] to bear the infirmities of the weak, and not to please ourselves" (Romans 15:1).

- **Making marriage decisions—** "But if any man think that he behaveth himself uncomely toward his virgin, if she pass the flower of her age, and **need** [*opheilo*] so require, let him do what he will, he sinneth not: let them marry" (I Corinthians 7:36).

- **Giving love in marriage—** "So **ought** [*opheilo*] men to love their wives as their own bodies. He that loveth his wife loveth himself" (Ephesians 5:28).

- **Being thankful for believers—** "We are **bound** [*opheilo*] to thank God always for you, brethren, as it is meet, because that your faith groweth exceedingly, and the charity of every one of you all toward each other aboundeth" (II Thessalonians 1:3).

Responsibility is not just doing what I said I would do, but doing what I *know* I should do.

"Confidence in an unfaithful man in time of trouble is like a broken tooth, and a foot out of joint."
—*Proverbs 25:19*

"You would not think any duty small if you yourself were great." —George MacDonald

Responsibility is doing what is expected and required. Profitability is doing what is extra and not anticipated.

Worry comes from assuming responsibilities that God never intended for us to have.

*T*he more responsible I am, the more freedom I will be given; the more freedom I am given, the more responsible I must be.

"Moreover it is required in stewards, that a man be found faithful."
—I Corinthians 4:2

*R*esponsibility is doing what I ought to do even when I don't want to do it.

"You can't escape the responsibility of tomorrow by avoiding it today."
—Abraham Lincoln

- **Suffering for believers—** "Hereby perceive we the love of God, because he laid down his life for us: and we **ought** [*opheilo*] to lay down our lives for the brethren" (I John 3:16).

- **Being in submission—** "For this cause **ought** [*opheilo*] the woman to have power on her head because of the angels" (I Corinthians 11:10).

- **Caring for children—** "The children **ought** [*opheilo*] not to lay up for the parents, but the parents for the children" (II Corinthians 12:14).

- **Walking in Christ's love—** "He that saith he abideth in him **ought** [*opheilo*] himself also so to walk, even as he walked" (I John 2:6). "Beloved, if God so loved us, we **ought** [*opheilo*] also to love one another" (I John 4:11).

- **Providing hospitality—** "Beloved, thou doest faithfully whatsoever thou doest to the brethren, and to strangers; . . . We therefore **ought** [*opheilo*] to receive such, that we might be fellow-helpers to the truth" (III John 5–8).

How Our Debt Requires Responsibility

In the same way that a citizen shares the debt load of his country, so every believer shares a debt of love to every other believer. Paul states, "**Owe** [*opheilo*] no man any thing, but to love one another: for he that loveth another hath fulfilled the law" (Romans 13:8). Jesus explained the necessity of paying that debt in His parable of the unjust servant.

Since we owe an unfathomable debt of love to Christ, the question comes, "How can we even *begin* to pay it?" Jesus explained that what we do to benefit others is actually done to Him. "Inasmuch as ye have done it unto one of the least of these my brethren, ye have done it unto me" (Matthew 25:40).

This same sense of indebtedness should carry over into our employment responsibilities, as explained by Paul. "Whatsoever ye do, do it heartily, as to the Lord, and not unto men; Knowing that of the Lord ye shall receive the reward of the inheritance: for ye serve the Lord Christ" (Colossians 3:23–24).

This gives further meaning to Christ's parable of the unprofitable servant.

"Which of you, having a servant plowing or feeding cattle, will say unto him by and by, when he is come from the field, Go and sit down to meat? And will not rather say unto him, Make ready wherewith I may sup, and gird thyself, and serve me, till I have eaten and drunken; and afterward thou shalt eat and drink?

"Doth he thank that servant because he did the things that were commanded him? I trow not. So likewise ye, when ye shall have done all those things which are commanded you, say, We are unprofitable servants: we have done that which was our **duty** [*opheilo*] to do" (Luke 17:7–10).

Personal Accountability for Responsibility

An important aspect of responsibility is being personally accountable for our thoughts, words, attitudes, and actions. These are to be consistent with the commands of Christ, because in the final judgement they will be exposed and evaluated on the basis of genuine love.

"He that saith, I know him, and keepeth not his commandments, is a liar, and the truth is not in him. But whoso keepeth his word, in him verily is the love of God perfected: hereby know we that we are in him. He that saith he abideth in him ought himself also so to walk, even as he walked" (I John 2:4–6).

• Responsibility for thoughts—

"Casting down imaginations, and every high thing that exalteth itself against the knowledge of God, and bringing into captivity every thought to the obedience of Christ" (II Corinthians 10:5).

• Responsibility for words—

"Every idle word that men shall speak, they shall give account thereof in the day of judgment. For by thy words thou shalt be justified, and by thy words thou shalt be condemned" (Matthew 12:36–37).

• Responsibility for actions—

"For we must all appear before the judgment seat of Christ; that every one may receive the things done in his body, according to that he hath done, whether it be good or bad" (II Corinthians 5:10).

• Responsibility for attitudes—

"Keep thy tongue from evil, and thy lips from speaking guile" (Psalm 34:13).

• Responsibility for motives—

"I the LORD search the heart, I try the reins, even to give every man according to his ways, and according to the fruit of his doings" (Jeremiah 17:10).

Personal Evaluation

How responsible are you?

- Do you accept responsibility for the debt of love that you owe every other believer?

- Do you have a special sense of gratefulness for the Jewish nation, because it is through them we have our spiritual heritage?

- Do you determine to set aside any personal pleasure that could cause a weak brother to stumble or be offended?

- Do you fulfill all your responsibilities in marriage?

- Do you fulfill your responsibility to pray for other believers?

- Do you look for practical ways to lay down your life for fellow believers?

- Do you accept personal responsibility for all your thoughts, words, actions, and attitudes?

- Do you purpose to fulfill your responsibilities to train up sons and daughters to be mighty in Spirit?

- Do you show responsibility for the practical needs of believers?

- Do you give support to those who minister to you in the Word?

- Do you take responsibility for your own health and well-being to better serve the Lord?

The **bald eagle** demonstrates responsibility by building enormous nests for the shelter of its young, by resting in the lifting power of the sun, and by remaining faithful to a single mate for an entire lifetime.

*T*hose who take responsibility surrender the luxury of being discouraged or depressed.

"Have not I commanded thee? Be strong and of a good courage; be not afraid, neither be thou dismayed: for the LORD thy God is with thee whithersoever thou goest." —Joshua 1:9

The test of security is how peaceful we are when our possessions are destroyed or taken away.

Jesus is all we need, but we will not know it until He is all we have. When our security is in the Lord, our desire will be for the advance of His Kingdom and the salvation of others.

Security is being free from the cares of this world because of the assurance of God's continual care for us.

"As long as I see any thing to be done for God, life is worth having; but O how vain and unworthy it is to live for any lower end."

—David Brainerd

Security
vs. Anxiety

Security is knowing that God will never leave us nor forsake us and that whatever we give to Him will become an eternal treasure.

Definition

The Greek word for *secure* is *amerimnos*. It means "freedom from anxiety and care." This was Paul's prayer for the church at Corinth: "I would have you without carefulness" (see I Corinthians 7:32). Another word for *security* is *confidence*. "In quietness and in confidence shall be your strength" (Isaiah 30:15). The Hebrew word for *confidence* is derived from *batach*, which means "to hasten for refuge and safety," both physically and emotionally.

The Value of Security

There is a deep longing for security in every person's heart. Unfortunately, we tend to look for security in temporal things that perish, such as money, possessions, or people, rather than eternal realities that cannot be taken away. Ironically, the very things we depend on for security produce insecurity and anxiety. "The sleep of a labouring man is sweet, whether he eat little or much: but the abundance of the rich will not suffer him to sleep" (Ecclesiastes 5:12).

It is also ironic that in a desperate attempt to find security, a woman will often sacrifice the strength of her purity for glib promises from a vain man, and a man will surrender his riches for a business scheme that he believes will provide for his future security. Yet "a gracious woman retaineth honour: and strong men retain riches" (Proverbs 11:16).

The Danger of False Security

The need for security is so great that many will latch on to whatever they think will produce it. This creates false security, which is not usually discovered until a trial comes and our sense of security collapses. For example, the consequences of looking to riches for security is explained in Proverbs 11:28, "He that trusteth [*batach*] in his riches shall fall."

False security produces a spirit of carelessness. Careless people appear to be secure but are on their way to destruction. "Therefore hear now this, thou that art given to pleasures, that dwellest carelessly [*betach*—derived from *batach*], that sayest in thine heart, I am, and none else beside me . . . . For thou hast trusted [*batach*] in thy wickedness . . . . Therefore shall evil come upon thee; thou shalt not know from whence it riseth" (Isaiah 47:8, 10–11).

Man has a built-in tendency to attach divine powers to inanimate objects fashioned by men. These objects are then revered as sources of security. "The idols of the heathen are silver and gold, the work of men's hands. They have mouths, but they speak not; eyes have they, but they see not; They have ears, but they hear not; neither is there any breath in their mouths. They that make them are like unto them: so is every one that trusteth [*batach*] in them" (Psalm 135:15–18).

Severe consequences come to the person who turns away from the Lord and puts his confidence in other people. "Thus saith the LORD; Cursed be the man that trusteth [*batach*] in man, and maketh flesh his arm, and whose heart departeth from the LORD. For he shall be like the heath in the desert, and shall not see when good cometh; but shall inhabit the parched places in the wilderness, in a salt land and not inhabited" (Jeremiah 17:5).

The Rewards of Making the Lord Our Security

1. Strength and help

"In quietness and in confidence shall be your strength" (Isaiah 30:15). "The LORD is my strength and my shield; my heart trusted [*batach*] in him, and I am helped" (Psalm 28:7).

2. Freedom from fear

"The LORD is my light and my salvation; whom shall I fear? the LORD is the strength of my life; of whom shall I be afraid? When the wicked, even mine enemies and my foes, came upon me to eat up my flesh, they stumbled and fell. Though an host should encamp against me, my heart shall not fear:

though war should rise against me, in this will I be confident [*batach*]" (Psalm 27:1–3).

3. Inward peace and joy

"Thou wilt keep him in perfect peace, whose mind is stayed on thee: because he trusteth [*batach*] in thee" (Isaiah 26:3). "Whoso trusteth [*batach*] in the LORD, happy is he" (Proverbs 16:20).

4. Stability and fruitfulness

"They that trust [*batach*] in the LORD shall be as mount Zion, which cannot be removed, but abideth for ever" (Psalm 125:1). "Blessed is the man that trusteth [*batach*] in the LORD, and whose hope the LORD is. For he shall be as a tree planted by the waters, and that spreadeth out her roots by the river, and shall not see when heat cometh, but her leaf shall be green; and shall not be careful in the year of drought, neither shall cease from yielding fruit" (Jeremiah 17:7–8).

Foundations of Security

Every believer has the security of the Lord in the following specific ways:

1. Secure in His love

"For I am persuaded, that neither death, nor life, nor angels, nor principalities, nor powers, nor things present, nor things to come, Nor height, nor depth, nor any other creature, shall be able to separate us from the love of God, which is in Christ Jesus our Lord" (Romans 8:38–39). "The LORD hath appeared of old unto me, saying, Yea, I have loved thee with an everlasting love: therefore with lovingkindness have I drawn thee." (Jeremiah 31:3).

*G*od created us with insecurities that He delights to address through a growing relationship of love.

"Be careful for nothing; but in every thing by prayer and supplication with thanksgiving let your requests be made known unto God. And the peace of God, which passeth all understanding, shall keep your hearts and minds through Christ Jesus."
—Philippians 4:6–7

Kangaroos give birth after a one-month gestation period. The helpless young kangaroo, called a joey, is only the size of a lima bean. It finds security in its mother's pouch, where it receives protection, food, and warmth for up to a year.

Insecurity is the result of expecting from people or things what only God can give.

"Some trust in chariots, and some in horses: but we will remember the name of the LORD our God."

—Psalm 20:7

The remedy for insecurity is realizing that Christ is the vine and we are the branches that hold the fruit He produces.

"Anxiety does not empty tomorrow of its sorrows, but only empties today of its strength."   —C. H. Spurgeon

2. Secure in His fellowship

"Go ye therefore, and teach all nations, baptizing them in the name of the Father, and of the Son, and of the Holy Ghost: Teaching them to observe all things whatsoever I have commanded you: and, lo, I am with you alway, even unto the end of the world. Amen" (Matthew 28:19–20). "For he hath said, I will never leave thee, nor forsake thee" (Hebrews 13:5). "God is faithful, by whom ye were called unto the fellowship of his Son Jesus Christ our Lord" (I Corinthians 1:9). "Truly our fellowship is with the Father, and with his Son Jesus Christ" (I John 1:3).

3. Secure in His Spirit

"Who hath also sealed us, and given the earnest of the Spirit in our hearts" (II Corinthians 1:22). "For ye have not received the spirit of bondage again to fear; but ye have received the Spirit of adoption, whereby we cry, Abba, Father" (Romans 8:15). "In whom ye also trusted, after that ye heard the word of truth, the gospel of your salvation: in whom also after that ye believed, ye were sealed with that holy Spirit of promise" (Ephesians 1:13).

4. Secure in His hand

"My Father, which gave them me, is greater than all; and no man is able to pluck them out of my Father's hand" (John 10:29). "Fear thou not; for I am with thee: be not dismayed; for I am thy God: I will strengthen thee; yea, I will help thee; yea, I will uphold thee with the right hand of my righteousness" (Isaiah 41:10). "I the LORD have called thee in righteousness, and will hold thine hand, and will keep thee, and give thee for a covenant of the people, for a light of the Gentiles" (Isaiah 42:6).

5. Secure in His protection

"For the which cause I also suffer these things: nevertheless I am not ashamed: for I know whom I have believed, and am persuaded that he is able to keep that which I have committed unto him against that day" (II Timothy 1:12). "He that dwelleth in the secret place of the most High shall abide under the shadow of the Almighty. I will say of the LORD, He is my refuge and my fortress: my God; in him will I trust [*batach*]. Surely he shall deliver thee from the snare of the fowler, and from the noisome pestilence. He shall cover thee with his feathers, and under his wings shalt thou trust: his truth shall be thy shield and buckler. Thou shalt not be afraid for the terror by night; nor for the arrow that flieth by day; Nor for the pestilence that walketh in darkness; nor for the destruction that wasteth at noonday" (Psalm 91:1–6). "But the Lord is faithful, who shall stablish you, and keep you from evil" (II Thessalonians 3:3).

6. Secure in His Body

"So we, being many, are one body in Christ, and every one members one of another" (Romans 12:5). "There is one body, and one Spirit, even as ye are called in one hope of your calling; One Lord, one faith, one baptism, One God and Father of all, who is above all, and through all, and in you all. But unto every one of us is given grace according to the measure of the gift of Christ" (Ephesians 4:4–7).

7. Secure in His family

"For whom the Lord loveth he chasteneth, and scourgeth every son whom he receiveth. If ye endure chastening, God dealeth with you as with sons; for what son is he whom the father chasteneth not?" (Hebrews 12:6–7). "Like as a father pitieth his children, so the LORD pitieth them that fear him" (Psalm 103:13). "The Spirit itself beareth witness with our spirit, that we are the children of God: And if children, then heirs; heirs of God, and joint-heirs with Christ; if so be that we suffer with him, that we may be also glorified together" (Romans 8:16–17).

The Key to Security

Security is building our life around that which can never be destroyed or taken away. On this basis, only God, His Word, and eternal things qualify.

By believing on the Lord Jesus Christ, we have His presence within us, as well as the Holy Spirit Who confirms with our spirits that we are children of God. (See Romans 8:16.) Then, as spiritual infants, we are to desire the Word of God so that we can grow to maturity.

To most people, building security is collecting possessions and money, yet to the believer, it is just the opposite. Security comes by giving to the needs of the poor. "A good man sheweth favour, and lendeth: he will guide his affairs with discretion. Surely he shall not be moved for ever: the righteous shall be in everlasting remembrance. He shall not be afraid of evil tidings: his heart is fixed, trusting [*batach*] in the LORD" (Psalm 112:5–7). Such generosity is based on a proper fear of the Lord. Those who fear the Lord will not fear man. "By humility and the fear of the LORD are riches, and honour, and life" (Proverbs 22:4).

Personal Evaluation

How secure are you?

- Do you concentrate on winning others to Christ rather than building a bank account?

- Do you give to the needs of the poor so that you do not fear evil tidings?

- Do you reject the false notion that good things come from objects made by man?

- Do you put your confidence in your Heavenly Father's love for you?

- Do you focus on the things of the Lord throughout the day?

- Do you have fellowship with God's Spirit, and does He control your life?

- Do you function effectively in the Body of Christ?

- Do you pray for a closer walk with the Lord rather than material things?

- Do you concentrate on spiritual strength rather than on building physical strength?

- If you lost all your possessions, would you still sense a completeness in Christ?

ecurity is knowing that God will never leave us nor forsake us.

"Yet will I not forget thee. Behold, I have graven thee upon the palms of my hands." —Isaiah 49:15–16

It is an act of God's love to remove from our lives the people or possessions that become objects of false security.

"Whom have I in heaven but thee? and there is none upon earth that I desire beside thee." —Psalm 73:25

"For thou hast been a shelter for me, and a strong tower from the enemy." —Psalm 61:3

"When everything in our lives and experience is shaken that can be shaken, and only that which cannot be shaken remains, we are brought to see that God only is our rock and foundation and we learn to have our expectation from Him alone." —Hannah Whitehall Smith

Self-control is transforming desires to please self into desires to please God.

"And be not conformed to this world: but be ye transformed by the renewing of your mind, that ye may prove what is that good, and acceptable, and perfect, will of God."

—Romans 12:2

The success from meditation includes the secrets of self-control.

"Meditate upon these things; give thyself wholly to them; that thy profiting may appear to all."

—I Timothy 4:15

"Always do something you don't need to do for the sake of doing it—it keeps you in moral fighting trim."

—Oswald Chambers

Self-Control
vs. Self-Indulgence

Self-control is the power of the Holy Spirit that results from passing the tests of the Spirit.

Definition

The Biblical term for *self-control* is *temperance*. The Greek word for *temperance* is *egkrateia*. It means "inward strength and restraint." It is the virtue of one who masters his desires and passions. Self-control is the inward strength to bring all physical appetites under the control of the Holy Spirit. A derivative of *egkrateia* is *egkrateuomai* which describes the rigid self-discipline practiced by athletes who are intent on winning the prize. Another Biblical word is *incontinency* and, by extension *continency*, meaning "to have power over oneself." (See I Corinthians 7:5 and II Timothy 3:3.)

The Vital Importance of Self-Control

Self-control is essential for any believer who wants to excel in the Christian life and receive honor from the Lord. Paul used the analogy of a runner in a race. "Know ye not that they which run in a race run all, but one receiveth the prize? So run, that ye may obtain. And every man that striveth for the mastery is **temperate** [*egkrateuomai*] in all things" (I Corinthians 9:24–25).

Paul then emphasized the eternal value of self-control and the personal sacrifice he was making to achieve it. "Now they

do it to obtain a corruptible crown; but we an incorruptible. I therefore so run, not as uncertainly; so fight I, not as one that beateth the air: But I keep under my body, and bring it into subjection: lest that by any means, when I have preached to others, I myself should be a castaway" (I Corinthians 9:25–27).

Any believer who desires to be a leader in the church must have self-control. "A bishop must be blameless, as the steward of God; not selfwilled, not soon angry, not given to wine, no striker, not given to filthy lucre . . . **temperate**" (Titus 1:7–8).

Because of their age and experience, older men are looked to for counsel and leadership; therefore, they also are to excel in temperance. "Speak thou the things which become sound doctrine: That the aged men be sober, grave, **temperate**, sound in faith, in charity, in patience" (Titus 2:1–2).

The Opposite of Self-Control

The Biblical antonym of *egkrateia* (temperance) is *akrates*. It means "to be powerless; incontinent; unable to withstand or resist the desires and passions of human appetite." Paul describes this condition: "That which I do I allow not: for what I would, that do I not; but what I hate, that do I. . . .

For the good that I would I do not: but the evil which I would not, that I do. . . . O wretched man that I am! who shall deliver me from the body of this death?" (Romans 7:15, 19, 24).

How Did Paul Develop Self-Control?

1. Joining God's Family

Paul's first step to conquer the powerful lusts of the flesh was to enter in to the family of God through faith in Jesus Christ. "There is therefore now no condemnation to them which are in Christ Jesus, who walk not after the flesh, but after the Spirit" (Romans 8:1).

When Paul became a believer, he, like all believers, received the indwelling of the Holy Spirit. "For as many as are led by the Spirit of God, they are the sons of God" (Romans 8:14). It is walking in obedience to the leading of God's Spirit that produces self-control, because self-control is the work of the Holy Spirit. "The fruit of the Spirit is love, joy, peace, longsuffering, gentleness, goodness, faith, Meekness, **temperance**" (Galatians 5:22–23).

2. Obeying the Holy Spirit

Self-control comes by instant obedience to the guidance of the Holy Spirit. "For what the law could not do, in that it was weak through the flesh, God sending his own Son in the likeness of sinful flesh, and for sin, condemned sin in the flesh: That the righteousness of the law might be fulfilled in us, who walk not after the flesh, but after the Spirit. . . . Because the carnal mind is enmity against God: for it is not subject to the law of God, neither indeed can be. So then they that are in the flesh cannot please God" (Romans 8:3–4; 7–8).

3. Listening to God's Spirit

Through the leading of God's Spirit, Paul learned how to conquer wrong desires. Paul stated, "Therefore, brethren, we are debtors, not to the flesh, to live after the flesh. For if ye live after the flesh, ye shall die: but if ye through the Spirit do mortify the deeds of the body, ye shall live" (Romans 8:12–13).

The word *mortify* is *thanatoo*. It means to cause to be put to death. The same instruction is given in Colossians 3:5: "Mortify therefore your members which are upon the earth; fornication, uncleanness, inordinate affection, evil concupiscence, and covetousness, which is idolatry." The word *mortify* in this verse is *nekroo*, which means "to deaden, to subdue."

Paul described his program of mortifying the flesh in I Corinthians 9:27: "But I keep under my body, and bring it into subjection: lest that by any means, when I have preached to others, I myself should be a castaway."

The phrase *keep under* literally means "to beat black and blue, to smite so as to cause bruises and livid spots, like a boxer who buffets his body, to handle it roughly, to discipline by hardships." This kind of treatment seems startlingly brutal, and Paul is not saying that every believer should carry it out. The message He is emphasizing is that no sacrifice is too small or too big to win the race and avoid being disqualified. Jesus put it a different way when He taught His disciples, "I say unto you, That whosoever looketh on a woman to lust after her hath committed adultery with her already in his heart.

Self-control is responding to sin in the same way a dead man does.

"How shall we, that are dead to sin, live any longer therein? . . . Likewise reckon ye also yourselves to be dead indeed unto sin, but alive unto God through Jesus Christ our Lord.
—Romans 6:2, 11

Freedom from self comes by being a slave to righteousness.

"Know ye not, that to whom ye yield yourselves servants to obey, his servants ye are to whom ye obey; whether of sin unto death, or of obedience unto righteousness?"
—Romans 6:16

Begin to reform the world by first reforming yourself.

"Temperance is the best medicine—for it is a preventive and a preservative, as well as a cure."
—C. H. Spurgeon

*W*e must conquer self else we become a slave of self.

Self-control is more than moderation. It is absolute resolve to discontinue self-indulgence.

"True self-control means willingness to resign the small for the sake of the great, the present for the sake of the future, the material for the sake of the spiritual, and that is what faith makes possible."

—Hugh Black

Unlike brown bears, the **black bear** usually refrains from confrontation. Even when other bears enter its territory, it avoids conflict whenever possible.

"And if thy right eye offend thee, pluck it out, and cast it from thee . . . And if thy right hand offend thee, cut it off, and cast it from thee: for it is profitable for thee that one of thy members should perish, and not that thy whole body should be cast into hell" (Matthew 5:28–30).

There is one painful activity Paul stated that he engaged in often which has a direct correlation to self-control: *fasting.* "Giving no offense in any thing, that the ministry be not blamed: But in all things approving ourselves as the ministers of God, in much patience, in afflictions, in necessities, in distresses, In stripes, in imprisonments, in tumults, in labours, in watchings, in fastings" (II Corinthians 6:3–5).

How Does Fasting Produce Self-Control

Jesus did not say to His disciples *"If* you fast," but rather *"When* you fast." (See Matthew 6:16; emphasis added.) Fasting is denying the body of food for any period of time. It is a humbling process which God honors when done for the right reasons. David stated, "I humbled my soul with fasting" (Psalm 35:13). God gives grace to the humble, and it is grace that teaches us "that, denying ungodliness and worldly lusts, we should live soberly, righteously, and godly, in this present world" (Titus 2:12).

Fasting is painful, but it has many rewards, especially in developing self-control. When food appetites are brought under control through regular fasting, sexual appetites are greatly diminished, especially during longer fasts. This is true because after the second or third day of fasting, the metabolism of the body changes. Rather than receiving strength from food, it turns fat cells into nourishment for vital organs such as the heart, lungs, kidneys, and brain, while other systems become dormant, including sexual drives.

Perhaps this is why Paul gives the instruction to married couples to give proper physical affection to each other unless it be during a time of fasting. During that time they would not have a desire to do this. (See I Corinthians 7:5.)

The physical discomfort of fasting could well be included in Peter's admonition, "Forasmuch then as Christ hath suffered for us in the flesh, arm yourselves likewise with the same mind: for he that hath suffered in the flesh hath ceased from sin" (I Peter 4:1). When the disciples were unable to free a boy from unclean spirits, they asked Jesus why they were powerless against them. Jesus replied, "This kind goeth not out but by prayer and fasting" (Matthew 17:21).

The Power That Produces Self-Control

Scripture gives a clear sequence of spiritual steps that,

when followed, produce self-control. "Having escaped the corruption that is in the world through lust . . . giving all diligence, add to your faith virtue; and to virtue knowledge; And to knowledge temperance" (II Peter 1:4–6).

These steps are consistent with the functions of the Holy Spirit in a believer's life. When a person exercises faith in believing on the Lord Jesus Christ, he receives the indwelling of the Holy Spirit, then as a believer he can ask his Heavenly Father to be filled with the Spirit. "If ye then, being evil, know how to give good gifts unto your children: how much more shall your heavenly Father give the Holy Spirit to them that ask him?" (Luke 11:13).

Once we are filled with the Spirit, we will be taken through trials and testing which will require us to die to ourselves and our natural inclinations. Passing each test requires that we thank God for His purposes in allowing the tests, then rejoice in them by looking for benefits, and then cry out to God if there is need for deliverance. To the degree that this is done, the believer experiences the power of the Holy Spirit.

The resurrection power of the Spirit produces self-control. Paul refers to this in Romans 8:11: "If the Spirit of him that raised up Jesus from the dead dwell in you, he that raised up Christ from the dead shall also quicken your mortal bodies by his Spirit that dwelleth in you."

Experiencing this power was Paul's great goal, and for it he was willing to go through whatever suffering was necessary. (See Philippians 3:8–10.)

The Prayer That Is Producing Self-Control

Paul said that when he was weak, then he was strong. (See II Corinthians 12:10.) When we acknowledge our weakness, we are in a position to experience God's power. Jabez was more honorable than his brothers, and he understood his weakness. Therefore, he "called on the God of Israel, saying, Oh that thou wouldest bless me indeed, and enlarge my coast, and that thine hand might be with me, and that thou wouldest keep me from evil, that it may not grieve me! And God granted him that which he requested" (I Chronicles 4:10). The Hebrew word for *called* in this passage is *qara'*. It means to "cry out."

Young men who have been unable to conquer the lusts of the flesh are adding this prayer to the other steps described above and for the first time are experiencing a new power over lust through self-control.

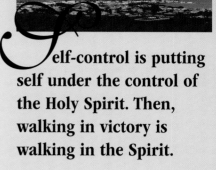

*S*elf-control is putting self under the control of the Holy Spirit. Then, walking in victory is walking in the Spirit.

"Walk in the Spirit, and ye shall not fulfil the lust of the flesh."
—Galatians 5:16

*I*t is the Scripture that cleanses our hearts and builds the shields that quench the darts.

Fiery darts are surges of anger, grief, or lust.

"Thy word have I hid in mine heart, that I might not sin against thee." "Above all, taking the shield of faith, wherewith ye shall be able to quench all the fiery darts of the wicked."
—Psalm 119:11; Ephesians 6:16

Personal Evaluation

How much self-control do you have?

- Do you give more time to spiritual pursuits than to the pleasures of the world?
- Do you bring every thought into captivity to the obedience of Christ?
- Do you control your eating or indulge in foods you know are unhealthy?
- Do you acknowledge your weakness so you can experience the power of Christ?
- Do you literally cry out to God for deliverance from addictions?
- Do you have a wise and Biblical program for fasting?
- Have you asked your Heavenly Father to fill you with His Spirit?
- Do you respond to each test of the Spirit by thanking God for His purposes and then look for benefits if you respond correctly?
- Do you ever erupt in uncontrollable anger?
- Do you remove provisions for indulgences so you will not fulfill them?

*S*ensitivity is perceiving the true feelings of others and adapting our responses to them.

"Rejoice with them that do rejoice, and weep with them that weep."
—*Romans 12:15*

*W*e earn the privilege of helping others by avoiding hurtful words and actions.

"There is that speaketh like the piercings of a sword: but the tongue of the wise is health." —*Proverbs 12:18*

*S*ensitivity is the communication of one spirit with the spirit of another.

"For what man knoweth the things of a man, save the spirit of man which is in him? even so the things of God knoweth no man, but the Spirit of God." —*I Corinthians 2:11*

Sensitivity

vs. Callousness

Sensitivity is being aware of the pain in others because of the healing we have received from God for similar hurts.

Definition

The Biblical word for *sensitivity* is *tenderheartedness*. Scripture instructs us: "Be ye kind one to another, **tenderhearted**, forgiving one another, even as God for Christ's sake hath forgiven you" (Ephesians 4:32).

The Greek word for *tenderhearted* is *eusplagchnos*. It comes from *eu* meaning "well and good" and *splagchnon* which literally means "spleen" or "intestines." Figuratively, it means "to be pitiful" and "to have bowels of compassion."

This same Greek word is translated *pitiful* in I Peter 3:8: "Finally, be ye all of one mind, having compassion one of another, love as brethren, be **pitiful**, be courteous."

God rewarded King Josiah for having a tender heart: "Because thine heart was **tender**, and thou hast humbled thyself before the LORD. . . . thine eyes shall not see all the evil which I will bring upon this place" (II Kings 22:19–20).

The Hebrew word for *tender* is *rakak* and means "to be soft." The antonym of *tenderheartedness* is therefore *hardheartedness*. The Psalmist wrote, "Harden not your heart, as in the provocation" (Psalm 95:8). This instruction is repeated by the writer of Hebrews. "Harden not your hearts, as in the provocation, in the day of temptation in the wilderness" (Hebrews 3:8). "While it is said, Today if ye will hear his voice, harden not your hearts, as in the provocation" (Hebrews 3:15).

The Hebrew word for *harden* is *quashah,* which means "to be dense, to be tough, severe, or cruel, to make grevious; to be stiffnecked." The Greek word for *harden* is *skleruno,* meaning "to be stubborn, hard, obstinate."

How Did a King Develop Sensitivity?

Josiah was only eight years old when he became the King of Judah. The biography that God wrote of his life concludes with an amazing tribute: "And like unto him was there no king before him, that turned to the LORD with all his heart, and with all his soul, and with all his might, according to all the law of Moses; neither after him arose there any like him" (II Kings 23:25).

According to the record, the key to his greatness was his tender heart. The account also explains how he developed it.

1. He purposed to please the Lord.

God's summary of the life and ministry of Josiah is "He did that which was right in the sight of the LORD" (II Kings 22:2).

As a boy, Josiah set his heart to follow the Lord in the same way that Daniel purposed in his heart that he would not defile himself by participating in heathen customs.

2. He chose a Godly role model.

It would have been easy for Josiah to follow the evil ways of his father and grandfather. Instead, he chose to "walk in all the ways of David his father" (II Kings 22:2). King Josiah used David's life as a pattern for righteous living, as David was known as "a man after God's own heart."

3. He kept his focus on the Lord.

Josiah maintained a Godly balance in his life as he diligently followed the Lord. He "turned not aside to the right hand or to the left" (II Kings 22:2).

4. He restored the place of worship.

At age eighteen, Josiah began a program to renovate the temple and restore the worship that was prescribed by God to take place in it. He began by collecting an offering "to repair the breaches of the house" (II Kings 22:5).

5. He humbled himself when he heard the Word of God.

In the process of repairing the House of God, a copy of the Scriptures was discovered and read to King Josiah. "It came to pass, when the king had heard the words of the book of the law, that he rent his clothes" (II Kings 22:11).

6. He acknowledged the iniquities of his forefathers.

Josiah realized that the judgment of God was upon the nation because his forefathers had rejected the ways of God. He said, "Great is the wrath of the LORD that is kindled against us, because our fathers have not hearkened unto the words

of this book, to do according unto all that which is written concerning us" (II Kings 22:13).

How God Rewarded a Tender Heart

When Josiah sent officials to inquire of the Lord concerning the evil that was to come upon the nation because of the transgression of his forefathers, God said to him, "Because thine heart was **tender**, and thou hast humbled thyself before the LORD, when thou heardest what I spake against this place, and against the inhabitants thereof, that they should become a desolation and a curse, and has rent thy clothes, and wept before me; I also have heard thee, saith the LORD. (II Kings 22:19).

—*Personal Evaluation*—

How sensitive are you?

- Do you seek the Lord with your whole heart?

- Do you allow bitterness or toleration of evil to cause callousness in your spirit?

- Do you close off communication with family members?

- Have you chosen a Godly role model to follow?

- Have you established a time and place to meet the Lord every day?

- Are you sensitive to the voice of God's Spirit as He speaks to you through Scripture?

- Do you exercise your spirit to be sensitive to the spirits of other people?

*W*here we harden our hearts, we lose the capacity to understand the hurts of others.

"And be ye kind one to another, tenderhearted . . . ." —Ephesians 4:32

"If we could read the secret history of our enemies, we should find in each man's life sorrow and suffering enough to disarm all hostilities."

—Henry W. Longfellow

The **varying hare** (snowshoe rabbit) changes color in response to the changing seasons. Its sensitivity to changing amounts of light conforms its hair to blend with the background of white snow in winter and the brown forest floor in the summer.

Sincerity is being as genuine on the inside as we appear to be on the outside.

*S*incerity is letting God shine through our blemishes rather than trying to cover them over.

"A broken and a contrite heart, O God, thou wilt not despise."

—Psalm 51:17

*S*incerity is acknowledging obvious faults for the healing prayers of others.

"Confess your faults one to another, and pray one for another, that ye may be healed. The effectual fervent prayer of a righteous man availeth much." —James 5:16

Definition

The word *sincere* comes from the Latin *sincerus*. The prefix *sine* means "without" and *cere* means "wax." According to legend, some unscrupulous old-world potters made expensive-looking clay pots by using an inferior clay that did not have all of the small rocks sifted out. When a pot was finished, these pebbles would fall out, creating indentations on the surface. Rather than reforming the pot, the potter would fill the defects with wax and paint over them. When the pots were used over a flame, the wax melted and ran down the pot. The merchants whose products were made with superior clay therefore wrote on the base of their pots *sine cera*— "without wax."

The Hebrew word for *sincerity* is *tamiym*. It means "without blemish, complete or whole, full, sound, wholesome, having integrity, completely in accord with truth and fact." The Greek *eilikrines*, is translated *sincere*. Paul wrote, "This I pray, that your love may abound yet more and more in knowledge and in all judgment; That ye may approve things that are excellent; that ye may be **sincere** [*eilikrines*] and without offense till the day of Christ; Being filled with the fruits of righteousness, which are by Jesus Christ, unto the glory and praise of God" (Philippians 1:9–11).

Eilikrines is made up of two Greek words, *heile*, which means "the sun's ray," and *krino*, meaning "to judge." The literal meaning of *sincere* could be rendered "to have our lives and actions judged by sunlight." Jesus explained, "Every one that doeth evil hateth the light, neither cometh to the light, lest his deeds should be reproved" (John 3:20).

The offering that Paul collected for the needy saints in Jerusalem shined light on the believers' sincerity and commended their wholehearted devotion to the needs of the church. (See II Corinthians 8:1–8.)

A close synonym of *sincerity* is the word *integrity*. It also means "completeness and fullness." "Judge me, O LORD; for I have walked in mine integrity: I have trusted also in the LORD; therefore I shall not slide" (Psalm 26:1).

How Sincerity Begins

The first two times *tamiym* is used in the Old Testament, it is translated *perfect*. "These are the generations of Noah: Noah was a just man and perfect [*tamiym*] in his generations, and Noah walked with God" (Genesis 6:9). "And when Abram was ninety years old and nine, the LORD appeared to Abram, and said unto him, I am the Almighty God; walk before me, and be thou perfect [*tamiym*]" (Genesis 17:1).

In Deuteronomy 18:13, God instructs all of His people to be perfect: "Thou shalt be perfect [*tamiym*] with the LORD thy God." In Psalm 15:2, *tamiym* is translated *uprightly*. "LORD, who shall abide in thy tabernacle? who shall dwell in thy holy hill? He that walketh uprightly [*tamiym*], and worketh righteousness, and speaketh the truth in his heart" (Psalm 15:1–2).

The Heart of Sincerity

The Hebrew word *shalem*—frequently translated *perfect*—describes sincerity and means "perfect and whole . . . complete." and comes from a root word meaning "to make amends." When Solomon dedicated the Temple, he prayed, "Let your heart therefore be perfect with the LORD our God, to walk in his statutes, and to keep his commandments, as at this day" (I Kings 8:61). However, Solomon failed to maintain sincerity and integrity. "For it came to pass, when Solomon was old, that his wives turned away his heart after other gods: and his heart was not perfect with the LORD his God, as was the heart of David his father" (I Kings 11:4).

Like Asa, one who fails to make wise decisions can still have a perfect heart, "The high places were not removed: nevertheless Asa's heart was perfect with the LORD all his days" (I Kings 15:14). On the other hand, a person can make right decisions but not have a perfect heart. "Amaziah was twenty and five years old when he began to reign, and he reigned twenty and nine years in Jerusalem. . . . And he did that which was right in the sight of the LORD, but not with a perfect heart" (II Chronicles 25:1–2).

We can discern whether our hearts are perfect by determining whether we worship other gods, either secretly or openly. "Now it came to pass, after that Amaziah was come from the slaughter of the Edomites, that he brought the gods of the children of Seir, and set them up to be his gods, and bowed down himself before them, and burned incense unto them" (II Chronicles 25:14). When we expect from things or people what only God can give, we make idols and lose the sincerity of our hearts.

Reward of Sincerity

God looks for sincere and perfect hearts through which to demonstrate His wisdom and power. "For the eyes of the LORD run to and fro throughout the whole earth, to shew himself strong in the behalf of them whose heart is perfect toward him" (II Chronicles 16:9). This statement was spoken to King Asa who won a great victory when he relied upon the Lord but suffered a great defeat when he relied upon a military ally.

One New Testament word for perfect is *teleioo*. Paul discovered that when he relied upon the Lord with all of his heart, even though he was weak, he experienced God's strength. The Lord said to him, "My grace is sufficient for thee: for my strength is made perfect in weakness. Most gladly therefore will I rather glory in my infirmities, that the power of Christ may rest upon me" (II Corinthians 12:9).

The Key to Sincerity

Another New Testament word translated *perfect* is *katartizo*, meaning "to complete thoroughly,

*S*incerity is using imperfections as reminders not to think more highly of ourselves than we ought.

One of the most respected men in history is Abraham Lincoln. According to tradition, when his portrait was being painted, the artist asked "Should I paint your cheek with or without the wart?" "With the wart," he answered.

Honey bees demonstrate unusual skill in communication. Using body language and uniquely formulated scents called pheromones, bees convey reliable messages describing danger, work assignments, and food sources.

*O*ur walk talks and our talk talks, but our walk talks louder than our talk talks.

"*I therefore . . . beseech you that ye walk worthy of the vocation wherewith ye are called.*"

—*Ephesians 4:1*

"**Are all the parts of our character and of our ways which no one can see as right as those which all can see? Are we true right through?**" —*Amy Carmichael*

*R*emove the mask of religious acts and let your true heart be seen.

*O*ur sincerity will be quickly revealed as we undergo fiery trials.

"*Beloved, think it not strange concerning the fiery trial which is to try you, as though some strange thing happened unto you.*"

—*I Peter 4:12*

---

to repair, to restore." Peter wrote, "The God of all grace, who hath called us unto his eternal glory by Christ Jesus, after that ye have suffered a while, make you perfect [*katartizo*], stablish, strengthen, settle you" (I Peter 5:10).

God takes all believers through fiery trials that expose hidden defects and imperfections. When believers thank God for these trials and rejoice in the purpose for which they are given, God grants a corresponding measure of the power of the Holy Spirit and a perfection of the fruit of the Spirit in believers' lives. (See I Peter 4:12–13.)

The Tragedy of Hypocrisy

Many people turn from the Lord because they observe hypocrisy in believers. Perhaps this is why Jesus was so harsh with hypocrites during His earthly ministry. "Woe unto you, scribes and Pharisees, hypocrites! for ye shut up the kingdom of heaven against men: for ye neither go in yourselves, neither suffer ye them that are entering to go in" (Matthew 23:13).

Hupokrites, the Greek word translated *hypocrite*, means "an actor, stage player, or pretender." The hypocrites of Jesus' day performed outward religious acts in order to get the praise of men, but were full of inward moral corruption. "Woe unto you, scribes and Pharisees, hypocrites! for ye are like unto whited sepulchres, which indeed appear beautiful outward, but are within full of dead men's bones, and of all uncleanness" (Matthew 23:27).

A hypocrite's root problem is that his whole heart is not devoted to the Lord. "Ye hypocrites, well

did Esaias prophesy of you, saying, This people draweth nigh unto me with their mouth, and honoureth me with their lips; but their heart is far from me" (Matthew 15:7–8).

A hypocrite focuses on details of righteousness while violating important issues. "Woe unto you, scribes and Pharisees, hypocrites! for ye pay tithe of mint and anise and cummin, and have omitted the weightier matters of the law, judgment, mercy, and faith: these ought ye to have done, and not to leave the other undone" (Matthew 23:23).

—*Personal Evaluation*—

How sincere are you?

- Are you the same on the outside as you are on the inside?

- Do you hide secret sins from the light of Christ?

- Do you judge others for things that you are guilty of?

- Do you obey outwardly, yet inwardly resist instruction?

- Do you seek the Lord with your whole heart?

- Do you do good deeds for the praise of men or the glory of God?

- Do you allow the strength of God to shine through your weaknesses?

- Do people see the light of Christ through your strengths and your weaknesses?

- Do you try to copy the achievements of others without their character?

Thoroughness

vs. Incompleteness

Thoroughness is carrying out each task in preparation for God's personal inspection and approval.

Definition

When David prayed, "Wash me throughly from mine iniquity, and cleanse me from my sin" (Psalm 51:2), he used the Hebrew word *rabah,* which occurs seventy-four other times in Scripture as *multiply*. He was asking God to cleanse him over and over so that there would be no trace of sin or iniquity left.

Thoroughness in cleaning is not accomplished by a "quick once-over" but by a deep cleaning and complete washing to make sure every bit of dirt or uncleanness is removed.

Thoroughness in Work

We have a tendency to do work as thoroughly as is necessary to pass the inspection of those who assign us the job. However, true thoroughness is motivated by the awareness that each job we do will be personally inspected by the Lord. This is the message of Colossians 3:22–24.

"Servants, obey in all things your masters according to the flesh; not with eye-service, as menpleasers; but in singleness of heart, fearing God: And whatsoever ye do, do it heartily, as to the Lord, and not unto men; Knowing that of the Lord ye shall receive the reward of the inheritance: for ye serve the Lord Christ."

The Greek word *psuche,* translated *heartily,* is used in fifty-eight other New Testament passages as *soul,* and forty times as *life*. This means that to be thorough requires that we put our whole soul into the work we do. This includes concentrating with the mind, directing the emotions, and using the will to do a complete and detailed job with excellence.

Because we are actually working for the Lord and not just for an earthly employer, we are to do a job consistent with God's character and standards, which will no doubt be higher than those of an employer. Therefore, if we pass the Lord's inspection, we should certainly *more* than pass an employer's expectations.

Thorough Cleansing

God's chief concern for our thoroughness is in the inward cleansing of our hearts. "Having therefore these promises, dearly beloved, let us cleanse ourselves from all filthiness of the flesh and spirit, perfecting holiness in the fear of God" (II Corinthians 7:1).

After listing sins that need to be cleansed from our lives, Scripture states: "If a man therefore purge himself from these, he shall be a vessel unto honour, sanctified, and meet for the mas-

*A*ttention to detail is the difference between mediocrity and excellence in the work we do.

God's commitment to thoroughness is illustrated in His insistence on the fulfillment of every "jot and tittle" of His Word. (See Matthew 5:18.)

A job is never really done until it is done right.

*D*o a job as if you will never have another chance to do it right.

"Whatsoever thy hand findeth to do, do it with thy might."—Ecclesiastes 9:10

"People forget how fast you did a job—but they remember how well you did it."
                                        —Howard W. Newton

*W*orking harder when the boss is watching is convicting evidence that you are a manpleaser rather than a pleaser of God.

"Not with eye-service, as menpleasers; but as the servants of Christ, doing the will of God from the heart."
                                        —Ephesians 6:6

The **American alligator** prepares a nesting spot that is not too high and not too low, not too wet and not too dry, not too hot and not too cold. Its nest is perfect in every respect.

ter's use, and prepared unto every good work" (II Timothy 2:21).

Based on the need for inward thoroughness, we should pray "Search me, O God, and know my heart: try me, and know my thoughts: And see if there be any wicked way in me, and lead me in the way everlasting" (Psalm 139:23–24).

When God thoroughly searches our hearts, He will reveal to us the hidden areas of sin and uncleanness. "Who can understand his errors? cleanse thou me from secret faults" (Psalm 19:12).

Outward Cleanliness

When thorough cleaning is not maintained, clutter and dirt accumulate. That was the case in the days of King Hezekiah, when "the priests went into the inner part of the house of the LORD, to cleanse it, and brought out all the uncleanness that they found in the temple of the LORD into the court of the house of the LORD. And the Levites took it, to carry it out abroad into the brook Kidron" (II Chronicles 29:16).

God also gave strict instructions to His people that they were to have no raw sewage in their camp when they went out to war, because it would breed disease and destruction among the soldiers. Their thoroughness in keeping the camp clean was also to be motivated by the fact that God would personally inspect it. "For the LORD thy God walketh in the midst of thy camp, to deliver thee, and to give up thine enemies before thee; therefore shall thy camp be holy: that he see no unclean thing in thee, and turn away from thee" (Deuteronomy 23:14).

Thorough Reformation

Thorough cleansing of our hearts and of our surroundings is not sufficient unless we also thoroughly change our ways to please the Lord. This was one of the requirements given by God through Jeremiah. "For if ye throughly amend your ways and your doings; if ye throughly execute judgment between a man and his neighbour; If ye oppress not the stranger, the fatherless, and the widow, and shed not innocent blood in this place, neither walk after other gods to your hurt: Then will I cause you to dwell in this place" (Jeremiah 7:5–7).

Personal Evaluation

How thorough are you?

- Are you committed to thoroughness in all you do?

- Would God be impressed with your thoroughness in hygiene: brushing teeth, washing hands, etc.?

- Do you picture God inspecting the jobs you do?

- Do you thoroughly examine your life before taking communion?

- Do you clean *around* items and also *under* them?

- When you paint, do you make sure there is adequate preparation, including drop cloths to protect floors and carpets?

- Do you complete all the necessary details of a job, or do you leave things for others to do, such as cleanup?

Thriftiness

vs. Extravagance

Thriftiness is multiplying my resources through wise investments so I have more to give back to God.

Definition

Thriftiness is the basis for wise stewardship. Therefore, the teaching of Jesus on stewardship provides an understanding of thriftiness.

The Greek word for *stewardship* is *oikonomia* and identifies one who manages the property of his master. His faithfulness is determined by how prosperous he becomes in the use and increase of the resources under his care.

The Importance of Thriftiness

When we meet the Lord at the end of our lives, He will give us an evaluation of our thriftiness. His highest commendation will be, "Well done, thou good and faithful servant: thou hast been faithful over a few things, I will make thee ruler over many things: enter thou into the joy of thy lord" (Matthew 25:21).

Requirements of Stewardship

Getting to Heaven is not achieved by our own good works. It is the gift of God to those who cry out to Him for salvation through faith in the Lord Jesus Christ. However, when a believer enters Heaven, he will be commended on the basis of his stewardship. Therefore, the account that Jesus gave of three stewards has significant applications to thriftiness.

"For the kingdom of Heaven is as a man travelling into a far country, who called his own servants, and delivered unto them his goods. And unto one he gave five talents, to another two, and to another one; to every man according to his several ability; and straightway took his journey.

"Then he that had received the five talents went and traded with the same, and made them other five talents. And likewise he that had received two, he also gained other two. But he that had received one went and digged in the earth, and hid his lord's money.

"After a long time the lord of those servants cometh, and reckoneth with them. And so he that had received five talents came and brought other five talents, saying, Lord, thou deliveredst unto me five talents: behold, I have gained beside them five talents more. His lord said unto him, Well done, thou good and faithful servant: thou hast been faithful over a few things, I will make thee ruler over many things: enter thou into the joy of thy lord.

"He also that had received two talents came and said, Lord, thou deliveredst unto me two

*T*hriftiness is the foundation of every generous deed.

"Every where and in all things I am instructed both to be full and to be hungry, both to abound and to suffer need.   —*Philippians 4:12*

"A man's treatment of money is the most decisive test of his character—how he makes it and spends it."

—James Moffat

*T*hriftiness is the skill of trading things of lesser value for things of greater value.

"The kingdom of heaven is like unto treasure hid in a field; the which when a man hath found, he hideth, and for joy thereof goeth and selleth all that he hath, and buyeth that field." —Matthew 13:44

*B*orrowing is the bane of thriftiness, because it turns the joy of saving into the bondage of survival.

"God's work done in God's way will never lack God's supply. He is too wise a God to frustrate His purposes with lack of funds; and He can just as easily supply ahead of time as afterwards, and He much prefers doing so."

—J. Hudson Taylor

talents: behold, I have gained two other talents beside them. His lord said unto him, Well done, good and faithful servant; thou hast been faithful over a few things, I will make thee ruler over many things: enter thou into the joy of thy lord.

"Then he which had received the one talent came and said, Lord, I knew thee that thou art an hard man, reaping where thou hast not sown, and gathering where thou hast not strawed: And I was afraid, and went and hid thy talent in the earth: lo, there thou hast that is thine.

"His lord answered and said unto him, Thou wicked and slothful servant, thou knewest that I reap where I sowed not, and gather where I have not strawed: Thou oughtest therefore to have put my money to the exchangers, and then at my coming I should have received mine own with usury" (Matthew 25:14–27).

It is obvious that the first two servants understood and practiced the principles of thriftiness. They used as few funds as possible for consumable items, and as much of their resources as possible on that which would bring greater returns.

How Thriftiness Differs From Stinginess

Thriftiness is using as few resources as possible for my own needs so that I will have greater resources for generosity to God and to others. Stinginess is keeping back what should be given to others so that I will have more for myself. God condemns stinginess. "He that by usury and unjust gain increaseth his substance, he shall

gather it for him that will pity the poor" (Proverbs 28:8).

"Behold, the hire of the labourers who have reaped down your fields, which is of you kept back by fraud, crieth: and the cries of them which have reaped are entered into the ears of the Lord of sabaoth" (James 5:4).

Aspects of Thriftiness

1. Thriftiness begins by being content with basics.

A person who believes that happiness is measured by personal possessions will not be capable of true thriftiness. He will use up valuable assets for things that neither profit nor satisfy. Jesus warned, "Take heed, and beware of covetousness: for a man's life consisteth not in the abundance of the things which he possesseth" (Luke 12:15).

On the other hand, a person who is content with the basic essentials of life will have the natural ability to be thrifty. "Having food and raiment let us be therewith content" (I Timothy 6:8).

2. Thriftiness is using creativity to increase assets.

Just as the faithful steward doubled his assets, so Jacob found creative ways to multiply the flocks that were entrusted to him. A thrifty man will understand how God designed things to work and will use this knowledge to increase productivity.

3. Thriftiness is protecting assets by putting up with irritations.

Life is filled with irritations and conditions that are less than ideal. Personal comfort often comes with a high price and is only temporary. A thrifty person will put up with temporary messiness that is necessary for productivity. "Where no oxen are, the crib is clean: but much increase is by the strength of the ox" (Proverbs 14:4).

4. Thriftiness is having only those personal possessions that are functional.

Jesus is the ultimate example of thriftiness. He owned only the things that were essential for life and ministry. When He sent out the twelve disciples, He "gave them power and authority over all devils, and to cure diseases. And he sent them to preach the kingdom of God, and to heal the sick. And he said unto them, Take nothing for your journey, neither staves, nor scrip, neither bread, neither money; neither have two coats apiece" (Luke 9:1–3).

Paul also understood how temporal things can be a hindrance to effectiveness in the work of the Lord. "But what things were gain to me, those I counted loss for Christ. Yea doubtless, and I count all things but loss for the excellency of the knowledge of Christ Jesus my Lord: for whom I have suffered the loss of all things, and do count them but dung, that I may win Christ" (Philippians 3:7–8).

5. Thriftiness is making offers rather than asking for quotes.

The wisdom that God gave Solomon included the ability to gain and retain riches. He compared a man's responsibility to preserve his riches with a woman's responsibility to maintain her purity. "A gracious woman retaineth honour: and strong men

retain riches" (Proverbs 11:16). Solomon provides a significant example of negotiating for the best buy through his business dealings with King Hiram.

First, Solomon reaffirmed the friendship that existed between his father, David, and King Hiram. Then he explained the importance of the building he was planning for the God of Heaven. He requested lumber from King Hiram's forests, but he himself supplied the labor, which greatly reduced the cost. Then he made his offer:

"Send me also cedar trees, fir trees, and algum trees, out of Lebanon: for I know that thy servants can skill to cut timber in Lebanon; and, behold, my servants shall be with thy servants, Even to prepare me timber in abundance: for the house which I am about to build shall be wonderful great. And, behold, I will give to thy servants, the hewers that cut timber, twenty thousand measures of beaten wheat, and twenty thousand measures of barley, and twenty thousand baths of wine, and twenty thousand baths of oil" (II Chronicles 2:8–10).

Solomon also advises the buyer that a seller will inflate the value of his products, and this must be counteracted in a gracious way. "It is nought, it is nought, saith the buyer: but when he is gone his way, then he boasteth" (Proverbs 20:14).

6. Thriftiness is gathering up the fragments after a project.

When Jesus fed the five thousand, He demonstrated thriftiness by not allowing the remaining food to go to waste.

Because **koalas** eat only eucalyptus leaves that contain very little nutritional value, they must conserve every bit of energy. To "get by" on less, koalas move very slowly and sleep most of the day.

*T*hriftiness is the personal discipline of those who are striving for the greatest rewards.

"While we look not at the things which are seen, but at the things which are not seen: for the things which are seen are temporal; but the things which are not seen are eternal."
—*II Corinthians 4:18*

*T*hriftiness is a way of life for those who enjoy the rewards of giving.

"I have shewed you all things, how that so labouring ye ought to support the weak, and to remember the words of the Lord Jesus, how he said, It is more blessed to give than to receive."   —Acts 20:35

A dollar saved is *more* than a dollar earned, because of the appreciating value of what we earn.

**"Earn all you can.
Save all you can.
Give all you can."**

—John Wesley

"A fool may make money, but it needs a wise man to spend it."

—C. H. Spurgeon

"And they did all eat, and were filled: and they took up of the fragments that remained twelve baskets full" (Matthew 14:20).

Thriftiness requires diligence, whereas extravagance breeds slothfulness. Solomon pointed out this when he wrote, "The slothful man roasteth not that which he took in hunting: but the substance of a diligent man is precious" (Proverbs 12:27).

7. Thriftiness is saving during times of plenty.

When a person's income increases, it is his tendency to also increase his standard of living, using up the increase with personal comforts and luxuries. This tendency is identified in Scripture. "When goods increase, they are increased that eat them: and what good is there to the owners thereof, saving the beholding of them with their eyes?" (Ecclesiastes 5:11).

On the other hand, Joseph demonstrated the wisdom of thriftiness when he gave a survival plan to Pharaoh. During the years of plenty, twenty percent of the harvest was stored, and then it was used during the lean years. (See Genesis 41.)

Thriftiness requires a long-range goal that is more important than immediate luxuries and conveniences. Our goal is to advance God's kingdom and please the Lord.

Three Requirements for Thriftiness

Because thriftiness is related to good stewardship, the requirements that Jesus gave to His disciples for faithfulness would apply. First, one must be faithful in little things. Second: being faithful in the use of money. Third: being faithful in that which belongs to another person.

┌─ **Personal Evaluation** ─┐

How thrifty are you?

- Do you keep detailed records of your resources so you know how they are being spent?

- Do you take time to evaluate the profitability of each investment you make?

- Do you plan out each day so you can make the wisest use of every hour?

- Do you use principles of negotiation so you can get the best buy and also help your suppliers save money?

- Do you save all you can so you can have available funds to give?

- Are you using your energies and resources primarily for yourself or for the needs of others?

- Do you study procedures to see how they can be more efficient and less costly?

- When your income increases, do you keep the same standard of living so you have more to give?

- When God reviews your investments of time, energy, and money, will He commend you for your thriftiness or condemn you for extravagance?

Tolerance
vs. Condemnation

Tolerance is making allowances for those who lack wisdom or maturity and praying that they will see and follow God's ways.

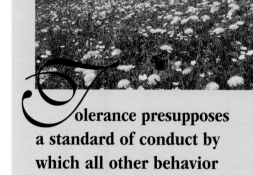

Definition

In a technical sense, tolerance is the amount of variation from a standard that will be accepted. Tolerance presupposes a precise standard of thinking and conduct by which other ideas and behavior can be evaluated as right or wrong.

Such a standard must be based on truth and fact. To form a conclusion or opinion before the facts are known is prejudice, and to tenaciously hold to ideas or behavior that disregards or is contrary to fact is bigotry.

In medical terms, tolerance is the ability of the body to withstand the effects of that which is detrimental to good health (e.g., extreme heat or cold, drugs, or unhealthy foods).

In mechanics, tolerance is determined by the difference between the allowable maximum and minimum sizes of a mechanical part. In each of these areas, tolerance has limitations beyond which consequences occur, because it is not being used according to its design.

A parallel Biblical word to tolerance is *longsuffering*. The Greek word most commonly translated *longsuffering* is *makrothumia*, which means "forbearance or fortitude."

Tolerance for Believers

Scripture makes a sharp distinction between the amount of tolerance believers are to have toward each other and the tolerance they are to have toward those who are unbelievers. Every true believer is a member of the Body of Christ. (See Romans 12:4–5.)

This Scriptural connection between the members of the Body of Christ occurs when a person becomes a believer. Communion was established by Jesus Christ as a time of regular examination to make sure that every believer is living in harmony with the standards of God's Word and is in fellowship with every other believer.

Such an examination is vital for the health of the Body of Christ, because as Paul pointed out, "There should be no schism in the body; but that the members should have the same care one for another. And whether one member suffer, all the members suffer with it; or one member be honoured, all the members rejoice with it. Now ye are the body of Christ, and members in particular" (I Corinthians 12:25–27).

The bonding and interaction that takes place between believers is powerfully affirmed in Paul's warning not to have immoral relationships. "Know ye not that your bodies are the members of

*T*olerance presupposes a standard of conduct by which all other behavior is measured.

"And we know that all things work together for good to them that love God. . . . to be conformed to the image of his Son." —Romans 8:28–29

There is an absolute standard for weights and measurements that is a constant reference for fairness and achievement in the world.

"But they measuring themselves by themselves, and comparing themselves among themselves, are not wise." —II Corinthians 10:12

*R*efusal to acknowledge or correct wrong decisions is not tolerance, but simple-mindedness.

*T*olerance is showing people that we are more concerned about communicating Christ's love than correcting wrong ideas or behavior.

"Charity suffereth long, and is kind."
—I Corinthians 13:4

*T*olerance is motivated by remembering how patient God has been with us in our failures.

"He hath not dealt with us after our sins; nor rewarded us according to our iniquities." —Psalm 103:10

"Compassion will cure more sins than condemnation."

—Henry Ward Beecher

Christ? shall I then take the members of Christ, and make them the members of an harlot? God forbid. What? know ye not that he which is joined to an harlot is one body? for two, saith he, shall be one flesh. But he that is joined unto the Lord is one spirit" (I Corinthians 6:15–17).

Because of the need for conformity to God's standards and for each member to demonstrate sincere love for each other, God has set up a structure of leadership in His church to strengthen the Body and also exercise discipline with those members who refuse to live by God's standards.

When Biblical discipline is administered through a local church, all the members of the Body are to support it. Therefore, the instructions are given, "not to keep company, if any man that is called a brother be a fornicator, or covetous, or an idolater, or a railer, or a drunkard, or an extortioner; with such an one no not to eat" (I Corinthians 5:11).

Because every believer is affected by what one believer does, the Bible gives a series of "one another" commands designed "for the perfecting of the saints, for the work of the ministry, for the edifying of the body of Christ: Till we all come in the unity of the faith, and of the knowledge of the Son of God, unto a perfect man, unto the measure of the stature of the fulness of Christ" (Ephesians 4:12–13).

Tolerance Toward Unbelievers

A believer is to have a greater tolerance for unbelievers than he has for fellow believers. Paul explains this in the same passage in which he warns believers not to have fellowship with other believers who violate God's standards.

"I wrote unto you in an epistle not to company with fornicators: Yet not altogether with the fornicators of this world, or with the covetous, or extortioners, or with idolaters; for then must ye needs go out of the world. . . .

"For what have I to do to judge them also that are without? do not ye judge them that are within? But them that are without God judgeth" (I Corinthians 5:9–10, 12–13).

A distinction must be made between unbelievers who violate the laws of the land and those who simply express opinions or actions contrary to God's ways. Crimes against society are not to be tolerated because a community will have as much crime as the neighborhood tolerates. Three times in Scripture, law officers are called the "ministers of God" for doing good and all citizens are to support and encourage them in their work of maintaining law and order. (See Romans 13:1–7.)

How to Show Tolerance

Tolerance is looking beyond the wrong ideas and behavior of a people and seeing the needs and struggles in their lives. One who is tolerant is more concerned about showing love to people than convincing them of the error of their ways.

To tolerate people means to not argue with them. This is consistent with the instruction of Scripture. "And the servant of the Lord must not strive; but be gentle unto all men, apt to teach, patient" (II Timothy 2:24.)

We are also to avoid foolish and unlearned questions, which produce unprofitable debate.

God's Narrow Tolerance Throughout History

Each time God establishes a new era in history, He lays down laws for its success and requires total adherence to those laws.

1. Tolerance at Creation

God gave Adam and Eve full freedom to investigate and discover everything in their environment except one item—the tree of the knowledge of good and evil. He warned them that harmony with Him and creation required zero tolerance of partaking of the fruit of this tree. The very moment they violated this standard, they and all those who came from them experienced the consequences of sin and death. (See Genesis 1–2.)

2. Tolerance with the Mosaic Law

When God gave Moses His laws and statutes, He required strict adherence to each one, because they were the basis of the health and prosperity of the nation. "Keep therefore and do them; for this is your wisdom and your understanding in the sight of the nations, which shall hear all these statutes, and say, Surely this great nation is a wise and understanding people. For what nation is there so great, who hath God so nigh unto them, as the LORD our God is in all things that we call upon him for?" (Deuteronomy 4:6–7).

Therefore, when a man was found breaking God's Law by picking up sticks on the Sabbath Day, he was brought into custody. Moses asked God what they should do, and God replied, "The man shall be surely put to death: all the congregation shall stone him with stones without the camp" (Numbers 15:35).

3. Tolerance in the New Testament Church

The spirit of love and sacrifice was so strong in the first-century church that many of the believers sold their possessions and distributed the money through the apostles to the poor and needy. When Ananias and Sapphira secretly determined to give the public appearance of generosity but retained part of the proceeds of the sale of their property, God did not tolerate such dishonesty. Peter said to them, "Whiles it remained, was it not thine own? and after it was sold, was it not in thine own power? why hast thou conceived this thing in thine heart? thou hast not lied unto men, but unto God. And Ananias hearing these words fell down, and gave up the ghost: and great fear came on all them that heard these things" (Acts 5:4–5).

Because the laws of God and the laws of nature are constant, those who violate them will experience the predicted results. Every deed and word will be judged according to the laws of the harvest. "Be not deceived; God is not mocked: for whatsoever a man soweth, that shall he also reap. For he that soweth to his flesh shall of the flesh reap corruption; but he that soweth to the Spirit shall of the Spirit reap life everlasting" (Galatians 6:7–8).

The Tolerance of God in Divorce and Remarriage

The Mosaic Law contains a tolerance for a man to divorce his wife if he finds some "unclean-

*T*olerance is not changing God's standards but living them out in such a way that others will want to follow them.

"Be ye followers of me, even as I also am of Christ." —I Corinthians 11:1

*N*ever mistake God's tolerance for a sinner as tolerance for sin.

"The Lord is not slack concerning his promise, as some men count slackness; but is longsuffering to us-ward, not willing that any should perish, but that all should come to repentance." —II Peter 3:9

*T*here is an important distinction between tolerance of immaturity and our responsibility to reprove evil.

"And have no fellowship with the unfruitful works of darkness, but rather reprove them." —Ephesians 5:11

"How far you go in life depends on you being tender with the young, compassionate with the aged, sympathetic with the striving, and tolerant of the weak and strong. Because some day in life you will have been all of these."

—George Washington Carver

The **Eastern box turtle** rests in the security of its protective covering. It endures the irritations of curious predators as they vainly try to pry open its hinged shell. Once the irritation is gone, the turtle confidently continues about its business.

ness" in her after marriage. (See Deuteronomy 24:1.) During Christ's ministry, there was much debate on what "uncleanness" was required for a man to divorce his wife. One school of Pharisees was more tolerant and gave a wide definition of uncleanness. Another school was less tolerant and gave few reasons to divorce.

When Jesus gave His strict standard on marriage, the Pharisees countered with the law of Moses: "They say unto him, Why did Moses then command to give a writing of divorcement, and to put her away? He saith unto them, Moses because of the hardness of your hearts suffered you to put away your wives: but from the beginning it was not so. And I say unto you, Whosoever shall put away his wife, except it be for fornication, and shall marry another, committeth adultery: and whoso marrieth her which is put away doth commit adultery" (Matthew 19:7–9).

Christ's standard was based on creation design rather than on Mosaic law because Christ was not only concerned for the happiness within marriages, but He was concerned for the welfare of future generations and the survival of civilizations which are dependent on strong marriages and families.

The Tolerance of Postponed Consequences

Although God cannot tolerate the violation of His laws, He can, upon repentance, postpone the temporal consequences of those violations. "Despisest thou the riches of his goodness and forbearance and longsuffering; not knowing that the goodness of God leadeth thee to repentance?" (Romans 2:4).

God also postpones judgment to demonstrate His power and the riches of His grace. "What if God, willing to shew his wrath, and to make his power known, endured with much longsuffering the vessels of wrath fitted to destruction: And that he might make known the riches of his glory on the vessels of mercy, which he had afore prepared unto glory" (Romans 9:22).

The Need and Purpose of Tolerance

One of the consistent traits of human nature is to be intolerant of the faults in other people that are similar to our own weaknesses. Therefore, the need for tolerance in others should be viewed as God's motivation for us to examine ourselves in that same area and correct any deficiencies, so that we can clearly and lovingly see how to help others.

1. Israel's rejection of the Promised Land

When the nation of Israel refused to enter the Promised Land, God determined to destroy them. However, Moses appealed to God to be longsuffering and have tolerance. God listened to Moses but stated that all those who rebelled would die and that only their children would see the land. (See Numbers 14:11–30.)

2. David's sin with Bathsheba

When David committed adultery with Bathsheba and then killed her husband in an attempt to cover it up, God forgave David when he repented. David praised

God for His tolerance. "Thou, O Lord, art a God full of compassion, and gracious, longsuffering, and plenteous in mercy and truth" (Psalm 86:15).

However, the temporal consequences of David's sin were still to come. "Wherefore hast thou despised the commandment of the LORD, to do evil in his sight? thou hast killed Uriah the Hittite with the sword, and hast taken his wife to be thy wife, and hast slain him with the sword of the children of Ammon. Now therefore the sword shall never depart from thine house; because thou hast despised me, and hast taken the wife of Uriah the Hittite to be thy wife.

"Thus saith the LORD, Behold, I will raise up evil against thee out of thine own house, and I will take thy wives before thine eyes, and give them unto thy neighbour, and he shall lie with thy wives in the sight of this sun. For thou didst it secretly: but I will do this thing before all Israel, and before the sun.

"And David said unto Nathan, I have sinned against the LORD. And Nathan said unto David, The LORD also hath put away thy sin; thou shalt not die. Howbeit, because by this deed thou hast given great occasion to the enemies of the LORD to blaspheme, the child also that is born unto thee shall surely die" (II Samuel 12:9–14).

3. Nineveh's corruption by wickedness

The great city of Nineveh is remembered for its corruption and cruelty. Therefore, God determined to destroy it. When Jonah warned the people that judgment would come in forty days, they all repented in sackcloth and ashes. God heard their cry and withheld destruction for over one hundred years. (See Jonah 3:4–9.)

God postpones the consequences of sin in order to motivate those who are breaking His laws to repent and turn back to His ways.

Personal Evaluation

How tolerant are you?

- Do you view each person as an individual rather than as a member of a race, culture, or group?

- Do you evaluate ideas and behavior based on the laws of nature and God's Law?

- Do you make allowances for those who are not as wise and mature as they should be?

- When you see faults in others does it motive you to be an example of Godly living before them?

- Do you look for common ground with people of different viewpoints and behavior rather than focusing on differing opinions and standards?

- Do you make greater allowances for unbelievers than you do for believers?

- Do you remind yourself that tolerance is based on God's right to rule His world and that He has not given that right to anyone outside His delegated authorities?

- Do you serve people regardless of their viewpoints and ask God to change those who need changing?

A parent wanting to learn tolerance needs only to consider God's care of His children.

"Like as a father pitieth his children, so the LORD pitieth them that fear him." —Psalm 103:13

"To keep one's voice sweet, one's face bright, one's will steady, one's patience unperturbed, in the arena of the home, in the light of one's own family, is no light task." —Margaret Sangster

*T*olerance is taking others by the hand and leading them to maturity.

Irritations are opportunities to demonstrate tolerance.

"Let him know, that he which converteth the sinner from the error of his way, shall save a soul from death, and shall hide a multitude of sins." —James 5:20

We must speak the truth in our hearts before we speak it with our mouths.

"LORD, who shall abide in thy tabernacle? who shall dwell in thy holy hill? He that walketh uprightly, and worketh righteousness, and speaketh the truth in his heart." "For out of the abundance of the heart the mouth speaketh."

—Psalm 15:1–2; Matthew 12:34

"It is not so much 'holding the truth' as being held by the truth." —H. A. Ironside

Truth is the foundation upon which anything that stands is built.

"No man ever puts a stumbling block in the way of others by telling the truth." —Oswald Chambers

Truthfulness
vs. Deception

Truthfulness is communicating by life and word what is genuine and accurate.

Definition

One Hebrew word for *truth* is *'emeth*. It means "stability, certainty, right, sure." It is from the word *'aman*, which means "to build up or support; to foster as a parent or nurse; to be firm or faithful; permanent, steadfast, verified." When Jesus emphasized truth, He often said the word *verily* twice, as in John 3:3.

"Verily, verily, I say unto thee, Except a man be born again, he cannot see the kingdom of God."

Sources of Truth

1. **God is truth**—"Ascribe ye greatness unto our God. He is the Rock, his work is perfect: for all his ways are judgment: a God of truth and without iniquity, just and right is he" (Deuteronomy 32:3–4).

2. **Jesus is truth**—"Jesus saith unto him, I am the way, the truth, and the life: no man cometh unto the Father, but by me" (John 14:6). It is ironic that Pilate asked Jesus, Who is the Source of truth, "What is truth?" and then turned Him over to be crucified.

3. **The Holy Spirit is truth**—"And it is the Spirit that beareth witness, because the Spirit is truth" (I John 5:6).

4. **God's Word is truth**—"Sanctify them through thy truth: thy word is truth" (John 17:17).

5. **God's Law is truth**—"Thy righteousness is an everlasting righteousness, and thy law is the truth." "Thou art near, O LORD; and all thy commandments are truth" (Psalm 119:142, 151).

6. **The Gospel is truth**—"Whereof ye heard before in the word of the truth of the gospel; Which is come unto you, as it is in all the world" (Colossians 1:5–6).

What Does Truth Do?

There is power in truth, because it is the very essence of God and the means by which He carries out His work in the world.

1. Truth brings us into Christ—"Of his own will begat he us with the word of truth, that we should be a kind of firstfruits of his creatures" (James 1:18).

2. Truth brings us to the light—"But he that doeth truth cometh to the light, that his deeds may be made manifest, that they are wrought in God" (John 3:21).

3. Truth purifies our souls—"Seeing ye have purified your souls in obeying the truth through the Spirit unto unfeigned love of the brethren, see that ye love one another with a pure heart fervently" (I Peter 1:22).

4. Truth frees us—"And ye shall know the truth, and the truth shall make you free" (John 8:32). Truth frees us by tearing down false ideas and conclusions that keep us in fear and bondage. "(For the weapons of our warfare are not carnal, but mighty through God to the pulling down of strong holds;) Casting down imaginations, and every high thing that exalteth itself against the knowledge of God, and bringing into captivity every thought to the obedience of Christ" (II Corinthians 10:4–5).

5. Truth leads us in the right way—"O send out thy light and thy truth: let them lead me" (Psalm 43:3).

6. Truth allows us to worship God—"But the hour cometh, and now is, when the true worshippers shall worship the Father in spirit and in truth: for the Father seeketh such to worship him. God is a Spirit: and they that worship him must worship him in spirit and in truth" (John 4:23–24).

7. Truth cleanses us from iniquity—"By mercy and truth iniquity is purged: and by the fear of the LORD men depart from evil" (Proverbs 16:6).

Lust and addictions hold many in bondage. The control comes from a spirit of uncleanness. The first step of purging is crying out to God for mercy. "And call upon me in the day of trouble: I will deliver thee, and thou shalt glorify me" (Psalm 50:15). The second step is to confess and repent. "If we confess our sins, he is faithful and just to forgive us our sins, and to cleanse us from all unrighteousness" (I John 1:9).

The third step is to fill our hearts with God's truth and meditate on it day and night. "Wherewithal shall a young man cleanse his way? by taking heed thereto according to thy word. With my whole heart have I sought thee: O let me not wander from thy commandments. Thy word have I hid in mine heart, that I might not sin against thee" (Psalm 119:9–11).

We may also need to acknowledge the iniquities of our forefathers (Daniel 9:16), regain surrendered ground (Ephesians 4:27), and engage in serious fasting and prayer (Isaiah 58:6). When the disciples were unable to deliver a boy from an unclean spirit, they asked Jesus why they were ineffective, and Jesus replied, "This kind can come forth by nothing, but by prayer and fasting" (Mark 9:29).

8. Truth preserves leaders—"Mercy and truth preserve the king: and his throne is upholden by mercy" (Proverbs 20:28).

It is significant that the throne is not established by truth and justice but by truth and mercy. When people violate truth, it is natural to be harsh, but loyalty is built when a leader teaches truth and demonstrates qualities of kindness, gentleness, patience, meekness, and self-control. Therefore, we are instructed to speak the truth in love.

How Can We Learn Truth?

We naturally tend to accept false ideas because the ways of death appeal to our human reasoning. "There is a way which seemeth right unto a man, but the end thereof are the ways of death" (Proverbs 14:12). Therefore, it is easy

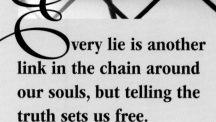

Every lie is another link in the chain around our souls, but telling the truth sets us free.

"Ye shall know the truth, and the truth shall make you free."—John 8:32

Saying whatever comes to mind is not truthfulness, but a lack of discretion.

Telling a lie is like pounding a nail in the wall of one's character. Telling the truth removes the nail, but leaves the mark.

Lions don't lie. They always speak the truth. Lions clearly reveal their intentions with the positions of their ears, the postures of their tails, the shapes of their mouths, and the sounds of their roars.

*I*n the continuing conflict between good and evil, truth is the weapon that wins the war.

"For we can do nothing against the truth, but for the truth."
—II Corinthians 13:8

"When he [Satan] speaketh a lie, he speaketh of his own: for he is a liar, and the father of it." —John 8:44

*T*hose that are closest to truth are closest to God.

"God is a Spirit: and they that worship him must worship him in spirit and in truth."
—John 4:24

to believe lies, which come from Satan, since he is a liar and the father of lies. "When he speaketh a lie, he speaketh of his own: for he is a liar, and the father of it" (John 8:44). Furthermore, if a person rejects the truth, God will send him strong delusions, and he will believe a lie. (See II Thessalonians 2:11.)

To learn truth, we need initiative and diligence in these areas:

1. By filling our soul with truth—"Wherefore lay apart all filthiness and superfluity of naughtiness, and receive with meekness the engrafted word, which is able to save your souls" (James 1:21).

2. By studying the meaning of truth—"Study to shew thyself approved unto God, a workman that needeth not to be ashamed, rightly dividing the word of truth" (II Timothy 2:15).

3. By learning to answer with truth—"Bow down thine ear, and hear the words of the wise, and apply thine heart unto my knowledge. . . . Have not I written to thee excellent things in counsels and knowledge, That I might make thee know the certainty of the words of truth; that thou mightest answer the words of truth to them that send unto thee?" (Proverbs 22:17–21).

4. By walking in fellowship with others—"If we say that we have fellowship with him, and walk in darkness, we lie, and do not the truth" (I John 1:6; see also I John 3:16–24).

5. By designing good works—"But mercy and truth shall be to them that devise good." (Proverbs 14:22). Therefore, "let us consider one another to provoke unto love and to good works" (Hebrews 10:24).

6. By testing the spirit—"Beloved, believe not every spirit, but try the spirits whether they are of God: because many false prophets are gone out into the world. Hereby know ye the Spirit of God: Every spirit that confesseth that Jesus Christ is come in the flesh is of God" (I John 4:1–2). We must beware of the following:

- False prophets (Matthew 7:15)
- False christs (Matthew 24:24)
- False apostles (II Corinthians 11:13)
- False teachers (II Peter 2:1)
- False brethren (II Corinthians 11:26)
- False accusers (II Timothy 3:3)
- False witnesses (Matthew 26:60)

Personal Evaluation

How truthful are you?

- Do you ask others to point out your blind spots?
- Do you confront your blind spots with Scripture?
- Do you believe that you have no serious faults and think you are better than you are?
- Do you exaggerate your achievements to others?
- Do you lie or tell only part of the truth to escape the consequences of your actions?
- Do you flatter people to gain their approval?
- Do you misrepresent the Lord with inconsistent or negative attitudes?
- Do you give damaging reports of others to make yourself look good?
- Do you guard against false teachings by checking everything you hear with the truth of Scripture?

Virtue
vs. Weakness

Virtue is the power of a life that is in harmony with the holy standards of God.

Definition

The Hebrew word for *virtuous* is *chayil*. It is translated only four times as *virtuous* and more than two hundred times as *man of valor, valiant, strength, power, might, strong, army, host, forces, riches, wealth, substance,* and other similar words.

Two Greek words are translated as *virtue: dunamis* and *arete*. *Dunamis* is translated only three times as *virtue* but more than one hundred times as *power, might, miracle, strength, mighty,* and *mighty work*. Virtue is the Godly influence of a life that is in a right relationship with the Lord and filled with the power of the Holy Spirit.

The Power of Virtue

Virtue is like static electricity that builds up in a person's body after walking on carpet in a dry atmosphere. If someone touches that person, there will be an electrical shock. In a similar manner, Christ was filled with the Holy Spirit and then led into the barren wilderness, where He was tested and tempted for forty days. He returned "in the power [*dunamis*] of the Spirit," (Luke 4:14), and He began to minister to the multitudes. The people soon realized that the power of God was

in Him; therefore, "the whole multitude sought to touch him: for there went virtue [*dunamis*] out of him, and healed them all" (Luke 6:19).

It is the will of God for every believer to experience this same power of virtue and use it to benefit others, who in turn will glorify God.

- "The kingdom of God is not in word, but in power [*dunamis*]" (I Corinthians 4:20).

- "Now unto him that is able to do exceeding abundantly above all that we ask or think, according to the power [*dunamis*] that worketh in us" (Ephesians 3:20).

- "According as his divine power [*dunamis*] hath given unto us all things that pertain unto life and godliness, through the knowledge of him that hath called us to glory and virtue" (II Peter 1:3).

How the Power of Virtue Is Lost

When virtue is defiled through lust and immorality, there is a loss of power. Thus, Scripture warns young men, "Give not thy strength [*chayil*] unto women, nor thy ways to that which destroyeth kings" (Proverbs 31:3).

Solomon warned his son, "The lips of a strange woman drop

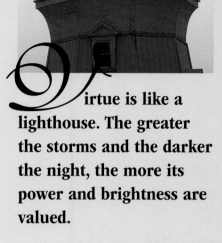

*V*irtue is like a lighthouse. The greater the storms and the darker the night, the more its power and brightness are valued.

"Arise, shine; for thy light is come, and the glory of the LORD is risen upon thee. For, behold, the darkness shall cover the earth, and gross darkness the people: but the LORD shall arise upon thee, and his glory shall be seen upon thee."
—Isaiah 60:1–2

*T*he power of virtue is a great threat to Satan's kingdom. Therefore, he will unleash his most attractive temptations to destroy it.

The wisest man who ever lived praised virtue, though he himself lost his virtue by associating with the kind of women he warned his sons to stay away from. (See I Kings 11:1–10.)

"Who can find a virtuous woman? for her price is far above rubies. . . . Favour is deceitful, and beauty is vain: but a woman that feareth the Lord, she shall be praised."—Proverbs 31:10, 30

Virtue is the power of the Holy Spirit energizing the lives of those touched by it.

"That he would grant you, according to the riches of his glory, to be strengthened with might by his Spirit in the inner man."
—Ephesians 3:16

as an honeycomb, and her mouth is smoother than oil: But her end is bitter as wormwood, sharp as a two edged sword. . . . Remove thy way far from her, and come not nigh the door of her house: Lest thou give thine honour unto others, and thy years unto the cruel: Lest strangers be filled with thy wealth; and thy labours be in the house of a stranger; And thou mourn at the last, when thy flesh and thy body are consumed" (Proverbs 5:4–8).

How the Power of Virtue Is Gained

When Peter wrote to all those who have "obtained like precious faith with us through the righteousness of God and our Saviour Jesus Christ," he stated, "add to your faith virtue" (II Peter 1:1, 5).

Paul explains the process by which virtue is added to faith. "For God, who commanded the light to shine out of darkness, hath shined in our hearts, to give the light of the knowledge of the glory of God in the face of Jesus Christ. But we have this treasure in earthen vessels, that the excellency of the power [*dunamis*] may be of God, and not of us. We are troubled on every side, yet not distressed; we are perplexed, but not in despair; Persecuted, but not forsaken; cast down, but not destroyed;

"Always bearing about in the body the dying of the Lord Jesus, that the life also of Jesus might be made manifest in our body. For we which live are alway delivered unto death for Jesus' sake, that the life also of Jesus might be made manifest in our

mortal flesh. So then death worketh in us, but life in you" (II Corinthians 4:6–12). The more Paul successfully responded to trials and tribulations, the more power he had to give the life of Christ to others.

In this same letter, Paul describes how he discovered the source of this power. "There was given to me a thorn in the flesh, the messenger of Satan to buffet me, lest I should be exalted above measure. For this thing I besought the Lord thrice, that it might depart from me.

"And he said unto me, My grace is sufficient for thee: for my strength [*dunamis*] is made perfect in weakness. Most gladly therefore will I rather glory in my infirmities, that the power [*dunamis*] of Christ may rest upon me.

"Therefore I take pleasure in infirmities, in reproaches, in necessities, in persecutions, in distresses for Christ's sake: for when I am weak, then am I strong." (II Corinthians 12:7–10).

This sequence of rejoicing in suffering in order to experience the power of virtue is repeated several times in Paul's epistles. He said to the believers in Philippi, "That I may know him, and the power of his resurrection, and the fellowship of his sufferings, being made conformable unto his death" (Philippians 3:10).

To the believers in Colosse he said, "That ye might walk worthy of the Lord unto all pleasing, being fruitful in every good work, and increasing in the knowledge of God; Strengthened with all might, according to his glorious power, unto all patience and longsuffering with joyfulness" (Colossians 1:10–11).

The Power of Virtue Illustrated

Proverbs 31:10–31 gives a marvelous tribute to the virtuous woman. She is praised by her husband and her children and by all who read about her. The following list of her virtuous character qualities is matched to the types of power that each quality brings about.

Descriptions of Virtue	Types of Power
"The heart of her husband doth safely trust in her.	The power of protection
"He shall have no need of spoil.	The power of provision
"She will do him good and not evil all the days of her life.	The power of endurance
"She seeketh wool, and flax, and worketh willingly with her hands.	The power of diligent work
"She is like the merchants' ships; she bringeth her food from afar.	The power of creative procurement
"She riseth also while it is yet night, and giveth meat to her household, and a portion to her maidens.	The power of fulfilling all responsibilities
"She considereth a field, and buyeth it: with the fruit of her hands she planteth a vineyard.	The power of making wise investments
"She girdeth her loins with strength, and strengtheneth her arms.	The power of good health and vigor
"She perceiveth that her merchandise is good: her candle goeth not out by night.	The power of guarding valuable assets
"She layeth her hands to the spindle, and her hands hold the distaff.	The power of skillful productivity
"She stretcheth out her hand to the poor; yea, she reacheth forth her hands to the needy.	The power of love and generosity
"She is not afraid of the snow for her household: for all her household are clothed with scarlet.	The power of preparation
"She maketh herself coverings of tapestry; her clothing is silk and purple.	The power of personal elegance
"Her husband is known in the gates, when he sitteth among the elders of the land.	The power of a good name
"She maketh fine linen, and selleth it; and delivereth girdles unto the merchant.	The power of making wealth
"Strength and honour are her clothing; and she shall rejoice in time to come.	The power of contentment and true security
"She openeth her mouth with wisdom; and in her tongue is the law of kindness.	The power of wise counsel
"She looketh well to the ways of her household, and eateth not the bread of idleness.	The power of resourcefulness
"Her children arise up, and call her blessed; her husband also, and he praiseth her.	The power of leadership
"Many daughters have done virtuously, but thou excellest them all.	The power of affirmation
"Favour is deceitful, and beauty is vain: but a woman that feareth the LORD, she shall be praised.	The power of inner beauty
"Give her of the fruit of her hands; and let her own works praise her in the gates."	The power of official honors

Many have wondered how the great white egret keeps its feathers so brilliantly white. The secret lies in downy feathers that flake off to produce a continual supply of powdery dust. The dust adheres to dirt, oil, and other impurities. As the egret brushes the dust from its feathers, it brushes away the impurities as well.

*V*irtue is a birthright of moral power. Those who despise it will lose it, as Esau did, and later seek it with tears.

"For ye know how that afterward, when he would have inherited the blessing, he was rejected: for he found no place of repentance, though he sought it carefully with tears."—Hebrews 12:17

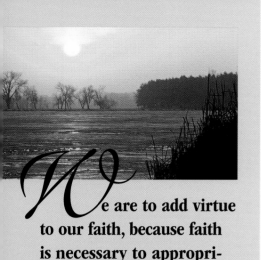

*W*e are to add virtue to our faith, because faith is necessary to appropriate the virtue of Christ.

(See II Peter 1:5.)

"Daughter, thy faith hath made thee whole; go in peace, and be whole of thy plague." —Mark 5:34

*T*hose who lose their virtue will ridicule those who have it, because they feel ashamed in the presence of its power.

"For the time past of our life may suffice us to have wrought the will of the Gentiles, when we walked in lasciviousness, lusts, excess of wine, revellings, banquetings, and abominable idolatries: Wherein they think it strange that ye run not with them to the same excess of riot, speaking evil of you:" —I Peter 4:3–4

The Requirement of Faith to Receive the Power of Virtue

"A certain woman, which had an issue of blood twelve years, And had suffered many things of many physicians, and had spent all that she had, and was nothing bettered, but rather grew worse, When she had heard of Jesus, came in the press behind, and touched his garment" (Mark 5:25–27).

Jesus immediately knew that the power of virtue had gone out of Him, so He turned around in the press of the throng and said, "Who touched my clothes?" (Mark 5:30). This question amazed the disciples, and they pointed out that the multitude thronged around Him and that many touched Him.

Yet one touched Him in faith, believing that she would receive the power of healing from that touch. "For she said, If I may touch but his clothes, I shall be whole. And straightway the fountain of her blood was dried up; and she felt in her body that she was healed of that plague" (Mark 5:28–29). It is, therefore, not enough just to touch Jesus, but rather to touch Him in faith. It is on this basis that Jesus often said, "Thy faith hath made thee whole."

The Consequence of Losing Virtue

There is a power of life that is lost when virtue is surrendered. It is this power that the evil woman seeks to destroy in simple young men who surrender to her. Therefore Solomon warns, "For by means of a whorish woman a man is brought to a piece of bread: and the adulteress will hunt for the precious life" (Proverbs 6:26). "For her house inclineth unto death, and her paths unto the dead. None that go unto her return again, neither take they hold of the paths of life" (Proverbs 2:18–19).

Such a loss should motivate us to repent and to cry out to God for His mercy and His grace.

Personal Evaluation

How virtuous are you?

- Do you value the power of virtue and do you have this power?

- Do people apologize for profanity or rudeness when you are around?

- Do others ask you for counsel for the problems they are facing in their lives?

- Do you help others conquer guilt, anger, fear, lust, and bitterness?

- Do others want to follow your example in living out the Christian life?

- Do you have the power to conquer the temptations Satan brings to you?

- Do you thank God for times of suffering and rejoice in them?

- Do you acknowledge your weaknesses to the Lord in order to experience His power?

- Do you demonstrate the qualities of a virtuous man or woman?

- Do others tell you how you have helped them in their walks with the Lord?

Wisdom

vs. Foolishness

Wisdom is seeing the hand of God in every experience of life.

Definition

The primary Hebrew word for *wisdom* is *chokmah*. It comes from a root word meaning "intelligent, skillful, or artful; to be cunning." A second Hebrew word for *wisdom* is *sekel*. It comes from the root word meaning "to be circumspect, to act prudently, to prosper and have good success, to be expert, to behave oneself wisely, to teach, to guide wittingly." The stated purpose of Proverbs is to "know wisdom [*chokmah*]" and "to receive the instruction of wisdom [*sekel*]." (See Proverbs 1:2–3.)

The basic Greek word for *wisdom* is *sophia*, which denotes practical skill and acumen. One Greek word for *wise* is *phronimos*, denoting one who is "thoughtful, sagacious, or discreet." It implies a cautious person.

God provides a description of wisdom [*sophia*] in James 3:17. "The wisdom that is from above is first pure, then peaceable, gentle, and easy to be entreated, full of mercy and good fruits, without partiality, and without hypocrisy."

How Is Wisdom Demonstrated?

When wisdom is first mentioned in Scripture, it involves the skillful making of things to benefit the work of God. First, there were the priestly garments.

"Thou shalt speak unto all that are wise-hearted, whom I have filled with the spirit of wisdom, that they may make Aaron's garments to consecrate him, that he may minister unto me in the priest's office" (Exodus 28:3).

Next, there was the wise construction of various buildings for the work of God. The man God chose to build the tabernacle was filled with wisdom. "I have filled him with the spirit of God, in wisdom, and in understanding, and in knowledge, and in all manner of workmanship, To devise cunning works, to work in gold, and in silver, and in brass, And in cutting of stones, to set them, and in carving of timber, to work in all manner of workmanship.

"And I, behold, I have given with him Aholiab, the son of Ahisamach, of the tribe of Dan: and in the hearts of all that are wise hearted I have put wisdom, that they may make all that I have commanded thee" (Exodus 31:3–6).

The theme of building continues throughout Scripture in connection with the wise. God gave Solomon great wisdom and understanding, and with it, he built the temple. In the Book of Proverbs, he stated, "Wisdom hath builded her house" (Proverbs 9:1). Again he explained, "Through wisdom is an house builded; and by understanding it is established" (Proverbs 24:3).

*W*isdom competes in the city streets for the eyes and ears of the simple.

"Wisdom crieth without; she uttereth her voice in the streets . . . How long, ye simple ones, will ye love simplicity?" —Proverbs 1:20–22

"Knowledge is proud that he has learned so much; wisdom is humble that he knows no more." —William Cowper

"Knowledge puffeth up, but charity edifieth." —I Corinthians 8:1

The ears of the **great horned owl** allow it to "see" from a second perspective. The owl's ears are offset so that it can hear in three dimensions. This allows an owl to recognize and track its prey using only the sounds of footsteps.

*T*aking information through the grid of God's presuppositions produces wisdom.

Philosophy is the love of wisdom, but without Christ it is void of both love and wisdom.

"For the wisdom of this world is foolishness with God." —I Corinthians 3:19

"Wisdom is the right use of knowledge. To know is not to be wise. . . . But to know how to use knowledge is to have wisdom." —C. H. Spurgeon

As a boy, Jesus grew in wisdom and in stature, and he was a carpenter in his father's shop. When he began his ministry, he used the analogy of a wise man building his house on a rock. Paul described his ministry by comparing himself to a wise master builder. (See Matthew 7:24 and I Corinthians 3:10.)

The function of wisdom is to build up, but the result of foolishness is to tear down. "Every wise woman buildeth her house: but the foolish plucketh it down with her hands" (Proverbs 14:1).

What Are Characteristics of a Wise Person ?

- A wise person will love one who rebukes him. "Rebuke a wise man, and he will love thee" (Proverbs 9:8).

- The wise will consider the lessons of nature. "Go to the ant, thou sluggard; consider her ways, and be wise" (Proverbs 6:6).

- A wise son delights the heart of his father. "A wise son maketh a glad father" (Proverbs 10:1).

- A wise person loves the law of God. "The wise in heart will receive commandments" (Proverbs 10:8).

- A wise person controls his tongue. "He that refraineth his lips is wise" (Proverbs 10:19).

- A wise person wins others to Christ. "He that winneth souls is wise" (Proverbs 11:30).

- A wise person listens to counsel and instruction. "He that hearkeneth unto counsel is wise" (Proverbs 12:15). "A wise son heareth his father's instruction" (Proverbs 13:1).

- A wise person makes friends with the wise. "He that walketh with wise men shall be wise" (Proverbs 13:20).

- A wise person knows how to use information in the right way. "The tongue of the wise useth knowledge aright: but the mouth of fools poureth out foolishness" (Proverbs 15:2).

- A wise person will avoid conflicts with leaders. "The wrath of a king is as messengers of death: but a wise man will pacify it" (Proverbs 16:14).

- A wise person will learn how to give precise answers. "The heart of the wise teacheth his mouth, and addeth learning to his lips" (Proverbs 16:23).

- A wise person knows how to give good counsel. "The lips of the wise disperse knowledge: but the heart of the foolish doeth not so" (Proverbs 15:7).

- A wise person will reform rebels. "A wise servant shall have rule over a son that causeth shame" (Proverbs 17:2).

Why Is Wisdom So Important?

In order to explain the superior value of wisdom, God compares it to the most precious things in life.

1. **It is more valuable than gold**— "My fruit is better than gold, yea, than fine gold; and my revenue than choice silver" (Proverbs 8:19).

2. **It is more precious than jewels**— "For wisdom is better than rubies; and all the things that may be desired are not to be compared to it" (Proverbs 8:11).

3. **It is more valuable than riches**—"Riches and honour are with me; yea, durable riches and righteousness" (Proverbs 8:18).

4. **It should be our first priority**—"Wisdom is the principal thing; therefore get wisdom: and with all thy getting get understanding" (Proverbs 4:7).

What Great Heroes of Faith Received Wisdom?

- **Joseph**
  "Pharaoh said unto Joseph, Forasmuch as God hath shewed thee all this, there is none so discreet and wise as thou art" and "he made him governor over Egypt and all his house" (Genesis 41:39; Acts 7:10).

- **Joshua**
  "Joshua the son of Nun was full of the spirit of wisdom; for Moses had laid his hands upon him: and the children of Israel hearkened unto him, and did as the LORD commanded Moses" (Deuteronomy 34:9).

- **Daniel**
  "God gave them knowledge and skill in all learning and wisdom: and Daniel had understanding in all visions and dreams. . . . And in all matters of wisdom and understanding, that the king enquired of them, he found them ten times better than all the magicians and astrologers" (Daniel 1:17, 20).

- **David**
  "David behaved himself wisely in all his ways; and the LORD was with him. Wherefore when Saul saw that he behaved himself very wisely, he was afraid of him. . . . David behaved himself more wisely than all the servants of Saul; so that his name was much set by" (I Samuel 18:14–15, 30).

- **Solomon**
  "God gave Solomon wisdom and understanding exceeding much, and largeness of heart, even as the sand that is on the sea shore. And Solomon's wisdom excelled the wisdom of all the children of the east country, and all the wisdom of Egypt. . . . And there came of all people to hear the wisdom of Solomon, from all kings of the earth, which had heard of his wisdom" (I Kings 4:29–30, 34).

- **Ezra**
  "And thou, Ezra, after the wisdom of thy God, that is in thine hand, set magistrates and judges, which may judge all the people that are beyond the river, all such as know the laws of thy God; and teach ye them that know them not" (Ezra 7:25).

- **Stephen**
  "Wherefore, brethren, look ye out among you seven men of honest report, full of the Holy Ghost and wisdom . . . and they chose Stephen, a man full of faith and of the Holy Ghost . . . And they were not able to resist the wisdom and the spirit by which he spake" (Acts 6:3–10).

How Do We Get Wisdom?

1. **By asking God for it**—"If any of you lack wisdom, let him ask of God, that giveth to all men liberally, and upbraideth not; and it shall be given him" (James 1:5).

2. **By studying God's law**—"Keep therefore and do them; for this is your wisdom and your understanding in the sight of the nations, which shall hear

A description of fools by the wisest man who ever lived:

1. **Simple fool**
   - Believes every word
   - Looks for a leader
   - Ignorant of cause and effect
   - Corrupted by scorning fools

2. **Silly fool**
   - Seeks "a good time"
   - Has fun breaking rules
   - Seeks wrong friends
   - Has guilt for wrongdoing

3. **Sensual fool**
   - Sneaks out with friends
   - Engages in immorality
   - Involved in drugs and bad habits
   - Skilled in deception

4. **Scorning fool**
   - Gets simple fools to do evil
   - Despises rules and authorities
   - Creates contention
   - Proud of evil exploits

5. **Committed fool**
   - Has a seared conscience
   - Believes wrong is right
   - Skilled in arguments
   - Seeks followers for self gain

*B*oth the wise and the foolish are known by the friends they choose.

*G*od identifies four animals as "exceeding wise" and explains why.

(See Proverbs 30:24–28.)

1. The ants are a people not strong, yet they prepare their meat in the summer.

2. The conies are but a feeble folk, yet make they their houses in the rocks.

3. The locusts have no king, yet go they forth all of them by bands.

4. The spider taketh hold with her hands, and is in kings' palaces.

all these statutes, and say, Surely this great nation is a wise and understanding people" (Deuteronomy 4:6).

3. **By keeping God's commandments with us**—"Thou through thy commandments hast made me wiser than mine enemies: for they are ever with me" (Psalm 119:98).

4. **Through the fear of the Lord**—"The fear of the LORD is the beginning of wisdom: and the knowledge of the holy is understanding" (Proverbs 9:10).

5. **By reading Proverbs**—"The proverbs of Solomon the son of David, king of Israel; To know wisdom and instruction; to perceive the words of understanding; To receive the instruction of wisdom, justice, and judgment, and equity" (Proverbs 1:1–3).

6. **By God's testimonies**—"The law of the LORD is perfect, converting the soul: the testimony of the LORD is sure, making wise the simple" (Psalm 19:7).

7. **By hearing instruction**—"Hear instruction, and be wise, and refuse it not" (Proverbs 8:33). "Give instruction to a wise man, and he will be yet wiser: teach a just man, and he will increase in learning" (Proverbs 9:9).

8. **By seeking it early**—"I love them that love me; and those that seek me early shall find me" (Proverbs 8:17).

9. **By listening to rebukes**—"Give instruction to a wise man, and he will be yet wiser: teach a just man, and he will increase in learning" (Proverbs 9:9).

10. **By seeking wise counsel**—"He that walketh with wise men shall be wise" (Proverbs 13:20).

Personal Evaluation

How wise are you?

- Do you go to sleep with thoughts of God so that your reigns can instruct you in the night seasons?

- Do you rise early in the morning to seek the wisdom of God?

- Have you developed skills so that you can make things with quality?

- Do you love those who rebuke you?

- Do you study the world of nature for insights and analogies?

- Are your parents pleased with your character and your actions?

- Have you searched for *rhemas* from Scripture and meditated upon them?

- Do you control your tongue because your heart is filled with truth?

- Are you skilled in winning others to Christ?

- Do you seek out the counsel of wise friends?

- Do you look for ways to apply the truths you have learned from God's Word?

- Do you value wisdom more than silver and gold?

- Do you study the testimonies in Scripture for application to your own life?

- Do you delight in the commandments of the Lord?

- Do you live in the reality that God is watching and evaluating everything you say and do?